STUDIES OF DEVELOPING COUNTRIES (formerly *Non European Societies*)

edited by

prof. dr. L. H. Janssen S.J. (Tilburg), dr. P. Kloos (Leiden), prof. dr. R. A. J. van Lier (Wageningen) and prof. dr. J. D. Speckmann (Leiden).

Thomas K. Fitzgerald, Editor

Nutrition and Anthropology in Action

1977

van Gorcum, Assen/Amsterdam

ISBN 90 232 1447 1

Printed in The Netherlands by Van Gorcum, Assen

Dedicated To
Dr. Leon Bryan Wolcott
friend

Contents

Preface

Audrey Richards, formerly Director of the Centre for African Studies, Cambridge University.

It has been forty-five years since I first made a study of nutrition in an African society. As a student of Malinowski, I used his institutional approach in analyzing the nutritional mechanisms of a group of Bantu people, being specifically concerned with the production, transport, preparation, and consumption of food. Malinowski was, at that time, engaged on a study which later appeared as "The Sexual Life of Savages" (1932); and, following his lead (but with a thesis on the nutritional systems of human societies) I began my work with the defiant statement that "Nutrition as a biological process is even more fundamental than sex!"

I chose some Bantu societies of South Africa, and this research is published in *Hunger and Work in a Savage Society* (1932). The book is not essentially a dietary study, since it primarily attempts to describe the economic processes by which some of the Southern Bantu produced their food. Yet, it deals with food as an object of exchange and as a symbol in ritual contexts. In other words, I tried to treat all aspects of the culture which seemed to affect their consumption of food.

I became more interested in diet itself and, subsequently, went into the field in Nothern Rhodesia, now Zambia. Diet and food customs were easy to observe since the villages were small, and cooking and eating were in the open. I became convinced that anthropologists could make a real contribution to the study of nutrition. For one thing, anthropology broadens the field of observation; in other words, anthropologists can ask questions not commonly occurring to dieticians working mainly in our society and thus having what Cattle (in this volume) calls a more "particularistic" approach.

There was considerable interest in nutrition in England at the time (1930-34), largely connected with a pre-war drive to raise the economic standards of various colonial people. (See chapter I for a summary). The subject of nutrition was very much in the air. I even decided to attempt to make some quantitative measures of food intakes, although in a somewhat amateurish fashion, in three villages. Food was weighed on a huge spring balance, usually hung on the most conveniently located tree. Samples of various food-stuffs were sent back to England for analysis. I even included some specimens of millet beer, which formed a large part of the diet of the older men of high status.

In spite of its imperfections, several interesting facts were revealed, e.g., the caloric intake of these villagers was about half that normally recommended by American or United Kingdom standards. It also showed some incredible seasonal changes in food intake and the negative results of dependence of people on a single crop (in this case finger millet).

The 1939 war put an end to field studies in the British Colonies, but the post-war period has witnessed major advances both in the scope and in the varieties of nutritional/anthropological techniques. One of the most important contributions that this book makes is its historical coverage (see Freedman) and its sophisticated treatment of the latest methodological techniques in nutrition and anthropology (see Wilson, Fitzgerald, Dewalt and Pelto). Also, the applied focus of this book is in no way limited, covering such wide geographical areas of the world as the British Solomons to Senegal, from Bolivia to Northern Mexico and Jamaica to Bangladesh. Through such ethnographic coverage, the reader can experience, at least second-hand, the theoretical and applied problems involved.

Certainly there have been changes in the nutritional surveys of the 1930's. In so-called "development" projects, for example, more general and unanticipated problems plagued the fieldworkers. Here the anthropologists, with their broader approach to the study of food and food production, have proved invaluable to the more specialized nutritionists. Another change in the scope of nutritional studies has been that anthropology has moved from the study of so-called "primitive" cultures to the study of contemporary, even urban communities – a change from the "exotic" to "back-yard" anthropology. In such work, the anthropologist is no longer a lone-wolf fieldworker but intimately in touch with nutritionists and other health-related scientists – borrowing and sharing their sophisticated research techniques. Those interested in this emerging field of inter- (really multi-) disciplinary effort are obviously in for a period of experiment and discussion. This book will help to focus on these current issues.

The authors of this book claim, at least implicitly, that there is now a new subject – "nutritional anthropology". A good case can probably be made for this "splitting off" or specialization, but many questions arise. Will the nutritional anthropologist continue to contribute to the wider knowledge of the social and economic aspects of given cultures, which have proved so valuable to those conducting nutritional surveys in the past? What is to be the division of responsibilities between representatives of different disciplines? Is the nutritional anthropologist to continue to be a fieldworker, and to what degree is participant observation feasible in a modern urban society?

Before concluding, one other comment seems in order. Although this book appears in the well known series, "Studies in Developing Countries", not all the papers in this volume deal specifically with nutritional/anthropological problems in developing countries (cf. Fitzgerald's conclusions with those of Dewalt and Pelto for such a contrast: the one is concerned with food habits in situations of maximum choice, i.e., in a middle-class industralized setting; the other deals with circumstances of minimal choice where economics overshadows "likes and dislikes" in food choices). All of the articles, however, are relevant – even by contrast – for a better understanding of peoples in developing countries. Certainly this is a most significant and valuable book. Specialists in many areas (sociology, medicine, food science, etc.) will be grateful to the writers of these papers for the theoretical, methodological, and applied issues they raise, as well as for the information given on diet in such varied cultural contexts.

Nutritional Anthropology:
An Overview

Robert L. Freedman, Consultant Child Nutrition Program, Department of Education, State of New Mexico, Santa Fe.

Introduction

Human culture, the focus of anthropological study, may be defined compositely as the sum total of a group's learned, shared behavior. This phenomenon of consistent transmittal, the *sharing* of experience through time, is apparently unique to our species and is also a basic type of positively reinforcing social behavior. From it arose the possibility for individuals and cultures to adapt to the natural environment and to begin the process of change and development some scholars have termed cultural evolution.

The series of articles which follows is concerned with three subjects of study fundamental to the successful survival of human culture. The first – nutrition – is a field of knowledge concerned with the effects of food upon individual biochemical and behavioral equilibrium. From observation of the effects of food upon the individual, extrapolation to the effects of nutrition upon social groups is not difficult (Brito 1948; Evans 1973).

Our second area of study is anthropology, which seeks to understand the laws governing the relationship of individuals with each other and to the cultures they have developed, as well as to explain processes which have evolved to satisfy basic physiological and psychological needs (Maslow 1943; Malinowski 1944: 52-84).

Our third (and perhaps most important) subject area is that of the *application* of knowledge to the solution of human problems, the success of which depends upon the comprehensive training of individuals in the many fields of academic endeavor; the development and refinement of technology and observational skills; the reinforcement of interdisciplinary communication; and the integration of all the foregoing into a guiding humanitarian ethic.

Applied nutritional anthropology may be defined, in one sense, as the application of anthropological data and methods to the solving of the cultural aspects of human nutritional problems, or as the study of the interrelationship between diet and culture and their mutual influence upon one another.

Nutritional problems may be of deficiency or of excess; may derive from inborn errors of metabolism or from cultural and/or environmental factors. Nutritional problems may require direct treatment of the individual, or direct or indirect change in the micro – or macro-social and/or natural envi-

1

ronments. Regardless of circumstance, however, the solution will almost always require some modification of a cultural habit. The job of the anthropologist in applied nutrition is to view a nutritional problem within its cultural context and, on the basis of analysis of both the problem and the culture, to suggest a plan of action which may be followed in such a manner that, whatever change must be brought about, the least resistance will be generated by the required intervention.

Interdisciplinary teamwork has proved effective in carrying out applied nutrition projects. This effectiveness is understandable, insofar as developments in both natural and social science over the past several decades have made clear that a holistic view of any portion of the physical or social world reveals a complex network of interrelationships. Therefore, one must expect that an awareness of this interrelatedness should be reflected in approaches to the solution of problems arising within the network. Examples of such teamwork are given later in this article.

A Brief Historical Background

Trémolières (1971: 7,8) has highlighted the history of food consumption surveys in Western Europe from the 17th through the 19th centuries. In this article, however, we will limit ourselves to consideration of studies in which ethnographic material is presented as an integral background for a fuller understanding of the nutritional milieu or vice-versa.

One of the earliest of these (Von Rechenberg 1890) looks at the diet of Saxon handweavers and uses questionnaires, direct observation, and interviews. Goss (1897) places the food habits of Spanish-Americans in New Mexico into socio-anthropological perspective, includes a nutritional analysis of several low-income diets, and compares this with dietary studies done by Atwater (1895) for other regions of the United States. The ethnography of Native American wild rice gatherers by Jenks (1900) also contains a nutrient analysis and considers the comparative nutritive value of the grain.

Wood and Mansfield's mini ethnography (1904) of a Maine lumber camp details food preparation techniques and includes nutritional and metabolic analyses of recorded diets. McCarrison (1928), a unique example of comparative nutritional ethnology, demonstrated the relative values of Sikh, Pathan, Bengali, and other Indian dietaries, by feeding these to laboratory animals. In this study, he concludes that "the striking differences in the physique of different Indian races are due, in the main, to differences in biological value of their national diets" (*ibid.* p. 323). Orr & Gilks (1931) performed extensive metabolic studies among two East African groups: the Masai (carnivores), and the Akikuyu (vegetarians) and pointed out the relationship between nutritional status and diet and the importance of anthropological factors influencing food intake. Richards' (1932) ethnology of the Bemba of Nothern Rhodesia marks the real beginning of anthropological studies of food habits. It employs the Malinowskian functionalist model

(Malinowski op cit.) to show diet in its interrelationship with other cultural institutions.

Formal collaboration between anthropologists and nutritionists was initiated in 1935, when the British International African Institute appointed a Diet Committee, composed of scholars of both disciplines, to investigate how anthropologists might contribute to field work in British Colonial Africa, by providing data upon which to construct comparative nutritional studies (see Fortes & Fortes 1936; Hellman 1936; Read 1938; and Ashton 1939; but especially Richards and Widdowson [1936] representing, in all probability, the first instance of formal association between an anthropologist and a biochemically-trained nutritionist). Richards' (1939) ethnography of the Bemba placed her dietary data in a comprehensive sociological framework and included nutritional information derived from the earlier work by Widdowson (Richards & Widdowson op. cit.).

Other pioneering studies are those of Price (1939), illustrating the effects of refined foods on the nutritional status of non-industrialized groups lately introduced to a Western diet; and Benedict & Steggerda (1937), showing the possible dietary factors responsible for high basal metabolic rates among Maya males in Yucatan.

Important developments in nutritional anthropology took place during the early 1940's, with the formation of the United States National Research Council's Committee on Food Habits, and as a consequence of the Southwest Project. These activities are taken up later in this article.

Bennett (1946) reviewed research in nutritional anthropology from ca. 1932 through 1944 and attempted to define the concepts of theoretical and applied research as these related to the study of food habits. The dissertation by Whiting (1958) signals a second growth phase in nutritional anthropology, characterized by emphasis on comparative ethnology and data-gathering techniques. Whiting's research is of particular importance for stressing the relationship between anthropology and public health nutrition. In Whiting's own words:

The nutritional data that have been compiled on these [118 cultural] groups are potentially useful for research in both public health and social science. In public health, there is considerable current interest in the comparative study of the diet and health of population groups accustomed to different levels of intake of specific nutrients, for example, in the relation of consumption of fat to coronary disease and in the importance of longitudinal studies for estimating human requirements of such nutrients as protein and calcium. In social science a theory concerning the relationship of variations in social organization to child training practices and to personality has been developed and tested through the comparative study of cultural groups. Nutritional practices are largely determined by basic customs which are interrelated with other aspects of the social organization such as basic economy. The nutritional data given here are now available for further study of these interrelationships (*ibid.* pp. vii, viii).

Dentan (1960) is a valuable guide for field research and anticipates the Human Relations Area Files' (H.R.A.F. 1964) survey of the food habits of 383 selected cultures. Chapter Four of the latter survey, titled "Nutritional Anal-

3

ysis", provides brief nutritional profiles of world geographic regions and indicates outstanding patterns of nutritional deficiencies. The regional studies in the Ecology of Malnutrition Series, edited by May & Jarcho (1961); May (1963, 1965, 1966, 1967); and May & McLellan (1968, 1970, 1971, 1972, and 1973), complement this research. McArthur (1960a, 1960b) also includes ethnographic background material in a study of Arnhem Land Aboriginal dietary behavior and nutritional status.

Others concerned with the integration of anthropology and nutrition include Read (1964), who considers the role of the anthropologist in nutrition programs with special reference to tropical areas; De (1967), who reviews the use of fermented foods in the Near East, Africa, and Asia; and Lee (1969), who analyzes the relationship between energy, time in-put and nutritional status in !Kung Bushman culture; as well as Ramanamurthy (1969), wherein laboratory experiments are described in an attempt to prove possible physiological bases underlying the hot/cold food classification system occurring in India. Knutsson (1970) shows how religious fasting affects nutritional status in Ethiopian infants of the Orthodox Christian faith; McCracken (1971) explores the ethnography and physiology of lactase deficiency; and Adams (1968), Klein & Yarbrough (1972) and Shneour (1974) each address themselves to the influence of nutrition upon intellectual development and learning ability. Regrettably, space limitations prevent a more complete review of other relevant studies.

Case Histories

Anthropological research in the area of food behavior is valuable because, as time passes, such data provide points of reference in terms of which persistence or change may be measured (Freedman 1973:15). The reports of Cassel (1955, 1957) on directed nutritional change in Polela, a Zulu community in Natal, Union of South Africa, are a useful illustration of how historical knowledge of a group's food habits may be used to advantage in promoting modification of prevailing dietary practices.

Among Polela's problems was acute malnutrition which further aggravated a variety of infectious diseases. Poor farming techniques had caused soil erosion, making agricultural self sufficiency impossible; and the relationship between faulty diet and ill-health was unfortunately not recognized. Efforts to encourage increased consumption of milk and eggs were resisted due to complex kinship rules and local concepts of practical economics.

Only members of the kin group of the head of a household could use milk produced by that man's cattle. When a married woman took up residence with her husband's kin group, this rule then prevented her from drinking milk produced in his household. During her menses, or when pregnant, a woman was thought to exert an evil influence on cattle and was not allowed to pass near the cattle enclosures or to partake of any milk. Thus, there was a double restriction for women in this culture.

4

As for eggs, three general beliefs prevailed: (1) to eat an egg, which would later hatch and become a chicken, was uneconomical; (2) eating eggs was a sign of greed; (3) eggs, when eaten by young girls, made the latter lascivious.

The Polela diet was also lacking in leafy green vegetables although, before the advent of soil erosion, wild greens had been gathered and eaten. Thus, the decision was made to exploit the similarity of garden greens to wild greens and thereby encourage the establishment of home gardens.

How were the cultural barriers to improved nutrition overcome? At the time of the project, the people of Polela maintained that their diet was the traditional one. At first, the public health team workers could not refute this contention. A search of the historical literature, however, revealed a contradiction.

Prior to the arrival of Europeans, the indigenous cereal had been millet. Maize, which supplanted it, was introduced and had been adopted owing to its greater yield potential. Millet was used only for brewing the native beer. Further, in time past, the Zulu had been a roving pastoral people owning large herds of cattle, with milk and meat constituting a significant proportion of their diet. "Once facts about the 'olden times' were presented," writes Cassel, "they were readily accepted by many of the older people. Almost in the same breath, however, they maintained that their present diet was traditional. Once they saw the anomaly, a certain measure of interest was aroused and cooperation finally achieved, particularly among the older people who were more likely to remember former conditions. This was of great importance in gaining acceptance for the new program. The assistance of the older group was gratifying in view of the fact that this group usually forms the most conservative element in any community" (1955:24).

Introducing milk into the diet of the women, especially those who were pregnant or lactating, was of prime importance, if infant malnutrition was to be alleviated. After careful consideration of the cultural complications, the decision was reached to introduce powdered milk. No secret was made that the powder was milk, but emphasis was placed on the fact that the milk did not originate from cows belonging to Bantu people. Polela folk themselves conceptualized the milk, in dried form, not as milk but rather as "powder" or "meal". Consequently the powder was accepted without protest.

Increasing egg consumption presented fewer difficulties than did milk. Ninety-five percent of the families in Polela kept poultry, and the health team decided that beliefs related to eating eggs derived more from economic considerations than from deep-seated cultural traditions. Therefore, efforts were directed at increasing egg yields so that enough were produced for eating as well as for hatching. The nutritional value and palatability of eggs were emphasized, and various methods were developed for incorporating eggs into familiar recipes.

Increasing consumption of green vegetables was accomplished in several ways. Nutritional value and similarity in taste to formerly-eaten wild greens were highlighted. But, most important, home gardens were encouraged; and the villagers were shown the financial savings these made possible. Demonstrations, too, were provided, showing the best ways of combining garden vegetables into the diet without destroying their nutrient values, while maintaining customary recipes and preparation methods. After approximately twelve years of the Polela health program, infant mortality decreased from 276 per 1,000 live births to 96. Pellagra and kwashiorkor were all but eliminated. Infant weights at the age of one year increased by an average of 2 pounds between ca. 1948 and 1954, and demand for powdered milk became so great that neither the Polela Health Centre nor the local retail store could satisfy it. To the great satisfaction of the Centre, permission was given, in a number of the more educated families, for women to consume milk from the family cows, without any marked reaction from the rest of the community.

When one considers the growth of nutritional anthropology in the United States, one is immediately reminded of the work accomplished by the National Research Council's Committee on Food Habits. In November, 1940, over a year before active involvement of the United States in global fighting, the National Research Council began to explore ways in which national defense potential could be heightened through improvement of the population's physical fitness. The primary role of nutrition in national health was recognized; yet it was known that an appreciable percentage of the U.S. population was suffering from one form or another of nutritional deficiency; and the fact was acknowledged that the improvement of this state of affairs would require not only the knowledge of the scientific facts of nutrition but also study and interpretation of the socio-cultural variables affecting the food folkways of the nation (NAS/NRC 1943:9). Therefore, the National Research Council was asked to set up two committees: one to focus on the biochemical and physiological aspects of nutrition; and the other upon the psychological and cultural patterns of diet – a committee on food habits – including particularly psychology and cultural anthropology. Anthropologists participating on the Committee on Food Habits included Margaret Mead, the Committee's Executive Secretary, and Ruth Benedict. Other committee members were selected from the fields of sociology, home economics, physiological psychology, and public health.

The Committee's work represents the first effort at coordinated interdisciplinary study of the variables involved in the directed change of food habits within an industrialized nation. Mead (1943) summarized the Committee's basic findings: anthropology, she observed, is useful in providing information as to how behavior may be changed; but she cautioned that the cultural anthropologist must have an awareness of the ramifications of change in other areas of life (see Merton 1936). Mead also noted that techniques have not been developed for setting in motion within a culture a type of behavior which is itself a form of prospective adaptation to change (Mead *op. cit.*).

One of the Committee's lasting contributions to applied nutritional anthropology is the well-known channel theory of Kurt Lewin (1943). All food, Lewin theorized, moves step by step, through "channels", the nature and number of which vary from culture to culture. Examples of such channels include hunters, farmers, means of transportation, wholesale and retail outlets (from simple markets in non-industrialized areas to metropolitan supermarkets); various processing, preparation, and storage activities (both industrial and domestic). Individual channels are, in turn, regulated by persons in the culture whom Lewin termed "gate-keepers" (*ibid.* p. 37). For the modification of food habits, within any group, it is important to know the gate-keepers and the channels they control. Lastly, the psychology of the gate-keeper – a factor which also varies from culture to culture along with the role and symbolism of food therein – is recognized as a basic factor in effecting change. Lewin also achived success experimentally in altering dietary behavior through the refinement of group decision-making techniques, by showing that consensus reached within a group was significantly more effective in facilitating change than an approach where the target group was passive as, say, in a lecture situation. These experimental results have been corroborated by Ross (1964), and by Sofer, Janis & Wishlade (1964).

The Committee on Food Habits also was responsible for the formulation of a procedural manual (NAS/NRC 1945) which was developed in order to "...set up preliminary standards for the collection of basic data on food habits from the perspectives of psychology, psychiatry, sociology, anthropology, or home economics" (*ibid.* p. 23). Included in the manual is an extensive review of the literature in anthropology, behavioral psychology, and physiology relating to cultural food behavior through the mid-1940's.

During the early 1940's, a series of regional food habits and nutrition surveys was made in the southwestern United States, as part of a project conducted jointly by the Office of Indian Affairs of the United States Department of the Interior, and the University of Chicago, under the technical direction of Professor Fred Eggan of the University's Department of Anthropology (Freedman 1971:174). According to Ms. Emma Reh, who participated in the Southwest Project, there were "... five regional surveys, three in Indian areas of the Southwest and two in Spanish-American communities of the Rio Grande Basin of New Mexico. The purpose was not only to throw light on the nutritional status of these populations, with a view to improvement, but also to shape general methods for investigation into food economics which might apply in Spanish American countries to the south or elsewhere" (1942:1). Pijoán (1942), the Project's medical nutritionist, emphasized that dietary change should be economically and psychologically feasible. Foods and preparation methods, therefore, should be familiar and acceptable, in order to provide some assurance of the permanent adoption of the change. "In conclusion", Pijoán wrote, "any nutritional program which has as its objective permanent changes in the culture pattern of a people should take into consideration the pre-existing ethnological background of the group involved. If possible, the people should be made aware of the evolutionary processes through which they have passed which make such changes necessary" (*ibid.* p. 243). Pijoán (NRC 1944) has also recounted some of the other problems met with during the Southwest Project. One such involved the premastication of infant food among Native Americans. Criticized as unhygienic, the practice was abandoned under pressure from European missionaries. With its disappearance, however, profound anemia developed in many Native American children. Why? Because premastication is a form of feeding, supplemental to natural breast milk, which often serves to increase the infant's iron intake – desirable because the child is unable to derive sufficient iron from prolonged and exclusive intake of human milk to make up for the primary physiological red blood cell destruction following birth. Was there a remedial step? "We put it up to the Indians," Pijoán writes, "we explained the situation to them. They told us the answer. It was to go back to their original supplemental feeding program and involved no economic adjustment" (ibid. p. 15; Pijoán; Elkin 1944). Owing to a high tuberculosis rate among Native Americans, however, there was concern that the baccilus might be transmitted from mother to infant. Health personnel decided, nonetheless, that contact between mother and child was sufficient to communicate infection regardless of premastication and "... it might be better for the child to be as healthy as possible, without anemia, and thus reduce the chances of having a fulminating disease" (loc. cit.). A similar return to traditional practices occurred in some Native American villages when outbreaks of botulism and gastro-intestinal disturbances resulted from failure to sterilize food during an innovative food preservation program. The villagers responded to the crises by simply resuming the old method of sun-drying vegetables, meat, and fish.

A final example of problems of cultural misunderstanding encountered in such projects includes the dramatic attempt to increase vitamin C intake by encouraging increased consumption of a popular traditional food, the fresh choke cherry (Prunus melanocarpa). Pijoán made the recommendation on the basis of Shoshone custom. Ten days later, a fourteen-year old woman was brought to the area hospital in a coma. Laboratory tests were unsuccessful in revealing the nature of the illness. The patient passed away after twenty-four hours; autopsy revealed huge quantities of fresh choke cherry seeds in the gastro-intestinal tract. The young woman had apparently spent several days in the mountains subsisting on choke-cherries and, in her hunger, had chewed the fresh seeds along with the fruit. Laboratory analysis indicated a breakdown of amygdalin to cyanide. Four similar cases occurred, though the victims were saved because the problem was by then understood (Pijoán 1942a). Pijoán concludes: "We were forced to advise the natives to beware of the seeds, little realizing that in doing so we were actually advising them not to touch the fruit as a whole. In tampering with their culture or advising them to do something which they did not understand, we had defeated our purpose and caused one death" (1944:17).

At about the same time, Oliver (1943) describes two cultures in the British Solomon Islands, their dietaries and the results of attempts to change these. The first group were mountain dwellers, nine-tenths of whose food intake by weight was comprised of taro (*Colocasia esculenta*), with insufficient supplementary calcium, and protein from nuts and animal sources to offset chronic rickets and other nutritional deficiencies. The women of the group were responsible for the planting, harvesting, cooking, and apportioning of the staple. Residence here was matrilocal and land inheritance matrilineal. Taro was the cultural symbol of well-being, and was used as a sacrament on ritual occasions.

In the second culture area, located in the southern part of Bougainville, taro was basic but not an exclusive staple. Sago, bananas, yams, greens, almonds, coconuts, fish, wild game, and pork all contributed to a well-balanced diet. In this culture, where patrilocality exists side by side with matrilocality, the men had taken over the preparation of some of the finer foods and were responsible for the introduction of new plants encountered in their travels about the island. Colonial administration, however, hoped to change the food habits of both groups. Oliver quotes one official: "In both places I handed out packets of seeds to the blighters' chiefs – even told them how to plant them. Warned them that their taro wasn't much good. Up there in the mountains the seeds weren't planted at all. They simply rotted in the chiefs' houses. In the south, they took hold in some places, but not in others" (*ibid.* p. 36).

What mistakes had been made? In the north, the fact had been ignored that, traditionally, women were the taro gardeners. Had this been recognized, the women might have been consulted, and a possible interest in new crops could have been created. Had the official been aware of the extent to which this culture valued taro, he would have avoided belittling it. In the south, the minimal success in introducing new crops was due to the fact that, in some communities, seed accidentally had been given to local leaders whose prestige was sufficient to stimulate a new food fashion. In other communities, tactless errors in the choice of recipients for seed had been made which so piqued the real leaders that none of the latter's followers dared plant the seeds.

In a different cultural context, Graubard (1944) reports how he was able to create an interest in nutrition education among labor unions in the United States during the early 1940's. In approaching the unions, the decision was made to avoid lectures and substitute instead historical anecdote. In Graubard's words: "To begin with, it (the historical approach) was rich in anecdotes which are interesting and novel. Besides, by pointing out how people maintained foolish habits in the past, the road was paved for aiding the audience in suspecting that they too might be blind victims of similar habits. . . . it was found soon enough that historical stories about milk, its uses among primitive tribes, its sources from a variety of animals, et cetera, did more to develop a favorable attitude than any number of discussions about its calcium or riboflavin" (*ibid.* p. 30).

"The first essential step to be taken must be to challenge as few beliefs as possible, provoke no suspicions, but concentrate upon weakening the grip of old belief by attacking the visible bonds which hold it together. In no wise must the impression be conveyed that resisting change by adherence to custom is a sign of stupidity. Rather it must be shown to be a common weakness but unfortunately all too human."

"The scientific truth can be ushered in only toward the end and at that gently and without implying that inability to accept it readily brands one as a half-wit or reactionary. The speed of this final process depends on the nature of the group, on the personality of the teachers, on the success of the preparatory effort of softening up the old beliefs and on many other intangible factors. In addition, special attention should be given throughout the process to the need for building up understanding within the group and the individual to loosen their grip on the old belief or practice, and for gaining enough fortitude to adopt the new one" (*ibid.* p. 30).

Following these guidelines, efforts were successful in overcoming an indifference or resistance to nutrition among various labor unions, and an unexpected cooperation was achieved which reinforced the national defense effort and greatly raised the prestige of labor in the eyes of numerous communities.

From nutrition education in an urban bureaucracy, we go with Apodaca (1952) to a small, Spanish-speaking farming town in New Mexico where, in 1946, a State Agricultural Extension Agent took steps to introduce a higher-yielding hybrid variety of maize. "The agent," Apodaca writes, "moved slowly and carefully, and only after a considerable period of observation and analysis of the specific local situation. He examined all the technical aspects of soil, growing conditions, and existing practices. A real need was felt for the new crop, and he was able to induce farmers to formulate that need among themselves. He utilized local leadership and made no start until the people thoroughly understood what was to be done. He demonstrated procedure and results. It cannot be said that he ignored any of the well-tried, and often-reiterated rules of extension procedure" (*ibid.* pp. 38, 39). But four years later, despite a threefold increase in yield, practically all of the farmers had gone back to the traditional seed corn. The reasons for this slowly came to light. Their wives, the farmers told him, had complained from the first. They did not like the texture of the hybrid maize. The meal made from it was not good for tortillas, and the color was different. Few cared for the flavor. The farmers continued planting the hybrid after the first year in the hope that their wives would grow accustomed to it and, also, because the higher yield provided abundant food for their livestock. After the third year, however, their wives would have no more of the new maize.

What were the errors? In the first place, the importance of food habits had been completely overlooked (especially the organoleptic factors). Also, the opinion of the women in the community should have been consulted. Under the circumstances, quality proved a greater concern than quantity. Upon reflection, the extension agent recalled that some of the farmers had doubts about the hybrid from the beginning. The customary courtesy of

10

these people, who were not accustomed to freely expressing themselves in the presence of "experts" had, however, led the farmers to a feeling that they should not discourage the extension agent's efforts.

Most of the examples showing the need for anthropological expertise in applied nutrition projects relate to programs of change or modification of food habits. Adams (1955), as a case in point, depicts culture in action within a clinical nutrition program carried out in a Central American community in 1951.

In order to ascertain serum levels of various nutrients, it was necessary to take blood samples in the field. One of the major hindrances encountered by the investigating team, however, was local beliefs about blood. As the Native Guatemalan interprets physiology, human blood once lost is not regenerated, and the individual is rendered permanently weaker. One informant told the anthropologist that the villagers simply could not understand why doctors, who claimed to know how to make people well, went around intentionally taking the blood of little children, thus making them weaker. The informant concluded that such doctors could not know very much about making people well. To overcome this difficulty, the anthropologist used the logic of the Native Guatemalan's own thinking: since blood was considered a measure of weakness or strength, predisposed a person to be sick or well, it would follow that the blood could also be a measure of sickness or well-being. Accordingly, the necessity for taking blood samples was explained in these terms. If a person had sick blood, he or she needed curing; if he or she had well blood, this was also important to know (*ibid.* pp. 446-448).

Introducing new ideas (or items) in a culture can have quite unintended results. In 1951, a yellow variety of Cuban maize was introduced into the Yungas and Santa Cruz regions of the Bolivian lowlands. The new maize had many apparent advantages. It grew well in the tropics, matured more rapidly, and had a higher oil content, was less subject to insect attack, and gave a higher yield than local varieties. In addition, it produced a very hard grain, a quality which made its storage easier but which also made it difficult to grind by hand; and local people were unwilling to take the time and trouble involved to haul the new maize to mills in nearby towns. The discovery was made, however, that the new variety was an excellent base for commercial alcohol which fetched high prices. Thus, a seemingly desirable innovation had the effect of reinforcing alcoholism rather than improving diet (Kelly 1959). Here, again, a failure to consider and compare *all* the qualities of the new maize with those of the traditional variety resulted in totally unanticipated consequence for the program planners. The result of the innovation was diametrically opposed to the original goal of the planned change.

Rosenstiel (1954:5) describes how the substitution of cassava for millet in Northern Rhodesia (now Zambia) produced another example of the unforeseen consequences of purposive social action (Merton *op. cit.*). Becuase millet is attacked by locusts and is affected by changes in climate, it is not very satisfactory as a commercial crop. Cassava, though, is much easier to grow and therefore more profitable. In southern Africa, however, millet is the most important indigenous crop, playing a vital role in the social and religious life of the Bantu people, as the basic ingredient of the ubiquitous millet beer. Further, however unsatisfactory it may be as a cash crop, millet is important nutritionally. Because the presence of the zoöphilic tse-tse fly makes cattle raising impossible, meat and milk are absent as sources of dietary fat. Millet, on the other hand, although it contains only small amounts of oil, possesses a greater percentage than cassava. Consequently, nutritional standards were lowered by the enforced change in diet. What is more, when the drinking of millet beer was forbidden by law, the problem of drunkenness developed as the local people were, themselves, obliged to substitute a new brew for the old. Called *skokian* and composed of methylated spirits and other substances which increased the alcohol content quickly, the new drink was not a satisfactory replacement for the milder millet beer. It aroused hostile reaction which, of course, simply created additional administrative difficulties.

Everyone likes a bargain, it is said. But, to the contrary there are those who will say that one should never receive something for nothing. In Chile, powdered milk, when first introduced at mothers' and children's health clinics, was provided without charge to needy families. Yet few mothers would use the milk. They suspected it was of poor quality or even harmful. Being free, it was perceived as valueless. Subsequently, after a nominal charge was made for the milk, and the mothers felt it had value in the eyes of the clinic personnel, the supply could scarcely keep up with the demand.

Sometimes, a change in food habits is well received but proves impractical for ecological reasons. Foster (1962:83) tells of the introduction of the legume, *Phaseolus vulgaris*, into the Helmand Valley of Afghanistan, as an inexpensive protein source for a region where little animal protein is eaten. The new food was liked and grew well; yet, there was resistance to its continued cultivation, because a natural shortage of fuel materials in the Helmand Valley placed a premium on quick-cooking foods. *P. vulgaris* was uneconomical in this regard. Another quicker cooking legume, the black-eyed, or cow pea (*Vigna unguiculata*), was substituted. It cooks in much less time than *P. vulgaris,* has a higher nutritive value, and has proved to be a successful innovation.

Apodaca (*op. cit.*) has shown how organoleptic factors affected the reception of a hybrid maize in a Spanish-speaking community in the United States. Kelly (1958) recounts a similar situation in the Republic of Mexico. Except for a few limited areas, white maize is the general preference among Mexicans for tortilla dough, a mixture of maize meal and water into which a small quantity of pulverized lime is traditionally dissolved. Yellow maize is considered food for animals. By sad coincidence, after cooking, tortillas made from yellow maize become exactly the same color as those made from white maize to which too much lime has been added. Consequently, no woman of the house wants to serve yellow maize tortillas because to do so would damage her reputation as a good cook (*ibid.* p. 206).

Kelly (*ibid.* p. 207) also reports of the prejudice, in many parts of Mexico, against eating cooked greens. "A woman of the house complains," writes Kelly, "that when serving the head of the family a plate of cooked greens, he says indignantly, 'I'm not a rabbit' ". Nevertheless, in this same community, the people of both sexes and of all ages enjoy eating raw carrots and beets. The solution here is not to insist too much on cooked greens; instead, the consumption of raw vegetables which are presently eaten with pleasure, should be reinforced.

The influence of technology on food habits is also strong. The presence or absence of efficient means for obtaining, transporting, processing, storing, and preparing food has a significant effect upon nutrient content and consequently upon nutritional status. Persons working for the improvement of health may make recommendations which are logically valid for a technologically sophisticated society but which cannot be readily followed in a less developed one without threatening traditional patterns. Burgess (1960) writes of an instance. "The Malay woman is usually a good cook. She handles food well, preparing it carefully for cooking with a minimum waste and spending considerable time in blending a variety of seasonings for the curry. Most of the women report using wood as the cooking fuel and boiling and frying as the methods of cooking. In view of the limitations imposed by cooking over an open wood fire, it is understandable that these women are not interested in preparing food in a variety of ways. Food is always cooked in the morning and well in advance of the time of the meal. By mid-day, the first has burnt down, and the house is more comfortable and the food is cool enough to be eaten with the fingers. For many reasons she does not readily accept the suggestion that vegetables should be prepared immediately before they are to be eaten in order to preserve their nutritive value. The Westerner cannot understand why meat and fish are cooked rather hard until he tries to take his food in Malay fashion. The typical Malay dishes, prepared and served in a home where forks and spoons are used, have a texture more nearly resembling that of Western food. But foods that are mushy are disliked by the Kampong women because they are difficult to eat with the fingers. This fact may help to explain their reluctance to prepare purées for weaning infants".

Some problem situations seem to suggest only a few anthropological variables. In others, quite a number of cultural factors are involved, and each must be carefully taken into account. The Chimbu are a case in point.

The Chimbu are subsistence gardeners living in the Eastern Highlands of New Guinea (see Brown 1972, for a general ethnography). Because protein malnutrition in the area has been an important clinical and public health problem affecting chiefly young children, and pregnant and lactating women, an experimental program was designed to introduce peanut butter as a protein supplement to the diet of all Chimbu infants aged six weeks and older.

In planning this program, an assessment was made of favorable and unfavorable factors which would influence food habits and directed nutritional change. On the favorable side, peanuts were a familiar food crop, so that no major adjustments in garden practice were required. In addition, peanuts are popular and eaten as a snack, rather than with any specific meal. They are not a status food, are not included in marriage payments or death exchanges, and have no magico-religious significance. Due to Chimbu concepts of sickness, however, the idea of promoting peanut butter as a "cure" for sick and malnourished infants was avoided. In Chimbu, when there is no obvious cause, illness is attributed to sorcery, an offended ancestral spirit, or failure to observe some ritual practice. Malnutrition, as such, does not seem to be recognized by the Chimbu. The infant who fails to thrive is usually considered to be the victim of malevolent spirits, sorcerers, inauspicious season or some other circumstance, although some Chimbu women know that their capacity for lactation is limited and sometimes relate lactational failure to a previous illness or other misfortune (Bailey 1964:10). On the other hand, the health value of certain foods is a concept congruent with Chimbu belief.

Because the Chimbu hold pigs in high esteem, and because pig fat has a high prestige food value, the decision was made to emphasize the oily nature of peanut butter which it was hoped would be associated with the likeness of the fat.

As far as cultivating peanuts was concerned, there was initial reluctance to give over valuable land used for the cash coffee crop. These difficulties were partially offset by the fact that the Chimbu have a high regard for agricultural workers, because these persons are concerned with one of the most important aspects of life in Chimbu: subsistence gardening. Agricultural personnel, therefore, were able to assist greatly in the peanut butter project by distributing seed and by advising on the best methods of cultivation.

In Chimbu, authority is vested in the male, and his acceptance of an idea is necessary before an extension worker can enlist the participation of the Chimbu mother. And, of course, it was essential to identify locally recognized leaders. A system of Local Government Councils exists as a means for fostering local political cohesion and community development; however, it often occurs that the local Councillor is only a go-between for the real leaders. It was with these "big men" that work was done to organize the peanut houses. These are simple structures, similar to the coffee houses which are centers of great interest, since it is in them that coffee buyers purchase locally-produced coffee crops. Generally, the peanut house is built on or close to the former ceremonial grounds. Members of a lineage or clan section, under the supervision of the recognized leader (or a Councillor) constructed small cane shelters to house a drum-top roasting stove, and a peanut grinder purchased by the people themselves. The fact that the group actually owned and maintained their own grinder contributed largely to their interest in the project (*ibid.* pp. 98-102).

Maximum effort was concentrated on encouraging the concept of peanut

14

butter as a baby food. This was an easy goal because its mushy texture, resembling indigenous weaning foods, made it unsuitable for grown men and women (*ibid*. p. 102). One problem remained. In Chimbu, all food, apart from breast milk is eaten out-of-hand. If a food is soft, such as boiled pumpkin, it is eaten on a leaf removed from a banana tree or other plant. These cultural practices initially militated against the introduction of spoons for feeding peanut butter to the infants. To solve the problem, the peanut butter was shaped into a ball about the size of an egg, before being given to the children. Another method was to spread the peanut butter inside a split banana, sandwich fashion. Both ways facilitated eating out-of-hand. Older infants, being accustomed to a handful of cooked sweet potato, took to the peanut butter ball and nut-butter sandwiches very well (Temgwe 1964:106).

The carefulness with which the infant feeding program in Chimbu was conducted is not characteristic of all programs of directed nutritional change. Although many solutions seem simple in retrospect, they are elusive. This elusiveness increases in direct ratio to absence of understanding of the culture in which the problem occurs.

Brito-Stelling (*n.d. in* Foster 1969: 8,9) also shows how oversight in planning can lead to temporary failure of a program. In order to encourage regular attendance at pre- and post-natal appointments, rural Venezuelan maternal and child health clinics used the inducement of giving free powdered milk to expectant mothers. While increased attendance was observed after several months, pregnancy complications and nutritional levels showed little improvement. A survey was made and the fact came to light that many of the mothers-to-be felt the powdered milk implied that their own breast milk was insufficient. The milk program threatened their image of themselves as women capable of fulfilling the role of motherhood through natural nursing of their infants. Other women in the program perceived as unfair the fact that only the very youngest in their families benefitted from the free milk. These women had developed the practice of exchanging the clinic milk for other foods, and even liquor, thereby assuring that everyone in their families, and especially the husbands, received a share. And the program also had overlooked the usefulness of demonstrating the easiest ways to mix the powdered milk and how it might be combined with other foods. To solve these problems, clinic nurses were instructed to open the tins of milk before distribution, thus making its exchange for other goods more difficult. Careful instructions in mixing and using the milk were incorporated into the clinic program, and prizes were given to the mothers who were the most proficient at the former and inventive at the latter. These remedial steps resulted in the originally anticipated increase in milk consumption and nutritional levels.

The Future of Nutritional Anthropology

The role which anthropological factors play in determining human food behavior and nutritional status has been examined and the effects of ecological variables on food preferences and preparation have been pointed out. We have seen also how efforts to introduce new foods have met with favorable or unfavorable responses, depending to a large extent on the degree of understanding of the cultural background of the client group. We have also tried to show that it is the job of the cultural and social anthropologist to provide the background for the understanding of human behavior necessary to permit desirable social engineering, and that there is good reason to believe that the successful application of nutritional knowledge can be facilitated by close collaboration of nutritionists with specialists in anthropology who have concentrated upon the study of human food habits. In 1943, the Committee on Food Habits observed that "A new science of food habits is developing. This will be a handmaid to, and of equal importance with, the biochemical science of nutrition in efforts for the prevention of disease and facilitating man's progress towards optimum health" (NAS/NRC 1943:3). The series of articles which follows, written thirty-three years later, confirms this prediction.

Foster (1969) notes the decrease in the number of anthropologists employed in technical aid programs by the United States and the various international agencies. At the same time, he comments on the increasing presence of anthropologists (in the United States, at least) in schools of public health, medicine, education, and social welfare, a trend which he feels might offset the former decline in the field of international development (*ibid.* p. 217). And it is true that anthropologists are now venturing afield to learn what they may about the sub-cultures of other scholarly disciplines and are beginning to involve themselves in the study of institutions devoted to the application of knowledge to the solution of problems of basic human welfare. Anthropologists are bringing their awareness of human bahavior to focus upon the problems of program planning and delivery-systems development in a wide range of social service areas, some of which Foster (*op. cit. vide supra*) has enumerated.

The field of nutrition impinges upon the foundations of human health, education, and well-being and offers the anthropologist a wide range of opportunities for collaboration with professionals in both the social and physical sciences (see Suchman 1963:155-174). In a recent series of workshops on applied nutrition, participants recognized this potential in their recommendation that (within university systems) "While respect for individual disciplines should be supported through appropriate administrative structures, opportunity for multidisciplinary majors should be developed" (U.S. Department of Agriculture & The Nutrition Foundation, Inc. 1973:88).

Perhaps no other field promises more possibility for satisfaction to the specialist in nutritional anthropology than does public health which, in the United States, is so highly characterized by its interdisciplinary nature. The role of the anthropologist in public health nutrition programs has been outlined in Dean & Burgess (1962:60-61; 142-145) and ranges from core faculty persons in schools of public health to key positions in institutes of nutrition; and as consultants, survey directors, and ethnographers, at various levels within applied public health nutrition projects. A need, at the governmental level, for specialists with an understanding of food habits, is also made clear (*ibid*. pp. 61; 152, 153). There is, furthermore, in public health, a mature appreciation of the relevance of the socio-cultural aspects of human life to the physical, psychological, and environmental problems which it works to resolve. For the anthropologist, the recognition in public health of the interconnecting nature of its component disciplines makes of it a fully "functionalist" field of academic endeavor.

It seems appropriate to close at this point, with two quotes. The first should be considered in the form of a question, a challenge to the public health nutritionist as well as to the anthropologist. It is taken from Trémolières' (1963:20) article "Nutrition and Public Health":

I made a survey in the *mellah* of a primitive village in the Atlas Mountains. After having examined the children I wished to see, I was invited by the head of the community to his home. I found that he had very little enthusiasm for the possibilities of distributing powdered milk in the village school. He considered this idea bizarre, and almost suspicious. In order to change the subject, I asked him what were his hopes and ambitions, and I saw that the interpreter failed to make clear my question and I realized that these words 'hopes', 'ambitions' had no meaning to my host. But upon leaving his home, he said to me: 'May God give you that which you can best ask for'. This probably was his ambition, and it was I who had no answer. He had thought about this question more profoundly than I had. The concept that one can work to improve one's fate hardly exists in a population where rain and the power of the feudal lord are the Heaven's will, and infinitely more powerful than the endeavors of the poor peasant.

The second quote may be seen as an answer to the first. Where Trémolières closes on a note of little optimism, Teulon's (1966) statement confidently indicates how success in applied nutrition may be achieved through the cooperation of the anthropologist:

Nous voulons surtout insister sur l'importance de l'étude socio-culturelle, qui devra mettre en lumière les racines profondes du problème. Celles auxquelles précisément l'éducation s'attaquera: cette étude est en rapport avec les habitudes, les attitudes et les tabous alimentaires. Seul une socio-ethnologue est en mesure de mener à bien une telle etude et il est dommage que l'on ne fasse pas appel plus souvent à ce spécialiste dont l'intervention pourrait éviter de nombreuse erreurs psychologiques, des fausses routes ou l'utilisation de motivations erronées (Teulon 1966:142). ('Above all, we want to insist on the importance of the socio-cultural investigation, which should shed light on the deep roots of the problem, those roots which must be attacked by education: the socio-cultural investigation puts us in touch with food habits, attitudes, and tabus. Only a social anthropologist is in the position to successfully undertake such an investigation and it is a shame that these experts – whose intervention could obviate numerous psychological errors, false avenues, or the operationalization of erroneous motives – are not called upon more often').

References

Adams, R. N.
1955   A Nutritional Research Program in Guatemala. *In* Health, Culture, and Community. Case Studies of Public Reactions to Health Programs. B. D. Paul and W. Miller, eds. New York: Russell Sage Foundation.
1968   Cultural Aspects of Infant Malnutrition and Mental Development. *In* Malnutrition, Learning and Behavior, N. S. Scrimshaw and J. E. Gordon, eds. Cambridge Massachusetts: MIT Press.

Ashton, E. H.
1939   A Sociological Sketch of Sotho Diet. Royal Society of South Africa. Transactions and Proceedings. 27:147-214.

Atwater, W. O.
1895   Methods and Results of Investigations on the Chemistry and Economy of Food. United States Department of Agriculture. Office of Experiment Stations. Bulletin No. 21.

Bailey, K. V.
1964   Protein malnutrition and Peanut Foods. *In* An Integrated Approach to Nutrition and Society. The Case of the Chimbu. E. H. Hipsley, ed. Report of the Symposium Held at the Thirty-seventh Congress of the Australian and New Zealand Association for the Advancement of Science, 20-24th January. New Guinea Research Unit Bulletin No. 9.

Benedict, F. G., and Steggerda, M.
1937   The Food of the Present-Day Maya Indians of Yucatan. Carnegie Institution of Washington. Publication 436. Contributions to American Archaeology 3:155-188.

Brito, J. C.
1948   La Pelagra y la Extinción de la Civilización Maya. Universidad de San Carlos, Ciudad de Guatemala. Publication Trimestral. 11:87-102.

Brito-Stelling, J.M.
n.d.   Communication. *In* Applied Anthropology. G. M. Foster. Boston, Massachusetts: Little, Brown & Company.

Brown, Paula
1972   The Chimbu: A Study of Change in the New Guinea Highlands. Boston: Schenckman Publishing Company.

Burgess, Anne
1960   Summary of a Report to the Government of the Federation of Malaya on Home Economics. *In* McKenzie (1967). (N.B. This quote is informally documented as being contained in a background paper prepared for the Cuernavaca Conference. Dean & Burgess (1962), which is a partial transcript of the Cuernavaca Conference, contains a list of 15 background papers, on pages 203-204. A paper by Burgess carrying this title is not listed therein.)

Burgess, Anne, and Dean, R. F. A., eds.
1962   Malnutrition and Food Habits. Report of an International and Interprofessional Conference. New York: The Macmillan Company.

Bennett, J. W.
1946   An Interpretation of the Scope and Implications of Social Scientific Research in Human Subsistence. American Anthropologist 48:553-573.

Cassel, J.
1955   A Comprehensive Health Program Among South African Zulus. *In* Health, Culture, and Community, B. D. Paul and W. Miller eds. New York: Russell Sage Foundation.
1957   Social and Cultural Implications of Food Habits. American Journal of Public Health 47:732-740.

De, S. S.
1967 Traditional Foods: Their Present Production and Use. Journal of Nutrition and Dietetics (Coimbatore) 4:331-341.

Dentan, R. ed.
1961 A Preliminary Guide to the Collection of Information on Food Behavior. Final Report. U.S.P.H. Grant No. A-3557. New Haven, Connecticut: Human Relations Area Files.

Evans, D. T.
1973 A Preliminary Evaluation of Tooth Tartar Among the Preconquest Maya at the Tayasal Area, El Peten. American Antiquity 38-489-493.

Fortes, M., and Fortes, S. L.
1936 Food in the Domestic Economy of the Tallensi. Africa 9:237-493.

Foster, F. M.
1962 Traditional Cultures: And the Impact of Technological Change. New York: Harper & Brothers.
1969 Applied Anthropology. Boston, Massachusetts: Little, Brown & Company.

Freedman, R. L.
1971 The State of Food Habits Research in the United States of America. Boletín Bibliográfico de Antropología Americana 33/34:167-193.
1973 Nutrition Problems and Adaptation of Migrants in a New Cultural Environment. International Migration 11:15-31.

Gilks, J. L., and Orr, J. B.
1931 Studies of Nutrition. The Physique and Health of Two African Tribes. Great Britain. Privy Council. Medical Research Council. Special Report Series No. 35. London: His Majesty's Stationery Office.

Goss, A.
1897 Dietary Studies in New Mexico in 1895. United States Department of Agriculture. Office of Experiment Stations. Bulletin No. 40.

Graubard, M.
1944 Nutrition Education in Labor Organizations. Applied Anthropology 3:26-37.

H.R.A.F. (Human Relations Area Files)
1964 Food Habits Survey. New Haven, Connecticut: Human Relations Area Files. 3 volumes. (Available on microfiche from Clearinghouse for Federal Scientific and Technical Information. National Bureau of Standards. Springfield, Virginia, U.S.A. 22151 Order No. AD817 507, 817 508, & 817 509. Cost = $ US 3.00).

Hellman, E.
1936 Urban Native Food in Johannesburg, Africa 9:277-290.

Hipsley, E. H.
1964 An Integrated Approach to Nutrition and Society. The Case of Chimbu. Report of the Symposium Held at the Thirty-Seventh Congress of the Australian and New Zealand Association for the Advancement of Science, 20-24th January. New Guinea Research Unit Bulletin No. 9.

Jenks, E. A.
1900 The Wild Rice Gatherers of the Upper Great Lakes. A Study in American Primitive Economics. United States. Bureau of American Ethnology. Nineteenth Annual Report, 1897. Part Two.

Kelly, Isabel
1958 Cambios en los Patrones Relacionadas con la Alimentacion. Boletín del Instituto Interamericano de Niño (Montevideo) 32:205-208.
1959 La Antrpología, la Cultura y la Salud Publica. La Paz, Bolívia: Institute for Inter-American Affairs, United States Mission to Bolívia. In Foster (1962:85). (Reprinted: 1960. Imprenta del SCISP (Ministry of Public Health and Social Welfare, Lima, Perú).

Klein, R. E., and Yarbrough, C.
1972 Some Considerations in the Interpretation of Psychological Data as They Relat-

ed to the Effects of Malnutrition. Archivos Latino-americános de Nutritión 22:40-48.

Knutsson, K. E., and Selinus, Ruth
1970 Fasting in Ethiopia. An Anthropological and Nutritional Study. American Journal of Clinical Nutrition 23:956-969.

Lee, R. B.
1969 !Kung Bushman Subsistence: An Input-Output Analysis. In Environment and Cultural Behavior. Ecological Studies in Cultural Anthropology. A. Vayda, ed. Garden City, New York: The Natural History Press.

Lewin, K.
1943 Forces Behind Food Habits and Methods of Change. In NAS/NRC (National Academy of Sciences. National Research Council 1943). The Problem of Changing Food Habits. Report of the Committee on Food Habits. 1941-1943. National Research Council. Bulletin 108. Washington, D.C.: National Academy of Sciences.

Malinowski, B.
1944 A Scientific Theory of Culture and Other Essays. Chapel Hill, North Carolina: The University of North Carolina Press.

Margen, S. ed.
1971 Progress in Human Nutrition, Volume 1. Westport, Connecticut: The AVI Publishing Company, Inc.

Maslow, A.
1943 A Theory of Human Motivation. Psychological Review 50:370-396.

May, J. M.
1963 The Ecology of Malnutrition in Five Countries of Eastern and Central Europe: East Germany, Poland, Yugoslavia, Albania, Greece. New York: Hafner Publishing Company.
1965 The Ecology of Malnutrition in Middle Africa: Ghana, Nigeria, Republic of the Congo, Rwanda, Burundi, and the Former French Equatorial Africa. New York: Hafner Publishing Company.
1966 The Ecology of Malnutrition in Central and Southern Europe: Austria, Hungary, Rumania, Bulgaria, Czechoslovakia. New York: Hafner Publishing Company.
1967 The Ecology of Malnutrition in Northern Africa: Libya, Tunisia, Algeria, Morocco, Spanish Sahara and Ifni, Mauretania. New York: Hafner Publishing Company.

May, J. M., and Jarcho, Irma S.
1961 The Ecology of Malnutrition in the Far and Near East: Food Resources, Habits, and Deficiencies. New York: Hafner Publishing Company.

May, J. M., and McLellan, Donna L.
1968 The Ecology of Malnutrition in the French Speaking Countries of West Africa and Madagascar: Sénégal, Guinea, Ivory Coast, Togo, Dahomey, Cameroun, Niger, Mali, Upper Volta, and Madagascar. New York: Hafner Publishing Company.
1970 The Ecology of Malnutrition in Eastern Africa: Equatorial Guinea, The Gambia, Liberia, Sierra Leone, Malawi, Rhodesia, Zambia, Kenya, Tanzania, Uganda, Ethiopia, and the French Territory of Afars and Issas, The Somali Republic and Sudan. New York: Hafner Publishing Company.
1971 The Ecology of Malnutrition in Seven Countries of Southern Africa and in Portuguese Guinea: The Republic of South Africa, South West Africa (Namibia), Botswana, Lesotho, Swaziland, Mozambique, Angola, Portuguese Guinea. New York: Hafner Publishing Company.
1972 The Ecology of Malnutrition of Mexico and Central America: Mexico, Guatemala, British Honduras, Honduras, El Salvador, Nicaragua, Costa Rica, and Panamá. New York: Hafner Publishing Company.

1973 The Ecology of Malnutrition in the Caribbean. The Bahamas, Cuba, Hispaniola (Haiti and the Dominican Republic), Puerto Rico, The Lesser Antilles, Trinidad and Tobago. New York: Hafner Publishing Company.

McArthur Margaret
1960a Report of the Nutrition Unit. *In* Records of the American-Australian Scientific Expedition to Arnhem Land, Volume Two. Anthropology and Nutrition. C. Mountford, ed. Melbourne, Australia: Melbourne University Press.
1960b Food Consumption and Dietary Levels of Groups of Aborigenes Living on Naturally Occurring Foods. *In* Mountford (1960).

McCarrison, R.
1928 Relative Values of the National Diets of Certain Indian Races. Far Eastern Association of Tropical Medicine. Seventh Congress in British India. Transactions. 3:322-323.

McCracken, R. D.
1971 Lactase Deficiency: An Example of Dietary Evolution. Current Anthropology 12:479-517.

McKenzie, J. C.
1967 Sociology as an Aid to Nutrition Change. *In* International Congress of Nutrition. Seventh. Hamburg, 1966. Proceedings. 3:269-275.

Mead, Margaret
1943 The Anthropological Approach to Dietary Problems. New York Academy of Sciences. Transactions. Series II. 5:177-182.

Merton, R. K.
1936 The Unanticipated Consequences of Purposive Social Action. American Sociological Review 1:894-904.

Moore, F.
1964 Methodologic Problems of Cross-Cultural Dietary Research. Journal of the American Dietetic Association 45:418-419.

Mountford, C. P. ed.
1960 Records of the American-Australian Scientific Expedition to Arnhem Land, 1948. Volume Two. Anthropology and Nutrition. Melbourne, Australia: Melbourne University Press.

NAS/NRC (National Academy of Sciences/National Research Council).
1943 The Problem of Changing Food Habits. Report of the Committee on Food Habits. National Research Council. Bulletin 108. Washington, D.C.: National Academy of Sciences.
1945 Manual for the Study of Food Habits. National Research Council. Bulletin 111. Washington, D.C.: National Academy of Sciences.

NRC (National Research Council (Committee on Food Habits).
1944 The Application of Anthropology to Problems of Nutrition and Population. Liaison Session. April 15. (N.B. These minutes were marked 'Not for Publication', on the original typescript, and the comments recorded therein indicated as 'off the record'. The Archives of the National Academy of Sciences has courteously provided a photocopy of same, and granted permission to reproduce portions thereof with the request that the aforementioned qualifications of the material quoted be given).

Oliver, D. L.
1942 A Case of Change in Food Habits in Bougainville, British Solomon Islands. Applied Anthropology 1:34-36.

Paul, B. D. and Miller, W.
1955 Health, Culture, and Community. Case Studies of Public Reactions to Health Programs, New York: Russell Sage Foundation.

Pijoán, M.
1942a Cyanide Poisoning from Choke-Cherry Seeds. American Journal of The Medical Sciences. 204:550-553.

21

1942b Food Availability and Social Function. New Mexico Quarterly Review 12:418-423.
1944 The Importance of a Cultural Approach in Ameliorating Nutritional Defects in the Southwest. *In* NRC (1944).
Pijoán, M., and Elkin, C. A.
1944 Secondary Anemia Due to Prolonged and Exclusive Milk-feeding Among Shoshone Indian Infants. Journal of Nutrition 27 : 67-75.
Price, W. A.
1939 Nutrition and Physical Degeneration. A Comparison of Primitive and Modern Diets and Their Effects. Privately Printed. (Reprinted 1972, Santa Monica, California: Price-Pottenger Foundation).
Ramanamurthy, P. S. V.
1969 Physiological Effects of "Hot" and "Cold" Foods in Human Subjects. Journal of Nutrition and Dietetics (Coimbatore) 6:187-191.
Read, Margaret H.
1938 Native Standards of Living and African Culture Change. Illustrated by Examples from the Ngoni Highlands of Nyasaland. Africa 11 (3).
1964 The Role of the Anthropologist. *In* Changing Food Habits. J. Yudkin and J. C. McKenzie, eds. London: MacGibbon and Kee.
Reh, Emma
1943 Diet and Nutrition of the Papago Indians. United States Department of the Interior. Office of Indian Affairs. Manuscript.
Richards, Audrey Isabel
1932 Hunger and Work in a Savage Tribe. A Functional Study of Nutrition Among the Southern Bantu. London: George Routledge & Sons.
1939 Land, Labor and Diet in Northern Rhodesia. An Economic Study of the Bemba Tribe. Oxford, England: Oxford University Press.
Richards, Audrey Isabel, and Widdowson, Elsie M.
1936 A Dietary Study in Northeastern Rhodesia. Africa 9:166-196.
Rosenstiel, Annette
1954 Long-Term Planning and Its Importance in the Effective Administration of Social Change. Human Organization 13:5-10.
Ross, June Anne
1964 Introducing Peanut Butter into Chimbu Infant Diet. *In* Hipsley (1964).
Shneour, E.
1974 The Malnourished Mind, Garden City, New York: Anchor Press/Doubleday.
Scrimshaw, N. S., and Gordon, J. E., eds.
1969 Malnutrition, Learning, and Behavior. Cambridge, Massachusetts: MIT Press.
Sofer, C., Janis, I., and Wishlade, L.
1964 Social and Psychological Factors in Changing Food Habits. *In* Yudkin and McKenzie (1964).
Spicer, E., ed.
1952 Human Problems in Technological Change. New York: Russell Sage Foundation.
Suchman, E. A.
1963 Sociology and the Field of Public Health. New York: Russell Sage Foundation.
Temgwe, N.
1964 Experiences of Peanut Feeding in the Chimbu District. *In* Hipsley (1964).
Teulon, H.
1966 La situation actuelle et les tendences devolution de l'alimentation des groupes dans les pays economiquement sous developpés et sur envoi de developpement. Seventh International Congress of Nutrition, Hamburg. Proceedings. Volume Four, pp. 654-657.
Trémolières, J.
1963 Nutrition and Public Health. World Review of Nutriton and Dietetics 4:1-24.

1971   Nutrition and Underdevelopment. *In* S. Margen (1971).

United States Department of Agriculture, & The Nutriton Foundation, Inc.
1973   Workshop on the Role of Land Grant Institutions in Applied Human Nutrition, Washington, D.C.: The Nutrition Foundation, Inc.

Vayda, A. P., ed.
1969   Environmental and Cultural Behavior. Ecological Studies in Cultural Anthropology. Garden City, New York: The Natural History Press.

Von Rechenberg, C.
1890   Die Ernährung der Handweber in der Amtshauptmannschaft Zittau. Gedrückt mit Unterstützungen. Königlich Sachsen Gesellschaft der Wissenschaften. Leipzig: Hirzel. (Cited *in* Atwater 1895).

Whiting, Marjorie Grant
1958   A Cross-Cultural Nutrition Survey of 118 Societies, Representing the Major Cultural and Geographic Areas of the World. Ph. D. Dissertation. School of Public Health, Harvard University: Cambridge, Massachusetts.

Woods, C. D., and Mansfield, E. R.
1904   Studies of the Food of Maine Lumbermen. United States Department of Agriculture. Office of Experiment Stations. Bulletin 149.

Yudkin, J. and McKenzie, J. C.
1964   Changing Food Habits. London: MacGibbon and Kee.

Food, Sex and Theory

Kurt W. Back, Department of Sociology, Duke University.

This paper will present a general point of view on the role of food in social organization. It will not be concerned with specific food habits and problems of introducing more rational or efficient ways of food production and consumption. Hunger and its satisfaction, as a fundamental human need, has an equivalent in the fundamental structure of social organization. We shall propose that this is identity, in contrast to the sex drive which is represented by interaction. The general understanding of the place of hunger in human society has mainly theoretical value, but it also provides a start in understanding the acceptance and resistance of change and the motivations of reformers as well as target populations.

One of the main tasks of anthropology is to look at man as a separate species. This is accomplished by viewing the similarities as well as the differences between the human and other species. The common heritage of all animal species can be considered the background of the study of man, while in the foreground we have those features which are peculiar to humanity through its use of technology, language, social forms – in essence, the basic structure of the human race. Various branches of anthropology and other social sciences study the links connecting the common biological heritage and the intricate social patterns of individual communities. Theory in each field can start with individual traits and derive social patterns from them, or can take social patterns as given and infer individual actions from them.

Individual Model

The individual approach begins with the study of needs necessary for the survival of the individual and the species, i.e., drives of the order of hunger and sex. These are common to all animal species; however, the tremendous food surplus which the human race has been able to accumulate makes the human species unique. This surplus allows a great variety in patterns of nutrition as well as in patterns of social behavior associated with eating. In observing these patterns one may overlook the needs for satisfaction of hunger in discussing the different varieties of food rituals. One may trace, for instance, the religious observances of feasts and fasts, food taboos or obligations. In fascination with these variations, one is likely to forget that each pattern must lead to at least minimal physical survival.

The main interest of social anthropological work, however, is in the cultural and social factors which determine a pattern of food consumption. Similarly, the control of sexual and family relationships may be interesting in the way they affect individuals' interpersonal relationships, but we also are dealing here with a drive which exists to assure the survival, as well as the evolutionary adaptation of the species. The working of these drives can be considered a constant, a given, something which is in common with the human species as well as the general biological heritage (Bates, 1967). Different social and cultural patterns connected with basic drives will keep the interest of social scientists engaged while they try to understand differences within human life. Different fields of anthropology, therefore, will trace the influences of prevading drives on human society.

In traditional statements, hunger, leading to survival of the individual, is treated as one of two main drives. The other is sex, leading to preservation of the species. The interest of social scientists in these two drives has led to different approaches. This difference fits into the development we have discussed above, namely, the juxtaposition of foreground and background.

Roughly speaking, the basic assumption is that food and the satisfaction of hunger needs are necessary for the survival of the individual. The social organization must be considered from the point of view of the individual's need. Thus food habits can be judged by rational standards. By contrast, sex and its satisfaction is considered to be the basic drive in the formation of society; and its social effects are considered to be paramount, not its individual consequences. Here cultural relativism is accepted. Thus in general discussions of food, one starts with geographic conditions which determine the availability of foods. Differences exist in climate, soil, and the relative abundance of food materials (meat or vegetable) that limit the capability and formation of the society. Further, we can find social conditions that restrict the consumption of food or lead to certain cultural preferences. In a fundamental study of food, we consider first the biological functions in a genaral ecological framework and then go on to mechanisms of social control.

The standard treatment of sex, however, begins from the opposite direction; it starts with a discussion of different patterns of family formations, of permission and prohibition of sexual relations and of the effects of these patterns on social organizations, symbolic representations and power relationships. The immediate social importance of sexual relations is taken as given and is little connected to its biological conditions, importance of the drive, and its possible consequences in evolutionary development. Little consideration has been given to satisfaction and variations of the sex drive itself.

A complementary relationship between hunger and sex discussed in most social science writing may be a function of the environmental control by the human race in general, or at least in those societies somewhat removed from subsistence level. The different point of view which anthropologists and other social scientists take toward the manifestation of the satisfaction of these

25

drives may be simply an exaggerated picture of the general cultural attitudes towards them in advanced civilizations; that is, anthropologists reflect the attitudes of their own societies. In this essay we shall attempt to show how food and hunger can also determine basic structures of society. This point of view might be helpful in better control and exploitation of existing food resources, but we must also recognize that the relation between food and sex may correspond to an actual difference in their relation between biology and society.

An example of this implicit hierarchy is presented in the framework of psychoanalytic theory. The attitude toward food in psychoanalytic theory is to subordinate it to the over-riding importance of sexual expression. Psychoanalytic theory acknowledges only that a need for food is the child's first need. It is immediately tied up with sucking and the child's relationship to his mother; but this relation is immediately interpreted sexually, and nursing leads to the oral erotic stage. The very primacy of the food need makes it inferior. The oral stage must be passed through to attain higher, more important stages: first the anal, more removed from food, then the genital, which is purely interested in sex. The personality of the child during the oral stage is interested in food and drink, and the desire for only that is considered infantile behavior. This hierarchy is also preserved in interpretation of neurotic and symbolic expressions. Food, starvation, and so on might symbolize corresponding sexual problems and failures, but not vice versa.

Some of the extremes to which this orientation can lead is shown in the case reported by Fenichel (1945). A patient in analysis reported a great amount of food imagery and associations. After several weeks' analysis, which discussed the possible meaning of this preoccupation, it was learned that the patient had trouble paying for his analysis and was practically starving himself to do so. Overlooking such a basic possibility could only occur in a society where actual hunger is not a primary need.

There is a curious reluctance in this framework of thought to accept hunger as the immediate and primary cause. Even cultural studies, which are closest to being concerned with the influence of hunger on the patterning of society (e.g., Du Bois 1944; Kardiner 1945), use the original hunger experience in a sublimated fashion. In the society where children are systematically exposed to harm, the inferences of this deprivation within the Freudian framework are shown to lead mainly to a feeling of abandonment and to a particular relationship to the parents, but not to any relationship to eating behavior. The primary inference of hunger on individual feeling symbolizations and reactions, as well as on interpersonal relations, is best shown in some incidences of immediate starvation which occurred as accidents or as part of research studies. In one of the more extensive studies, the Keys studies in Minnesota (1950), we can see the direct influence of hunger on dreams, hallucinations and sensations, and how hunger by itself can influence the different symbolizations of life. There is evidence that one can trace the influence of food and hunger on the individual psyche and from that, on a society; however, there is a tendency, also represented in social science theory, to consider this influence only as mediated through other symbolism, mainly sexual-interpersonal. However, the psycho-dynamic orientation represents drives connected with food as mainly individual and of little social consequence, while social relations are seen as influenced more by sexual drives.

Social Model

When society is taken as a given characteristic of humans, again the question arises as to the place of food in society. Here food generally fares better: eating patterns and family formation are given equal weight.

The structural approaches, which can be taken as representative of the social point of view, treat food as an important problem in itself. Levi-Strauss, for instance, has considered the use of fire and the preparation of food as the main step separating nature from culture. He believes that diverse ways of preparing food represent different ways of relating nature and culture. Lévi-Strauss states that food and sex are of coordinate importance to social organization, sexual and ritual distinction. While his original work, which establishes his theory, was an analysis of kinship structures (Lévi-Strauss 1949), his later work – the large-scale analysis of myth – discusses the patterns inherent in the preparation and consumption of food (Lévi-Strauss 1964-75). Structuralists, of course, are less interested in the nature of biological drives than in the basis of human categorization, and they take sexual organization as a fundamental principle fully as important as the organization for food collection and consumption.

In a sense, classification of food is shown in the theory as man's first task. Lévi-Strauss believes that one of the main achievements of mankind in the creation of culture in the Neolithic age was the categorization of all plants and animals according to their usefulness. This categorization has been so thorough that, since that time, there has been scarcely an addition to domesticated animals or cultivated plants or even new discoveries of edible sources. This intellectual feat was accomplished in conjunction with the development of social forms: family, tribal and political units. The consistent organization of prohibited and permitted foods, as well as of social relations, is simply a device to ease the effort in understanding the surrounding world by applying the same system to every context. It could be argued in this context that social forms are developed to correspond to the natural forms and not vice versa.

The expressive importance of food, food ritual, and food avoidances occurs not only in less developed societies, which Lévi-Strauss describes as dominated by the "savage mind" (Lévi-Strauss 1966). So-called rational dietary procedures also are expressed in current social structure. Mary Douglas (1966) has shown, for instance, a classification system designed according to what is "good" food and what is "unhealthy" food. This classification may later be rationalized through scientific findings. The rise and decline of food fads dependent on much publicized recent medical findings may be a case in point and can be studied as ritual. Structural patterns are shown also to lead to arbitrary decisions, which might look like personal whims. What constitutes a meal and what is the proper sequence for a meal shows an invariable pattern which is justified more by a feeling of rightness than by any other rational explanation.

Eating is a patterned activity, like language; and grammatical categories are quite constant in a society. English eaters consider the minimum structure for a proper meal to be one stressed (main) course and two unstressed courses (side dishes). This is shown in the meat with two vegetables, pudding with cream and biscuits, or even the canape with a cereal base, cheese and meat. By contrast, the French meal consists of a crescendo of savory dishes, climaxed by the main course, followed by a decrescendo of sweets, from chesse to coffee (Douglas 1973).

The Field of Nutritional Anthropology

Nutritional anthropology has a wider reach and greater unity than one would expect by looking at specific problems in different societies. We have considered two different ways in which theories have tried to integrate hunger and eating into studies of specific situations. In trying to build a hierarchy or a sequential developmental system of drives, most dynamic psychology led by psychoanalysis has subordinated hunger (considered an egotistical drive) to sex, which as a drive establishes interpersonal relations in society. On the other hand, structural theories view food in a different manner; they see it as a code which can be used to decipher other features of the society. Structuralists often go to the opposite extreme from psychoanalysis by considering societies and individuals in their relation to food as a purely cultural and social phenomenon.

Concentrating on the food drive itself, we must take into account the characteristics of the drive itself and the biological nature of man's relation to food as well as the possible social manifestations. By considering nutritional anthropology as a topic in itself, we may be able to impose a unity on the different manifestations of hunger and thereby study it in different social and cultural conditions.

There are some distinct traits of the hunger drive in its relation to human activity which become important in considering its cultural effects. Once we accept the obvious necessity of food supply and the fact that it originally determines or at least establishes limits on the development of material culture, there are several aspects which can be considered. The fact that man is omnivorous makes the human species adaptable to many environments. In contrast to other species, man does not have a particular niche, but has been able to adjust to almost all habitants on the globe even before extensive trading could augment food supply. In addition, the possibility of preparing surplus food has made human culture as we know it possible by permitting activities other than those for pure survival.

Control of the food supply as virtually a pre-condition of the development of human culture is just the characteristic which has given food its ubiquitous but modest place in the background. Because of its importance it has become intertwined with many other human activities and, therefore, is seldom considered a cultural activity in its own right. Mores about eating are part of religious and moral standards. Seemingly inrrational refusal of certain foods can be a characteristic of the human species. Other species act directly to the food stimulus. A case has been made for this view in a philosophical novel by Vercors (1953). Eating habits also define social relationships and the regulation of social activity. Through rules of dietary restraint, fear of pollution, or direct prohibition of people eating together, eating ritual has effectively separated human groups. Commensality may be the most important basis of human associations (Darlington 1969).

Another aspect of man's relation to hunger and food is the physical expression of its effect. Overindulgence in food, lack of it, and dietary deficiency, when occuring in the past or currently, leave a mark on a person. Violation of some rules on food consumption become immediately visible. Again, in comparison with the sex drive, we can realize that lechery does not leave as obvious a mark on a person as gluttony. And thus, moral judgment of a person's character can be easily made in relation to eating habits (Maddox, Back, and Leiderman 1968).

The outline of nutritional anthropology and eating can be found in this description of the effects of the hunger drive: the characteristics being its pervasiveness and its intermeshing with most other activities and institutions as well as its immediate effects on appearances and actions of people. It is this pervasiveness which has kept it in the background, yet it is an almost universal framework of all human activity. We can also define the hunger drive as an important ingredient for individual identity. The necessary satisfaction of hunger for survival and the visibility of overindulgence will show the greatest effects on self-perception of others. It may be that an understanding of the importance, especially the cultural importance of eating patterns, can be found in the interrelation which they have with individual identity. We shall trace a few of these possibilities.

Food and Identity

The distinction between a background and foreground position, in the effect of hunger and food, corresponds to two ways in which we can see the importance of food in human society. The first approach is an ecological, cultural position; it takes food and food production as an independent variable and shows its effects by some social conformations. Studies of this kind show how climate, soil condition, similar factors lead to certain patterns of agriculture and food production, which in turn lead to certain kinds of social or-

29

ganization and certain rituals which conform to the improvement of food production or adjustment of certain shortages. These studies may include such general distinctions as the fact that a hunting society can be nomadic while a society which raises grain must at least stay for one complete growing period in the same place. As another example, it can be shown that agriculture dependent on large irrigation projects is also dependent on the political-authoritarian structure because of the coordination of human labor involved (Wittfogel 1957). Others may trace the effects of specific and different kinds of food sources on complicated social interaction such as food rituals in New Guinea (Vayda 1969), or the fact that the use of wheat and rye which exhausts the soil will lead to a system where certain fields will lie fallow in alternating years, a situation conducive to the raising of cattle. Thus, the European countries which did concentrate on wheat and rye became great cattle raisers and meat consumers. Meat made it possible then to store relatively high food value in small spaces and thus made far-reaching navigation and exploration possible. This then assured or at least helped the pervasive influence of European culture on the entire globe (Braudel 1973). Effects of this kind can be multiplied and be shown in the effect of such foods as of the potato in Ireland or of the breadfruit in the West Indies.

A second approach may take food as the dependent variable. One does not look at the conditions in which food production constrains human action. Availability of more than sufficient food for survival is considered as given. The scientists' interest is in the choice of food and in the consequences of these choices. Nutrition becomes an assertion of identity.

We are led to the fact that, socially, the importance of the selection of food and ways of stilling the hunger drive are most intimately connected with the definition of identity. All the characteristics of hunger and eating we have discussed point in that direction. The literal as well as the symbolic meaning of eating, of incorporating alien matter and changing it into part of oneself, gives one indication of the meaning of eating. It is easy to identify oneself and others by what one eats. Some people believe that the character of a food animal will be transmitted to the eater: eating a lion's heart will give courage or a rabbit will give fertility. Even cannibalism is explained by a desire to acquire the slain enemies' strength. Although this may not be literally accepted in many societies, some indirect beliefs, based on some half-understood characteristics of the food, are still prevalent. Secondly, the amount of food consumed and the attitude of the sheer enjoyment of the quantity are important components of identity, which the psychoanalyst expresses as the oral character, although it can be considered in this way without any reference to psycho-sexual development. We can also distinguish some social attitudes toward food. Hilde Bruch (1957) gives one example based on Veblen's theories (1912) which shows the possibilities of this theoretical approach. Within the lower class, for example, the abilities to secure enough food and the resulting strengths promoted by sufficient food have a great positive value. Hence in this group, attention to food in quantity and resulting robustness of food consumed in quantity will be approved. The middle class reacts to lower-class values in its effort to show that it is not constrained by economic conditions and thus emphasizes the slimmer figure. It also emphasizes "dainty" foods, diets, slimming, and everything which shows that quantity of food is a matter of course and physical strength is no more an economic asset. The upper classes, however, do not have to complete in either direction. They know that they can afford food for strength and that they don't need to show in their figure that they do not have to do physical labor. Therefore, they eat heartily what they like.

A whole theory of stereotypes can be built up about indulgences in food and the resulting prototypes: the picture of the dour puritan and the jolly fat man have even been validated in some public opinion research (Stapel 1947-48). We must realize, however, that there may be a relationship between excessive or deficient interests in food and some personal characteristics. The reaction to the hunger drive is so visible in its effects that it is bound to have some social significance in the assignment of identity to the individual. Identity becomes, therefore, of paramount importance.

A third point lies in the fact that in almost all societies, eating is essentially a social activity. The way in which food is prepared and served, the food people eat together, the food they do not eat in companionship – all express the ways in which individuals in different societies project their identities. Different preferences in the preparing of food, different preferences and rejections of certain foods give an identity, not only in the simple sense of incorporation but in the sense of demanding attention in various social circumstances. In individual development it is recognized that the easiest way for a child to demand attention is by rejecting food or at least certain foods, and this pattern may exist throughout society. Adherence to a diet gives a person a certain aura and forces other people to at least show some concern. If the diet can be justified by some religious, ethical, or rational statements, then the social function of food becomes even more apparent. Sartre has pointed out in *The Portrait of the Anti-Semite* (1946) that it is easier to establish an identity expressing dislikes and rejection than by attraction or positive identification. The demarcation of self is quickly and best established by maintaining and exhibiting some contrast between oneself and others.

In studies of social movement and the formation of sects and dissident groups, the role of food cannot be underestimated. In adhering to some dietary rules, what to eat, when to eat, or when not to eat, groups maintain control over their members. They also require members to deviate from the general population when they venture outside their own group. This behavior then is one of the most effective ways of assuring adherence to special group codes. Vegetarianism, which has recently attracted a variety of individuals and been intimately connected with several modern social movements (Barkas 1975) might serve as an example. It is hard to find a common denominator among these groups, except that they are all in some way intent on establishing a difference and attracting attention to it. A more recent phenomenon seems to be the fad for "natural foods," which often corresponds to some political and social dogma and thereby serves to bring adherents together. Other current varieties of diets and food fads are ways of establishing solidarity with other people by fasting or refusing certain foods. Thus, there seems to be a continuous tradition of establishing group memberships through eating from the totemic feast of the past to the present day.

We can look at the development of national cuisines in searching for larger units for social significance of food. This depends on a variety of conditions: available food, as well as preferences, and the social organization for preparing and eating the food. The essence of a national cuisine, of course, is the fact that it becomes the "normal" food for a group. It is not recognized by its practitioners as an assertion of individuality. Like other social patterns, this is taken as given by members of the community, and only deviations from the norm are perceived as such. Recognition of national food and interest in it then correspond to a more cosmopolitan outlook. And this occurs when different groups come into contact with one another, as in metropolitan areas.

Food follows the development of ethnicity in the United States, as first sketched by Oscar Handlin (1951). National consciousness of immigrant groups developed in American cities, not in their European home lands. In Europe a peasant had only the identity of his community but no consciousness as such of being Polish, or Italian, or so on. Recognition of larger differences gave immigrants from different communities a sense of national solidarity in American cities. However, under those conditions, the development of national consciousness also includes the possibility of living closer to other nationalities. Thus, the urban-industrialized metropolitan society has led to an awareness of ethnic identity as well as a cosmopolitan consciousness. This social development of ethnic consciousness and cosmopolitan integration are also a part of the renewed interest in national and international cooking. There is also a great interest in correct national cuisine. Such concern defines not only the practitioner's identity; it also includes interest in a variety of national cuisines, corresponding to the multi-ethnic city. The cosmopolitan gourmet, however, becomes an attribute of a certain class, trying to distinguish himself consciously from the rest of the population which keeps unconsciously to its local food. Interest in the variety of foods from different sources corresponds to other patterns of sociability in a rapidly mobile middle-class group. We may date this whole pattern as starting around the beginning of the nineteenth century (Smith 1974). Food preferences and patterns of sociability gave a society its expression of identity.

We have stressed some of the food habits and rituals in current Western society in order to show their social importance and pervasiveness. People concerned with solving problems of global food needs and of hunger have found themselves frustrated by apparently unreasonable food requirements in other cultures. It is easy and common to adopt a curious intolerance in this regard, which contrasts with relatively open acceptance of variations in sexual behavior. There is in general a tendency to accord more respect toward differences in sexual patterns of other individuals and cultures than toward corresponding differences in eating habits. Where a social pattern is considered to be completely instrumental – and hence rational – less tolerance is shown. Thus, it may be exasperating for a relief worker in famine conditions to be thwarted by the rejection of perfectly nutritious and safe food. The irrationality of starving rather than eating unfamiliar food is quite apparent but may be deeply human. Therefore, it is important to stress the identity function rather than the survival function of food and to demonstrate the role of food in its total social framework. Food gives identity even in modern society which supposedly recognizes only a biochemical assessment of nutrition. As we have previously pointed out, patterns of nutrition have important aspects of identity. Further recognition and study of these patterns offers a more consistent theoretical model for the social anthropology of nutrition which may be unexpectedly helpful in many contexts.

References

Barkas, Janet
1975 The Vegetable Passion. New York: Scribner.
Bates, Marston
1967 Gluttons and Libertines; Human Problems of Being Natural. New York: Random House.
Braudel, Fernand
1973 Capitalism and Material Life 1400-1800. New York: Harper and Row.
Bruch, Hilde
1957 The Importance of Overweight. New York: W. W. Norton.
Darlington, Cyril D.
1969 The Evolution of Man and Society. New York: Simon and Schuster.
Douglas, Mary T.
1966 Purity and Danger; An Analysis of Concepts of Pollution and Taboo. New York: Praeger.
1972 Deciphering a Meal. Daedalus 101:61-82.
Du Bois, Cora A.
1944 The People of Alor; A Social-Psychological Study of an East Indian Island. Minneapolis: University of Minnesota Press.
Fenichel, Otto
1945 The Psychoanalytic Theory of Neurosis. New York: W. W. Norton.
Handlin, Oscar
1951 The Uprooted; the Epic Story of the Great Migrations that Made the American People. Boston: Little, Brown.
Kardiner, Abram
1945 The Psychological Frontiers of Society. New York: Columbia University Press.
Keys, Ancel
1950 The Biology of Human Starvation. Minneapolis: University of Minnesota Press.
Levi-Strauss, Claude
1966 The Savage Mind. Chicago: University of Chicago Press.
1969 (orig. 1949) The Elementary Structures of Kinship. Boston: Beacon Press.
1964-1974 Mythologiques. 4 vols. Paris: Plon.

Maddox, George L., Back, Kurt W., and Leiderman, Veronica R.
1968   Overweight as Social Deviance and Disability. Journal of Health and Social Behavior 9:287-298.
Sartre, Jean Paul
1946   Portrait of the Anti-Semite. New York: Partisan Review.
Smith, Thomas S.
1974   Aestheticism and Social Structure: Style and Social Network in Dandy Life. American Sociological Review 39:725-744.
Stapel, Jan
1947-48   The Convivial Respondent. Public Opinion Quarterly Winter: 524-529.
Vayda, Andrew P. (ed.)
1969   Environment and Cultural Behavior; Ecological Studies in Cultural Anthropology. Garden City, N.Y.: Natural History Press.
Veblen, Thorstein
1912   The Theory of the Leisure Class; An Economic Study of Institutions. New York: Viking.
Vercors (pseud.), Jean Bruller
1953   You Shall Know Them. Boston: Little, Brown.
Wittfogel, Karl A.
1957   Oriental Despotism; A Comparative Study of Total Power. New Haven: Yale University Press.

An Alternative to Nutritional Particularism

Dorothy J. Cattle, Department of Anthropology, The University of New Mexico.

Introduction

Nutritional problems of all dimensions have been the object of considerable scientific and social research conducted by diverse disciplines. This disciplinary diversity includes medical specialities, industrial, technical, and commercial concerns, consumer-oriented and public health interests, governmental and international agencies, and sociocultural, economic, and psychological fields. Within each separate sphere of interest, there is a general tendency to consider only a narrowly delimited set of nutritional problems. For example, the discipline of economics commonly focuses on nutritional problems of food production; price policies and implications; distribution, transportation, or marketing networks; and income and demand trends. Other examples of specialized foci can be readily cited. What emerges from a more lengthy recitation is a realization of the complexity of the subject matter and the multiplicity of particularistic perspectives. Such a situation exists even when the disciplinary field is limited to anthropology and nutrition.

In the following discussion, the current trend in nutritionally-related research is characterized as particularistic. Particularism is viewed as a perspective, an activity, and as a research result. Using this tridimensional viewpoint, it is noted that particularism fails to generate interdisciplinary cooperation; produces discrete, usually disconnected bodies of data; and results in "low-level" generalizations which lack potential for further development. In general, particularism as a dominant trend is inimical to theoretical development. Three underlying assumptions and attitudes of particularistic research are discussed. The first is labeled Western standards and cultural bias. It is suggested that the discipline of anthropology can offer considerable expertise in the recognition of cultural bias, in the study of the possible consequences of imposing Western standards and solutions on other sociocultural systems, and in the imaginative revision and rethinking of applied approaches. The two other underlying attitudes are institutional and disciplinary rivalries and advocacy and research *versus* application. Such underlying assumptions and attitudes are generally counterproductive to research and applied goals.

The adaptive model is proposed as a generally relevant alternative to the current particularistic research situation. The model presented here is assembled from four processes: biological, evolutionary, ecological, and socio-cultural. Process is defined and examples of the four are listed. It is noted that the processual categories are interrelated and refer back to the concept of adaptation and general evolutionary theory. A brief research example congruent with the proposed model is presented. The complexity of nutritional problems requires sustained analysis within a conceptual-theoretical framework which allows the organization and integration of diverse empirical data and incorporates the dynamic relationships of multiple variables, mechanisms, and processes of change. Explanatory synthesis of contributions from the various disciplines involved in nutritional research is an important goal which warrants greater attention.

Current Research Trend: Particularism as Perspective

Particularism as a perspective is characterized by special attention to disciplinary interests; as a research activity, it involves documentation of specific or unique items of information. As a research result, particularism emphasizes atheoretical propositions. In the first instance, a particularistic perspective fails to generate interdisciplinary cooperation, the development of which is necessary in the study and resolution of applied problems. Reduplication of research efforts and compartmentalization of information are frequent results of such a perspective.

In the second instance, particularistic documentation of information often produces a rich but discrete and disconnected corpus of data (Manners and Kaplan 1968: 3,7). The importance of such information cannot be evaluated or appreciated in a conceptual or theoretical vacuum. Furthermore, recognition of the importance or the usefulness of such discrete data may be dependent upon other bodies of data or advances in other disciplines. The relationship between scientific progress and a theoretical framework was pointed out in the volume *Biology and the Future of Man* (Handler 1970):

In general, science progresses by organizing observations that can fit on the conceptual framework and allow its further extension. Progress can be rapid when the conceptual framework is extensive and general enough in character to accommodate different kinds of observations, and when new observations can be made rapidly. Without such an intellectual framework, without the tools and methodology to make appropriate observations, knowledge grows slowly and only by accident. ... medicine has achieved success by outright empiricism, but the returns have been relatively poor and the price high (1970: 628).

The fruitfulness of nutritional research is dependent, in a similar way, on theoretical advances. These advances do not preclude refinements of data-gathering techniques or expansion of empirical observations. However, the latter should not proceed within the limitations of the various nutritionally-related specialties while conceptual advances are held in abeyance. Furtherance of nutritional understanding depends on the creative synergy of data and theory. Finally, the conclusions offered by particularistic research are

36

usually low-level or "localized" generalizations which can be characterized as repetitive and unexciting.

Particularism as Assumptions and Attitudes

There are several major underlying assumptions and attitudes that tend to perpetuate nutritional particularism. These preconceptions permeate, to a greater or lesser extent, all of the disciplines engaged in nutritional research. Three of these attitudes are discussed below. An awareness of this underlying complex and its implications is necessary for the further development of nutritional and anthropological research.

1) Western standards and cultural bias
2) Institutional and disciplinary rivalries and advocacy
3) Research *versus* application

1) Western Standards: Western standards are the criteria which are used to measure or assess such concepts as progress, efficiency, and well-being. The resulting "yardsticks" utilize Western populations as the exemplars and/ or as the bases of comparison. This utilization may be subtle or explicit.

Western standards and cultural bias are evident in research designs, methodologies, conclusions, and recommendations. For example, conclusions which include labels such as "technologically backward," "primitive sanitary conditions," "ignorance," "lack of motivation," and the like, have been reached by using Western standards for comparison and are often indicative of explicit or implicit ethnocentricism. Proposed recommendations that are based on such conclusions also include these prejudices. If such recommendations are then formalized into applied projects and implemented, this underlying assumption and attitude is perpetuated.

Examples can also be drawn from within the boundaries of several disciplines. Economics applies Western standards in discussions of economic or development progress, agricultural efficiency, quality and well-being (i.e., living standards) and so forth. Technology (largely Western) and technical solutions receive much attention, reemphasizing the Western tenet that more complicated and sophisticated technology will rescue our species from any dilemma we produce. Western standards and cultural bias are also apparent in the educational fields, including nutritional education. Institutional structures and organization, educational standards and curricula have been exported mainly by Western countries and imposed on very different sociocultural systems.

Similarly, the medical profession has been generally uncritical of this underlying attitude in its utilization of Western standards for medical training and curricula. Western medical training is often biased toward specialization and professionalism as opposed to more general perspectives and paraprofessional alternatives. Expertise in nutrition and its interrelationships with other fields is not possessed by the majority of Western doctors and yet, the medical profession has been in the front ranks in the design of health care delivery systems for non-Western countries. However, M.D. expertise and this forefront position are beginning to be questioned, criticized, and challenged by medical personnel and others in Third World countries and in industrialized nations which are facing critical food problems. A well-known contributor to nutritional research, D. Jelliffe, voiced his criticism as follows:

... the modes of delivering maternal and child health in developing countries are impossible. They are ludicrous. They have been imported from elsewhere and are being questioned even in the countries from which they have been imported. These models depend on expensive staff, on costly hospitals, on electronic gadgetry, and so forth (1973: 46).

Explicit recognition of cultural bias and the possible consequences on imposing Western standards on other sociocultural systems is precisely the area where anthropology can offer more expertise than any other discipline. Other fields have called upon anthropologists to contribute sociocultural information (György and Kline 1970) but have been slow to realize the broader contribution that anthropologists can make to nutrition and applied research.

2) Institutional Rivalry: Mohamed A. Nour in his summary of a paper presented by Barg (1973: 49-69), noted this point very clearly:

Because of its rather diffuse nature, nutrition has become, as it were, the baby of several foster parents. The doctor, the agriculturalist, the sociologist, the economist, and the educator rightly wish, each from his own vantage point, to contain nutrition within his respective institutional domain. The policymaker and the planner find this an unappealing situation of nebulous dimensions; as a result meager resource funds are apportioned to nutrition and it is fragmented among executing units at different governmental ministries (1973: 87).

Nour describes the vicious circle of limited funding and rivalry among disciplines for the available funds. Such meager funding is sometimes viewed as tokenism and the reaction of nutrition disciplines is to limit the scope of nutritional activities (Berg and Muscat 1973: 253). The circle is then completed with the next allocation of limited funds. To break such a circle, the disciplines investigating applied nutritional problems must put interdisciplinary nutritional concern first and foremost and institutional rivalries and concepts of professional prestige in the background. In the arena of prestige peddling, influential disciplines, of which anthropology is not one, usually end up acquiescing to politics and bureaucracy; that is to say, the practicalities of the arena often pressure these disciplines to produce quick and visible results. The discipline which "wins" because of its prestige or political influence is making a contribution which is of limited value to both nutritional research and to the firm establishment of national-level recognition of the importance of nutrition and related areas.

38

Anthropology has not been a strong opponent in disciplinary rivalries occurring within applied nutrition research. On the other hand, neither has it been a strong mediator in such disputes. It is my contention that this rivalry and particularistic advocacy is in part due to the lack of a conceptual or theoretical framework or orientation which would provide the basis for integrating the contributions of the diverse disciplines involved in nutritional research and applied problems. Without such a framework, the immediate situation seems to be that analytical problems are "fractured into so many pieces and parts that the scientific domain becomes a Balkanized region of research principalities" (Dubin 1969: 68). In the development of a theoretical framework, the establishment of effective, productive interdisciplinary collaboration merits serious consideration. Of course, interdisciplinary research teams and programs are nothing new, but have often faltered. Nutritional researchers are prone to call for an interdisciplinary approach and then leave it at that.

3) Research *versus* Appplication: Research and application are often separate entities competing for finite resources. Part of this separation and competition is institutionalized. The dichotomy is perpetuated by governments, international agencies, professional associations, publishing enterprises, and academic institutions. Differential prestige accorded to research and application also promotes the continuation of the separate but unequal status of these two entities. In the current climate of pressure to understand and solve human health problems, attention should not be focused primarily on determining the "lowest common denominator of discourse and mutual understanding" (Dubin 1969: 67) which may serve as the link between research and application. Rather, attention should be directed to the development of an overarching or general framework which includes both research and application. In addition, rather than homogenizing the diversity of research problems, goals, disciplinary expertise, and so forth, a shared framework would allow for systematic coordination, critical review, and exploitation of this diversity.

It is, in part, the underlying assumptions and attitudes discussed above that are influential in nutritional research. Investigators and planners have been slow to realize that many standards are culturally-based, not impartial criteria of measurement. Dr. Halfdan Mahler, Director-General of WHO, commented in a recent speech in Geneva that "unselective transfer" of such standards and the programs which incorporate them has resulted, for example, in financial and application difficulties and has even been counterproductive. Disciplinary rivalries have prevented the development of "a systematic means of coming up with what will probably be the best possible range of program solutions" (Berg and Muscat 1973: 271), and the most effective use of available data. As Berg and Muscat strongly pointed out: "To the extent that activities exist today in the field of nutrition, they more often than not are the result of the persistence and persuasiveness of the project advocate rather than of a thoughtful look at total needs and alternatives to meet these needs. . . a government interested in attacking the problem [malnutrition] in any short-term time-frame will have to think in broader scope than it has to date" (1973: 271). Not only will the disciplines involved in nutrition research have to integrate their activities and broaden their perspectives, especially in the areas of basic research and program design, but will also have to re-examine the implicit or explicit assumptions which underlie their fields. The discipline of anthropology can be effective in evaluating the use and challenging the abuse of Western standards and in pointing out attendant cultural bias. Anthropology can also contribute sociocultural information, but this need not be its central or only contribution to nutritional research and applied programs. Input from anthropology can and should be included in the areas of research perspectives and design, and the planning process, including evaluation of applied programs. Anthropologists can also be active in proposing alternatives to the current nutritional research situation, alternatives which would reverse the particularistic trend and lead to the development of a conceptual or theoretical framework relevant to all the disciplines involved in such research.

Theoretical Base

This section is an initial attempt directly to face the problems which were recognized above, and the general topic of nutrition and man. It is suggested that a general model is needed. This need is most adequately met by the adaptive model. The author assumes no credit for originating this model; the written stimulus of Alland (1967) is hereby acknowledged. In the process of writing this section, I made an unexpected discovery of a paper by Boyden (Boyden 1970: 190-209) which bears directly on the perspective taken here and lends support to the ideas presented. The value of the following discussion perhaps rests in its presentation within the context of applied research involving nutrition and anthropology. Useful references include Sahlins (1968); Dubos (1965); Boyden (1970); and Alland (1966).

The Adaptive Model – General Introduction: "The capacity to adapt to changing conditions is an essential property of living matter, and the fate of species in evolution and of individual organisms in their life times is determined largely by the degree of effectiveness of their adaptive processes" (Boyden 1970: 190). There are only two fates: to exist or to become extinct. "According to the Shorter Oxford Dictionary, 'adaptation' means 'the process of modifying so as to suit new conditions.' " Its use is restricted "to those changes which take place in populations or individual organisms that render them better suited to the environment and better able to cope with the conditions of life" (Boyden 1970: 190). As Cohen (1968: 9) points out, "adaptation never occurs in the abstract but only in relation to specific habitational pressures and challenges" (see Alland [1967: 125] for a similar statement). Freeman (1970: 214) has called adaptation "the master concept" or "a unifying concept." It is unifying in several respects. It encompasses all of life, all living systems. It is not bounded by culture nor specific to man. It directs attention to the interrelationships between living organisms and between systems of living organisms which share the same fates. The concept encompasses "all of the main determining variables" and parameters in "a single sustained analysis" (Freeman 1970: 214). It unites man's biology and culture, history and environment within a general evolutionary framework.

The adaptive model presented here is assembled from the following four processes: 1) biological; 2) evolutionary; 3) ecological; and 4) sociocultural. This four-fold categorization eliminates the dichotomy between physical and cultural problems or perspectives. It is felt that the four-fold classification presented here suggests the interrelatedness or linkage between the several processes. One category may be focused upon but not to the exclusion of the remaining three. The interfaces or articulation between these categories need investigative attention as well. It is a "holistic" approach not because research generates general functional statements about a whole complex system but rather because the approach assumes uniformities (in features, processes, mechanisms) that "are common to all the phenomena under consideration" (Alland 1967: 121). Constant attention is directed "to the way in which the various activities of living organisms contribute to their continued maintenance" (Young 1971: 120).

Following Alland (1967) and Binford (1972), process is defined here as "the interaction of variables and parameters" (Alland 1967: 195) or "the dynamic relationships (causes and effects) operative among the components of a system" (Binford 1972: 117). Examples of biological processes are aging, growth, and malnutrition. Evolutionary processes include gene mutation and natural selection. Degradation and succession are examples of ecological processes. Sociocultural examples include energy extraction (production and development), commerce and warfare (White 1949: 380) and socialization. It is apparent that these processual categories are interrelated and under the proposed model, all refer back to the concept of adaptation and general evolutionary theory.

As disciplines, nutrition and anthropology have recognized these various components of their respective subjects. Anthropology has traditionally included within its subdisciplines all the categories mentioned above but has largely failed to integrate them on a theoretical level. Nutrition is similar to anthropology in this respect. This parallelism has important implications for applied work involving these disciplines (as well as others). Applied work is synonymous with involvement in the dynamic processes of social change. Social change of course can be adaptive or maladaptive. In addition, social change alters the interactions between the components and processes of the system undergoing such change. Involvement in applied projects, whether as a research contributor or an "implementor", therefore necessitates an awareness of alterations to the balance of the system and final systemic outcomes. In other words, the state(s) and fate(s) of the system under study require sustained consideration during basic research, design and application and evaluation.

Alland (1967: 228) suggests four problem complexes involving the study of the process of adaptation. Other examples can be drawn from medical anthropology (see Alland 1966). The following example briefly illustrates the "state-fate" perspective in nutritionally-oriented anthropological research. It is a more circumscribed research problem and is not meant as an example of the application of the adaptive model *per se*. However, it is important because the problem and approach are congruent with the model. Therefore, the example given below is not a particularistic, isolated segment of research.

The study population is an isolated Miskito Indian village of 377 persons located on the east coast of Nicaragua. The dietary regime consists of local foodstuffs which are obtained from turtling (green sea turtles, *Chelonia mydas*, are captured by nets or harpoons), swidden agriculture, animal husbandry, hunting, fishing, and gathering and purchased food items which are obtained from several village stores. The only major source of cash income is provided by the commercial sale of green sea turtles to a foreign-owned company. One result of the commercialization of this subsistence resource is that turtle meat is often unavailable in the village. The coastal Miskito are obtaining cash instead of meat from a traditional subsistence resource. In general, conversion of this resource to cash results in a protein being exchanged for purchased carbohydrates such as rice and white flour. One purpose of the study was to examine the diversity of the annual dietary regime and to explore the measurement of dietary diversity. The major assumption was that the greater the dietary diversity (i.e., the number of different food items exploited), especially of local foodstuffs, the more secure the nutritional strategy of the Miskito Indians. (Security was defined in this study as the maintenance of the average intake of nutrients, although a more useful definition for studies concerned with nutritional assessment may be the maintenance of recommended or required intakes of nutrients.)

Ecologists, anthropologists, and others have been concerned with the problem of diversity, stability, and security. This study proposed that in order to evaluate correctly the implications of diversity, a broader view of the system of adaptation was necessary. This view was in contrast to considering diversity as a static, reliable indicator of stability and security.

The Shannon-Wiener function (Krebs 1972: 506-507) was used as the measure of dietary diversity. It includes two components of diversity: the number of items and their equitability (the proportions contributed by each item). Maximum dietary diversity can also be computed using this function. This measure of diversity can be presented in such a way as to demonstrate its fluctuations or stability throughout the year. A quantified measure of dietary diversity can serve as a basis for the assessment of nutritional strategies. It can be related to nutrient intake (security), as in this example or used in diachronic studies to monitor the impact of change on a group.

42

Application of this diversity measure on a limited number of examples leads to the conclusion that greater dietary diversity does not warrant the assumption of greater nutritional security in all situations. Two cases of high dietary diversity were suggested. The first occurs when the adaptive system is in equilibrium and the second occurs at a time of disequilibrium – and may indicate the last peak before the occurrence of large disruptions which force a restructuring of the system along different lines (Krebs 1972: 545 et seq.). The Miskito represent the latter case. The use of a standard measure of diversity, borrowed from ecology and applied to dietary information, illustrated one aspect of dietary disequilibrium. Attention was directed to the disruptive interaction between the cash economy and the traditional subsistence system. Cash income derived from the commercial exploitation of a basic subsistence resource was one factor that had upset the equilibrium of the adaptive system.

Although this research was not conducted with an applied goal in mind, the approach used is applicable and valuable to applied work. The introduction of a cash sector to a traditional non-monetary economy is a common development proposal and also a common "non-planned" occurrence in regions which have until recently been relatively isolated. The introduction of a cash sector to such economies requires adaptive adjustments. These adjustments affect subsistence and nutritional strategies, which were the focus of the Miskito study. Whatever the specific applied goals may be, consideration must be given to the present state of the system and the interrelationships among components, processes, and mechanisms of the system. Prediction of the future state and fate of the system after application of applied proposals is also necessary, but must be based on knowledge of present processes and the current system state. As Campbell and Roark similarly note in their discussion of systemic interaction:

Because all man-environment systems are dynamic, what we can learn about them in real time is the current condition of interacting elements or the state of the contemporary process. By judging the current outputs, we can perhaps make more reasonable efforts to alter the quality of the process. So instead of specifying the design of some future concrete entity (as is so often the case with city planning), it is possible to think of specifying changes in present processes (1974: 98).

With regard to the research example presented above, the investigation of diversity, stability, and security is a general problem which can be studied by the various disciplines involved in nutritional research. It is felt that such conceptual coordination which serves as investigative foci is a fruitful approach for interdisciplinary research. These types of studies are based on general principles (in the above example, ecological) explicitly stated and have the potential for answering fundamental questions resulting in a better understanding of the adaptive process and the implications of applied work. Development of a general model is a more comprehensive way of integrating the research contributions and specialized expertise of the diverse disciplines.

Notes

1 Special thanks are due to my colleagues Randall Schalk and David E. Stuart with whom I have discussed some of the ideas presented here. Appreciation is also extended to Stephen Beckerman for suggestions made after reading a preliminary draft of this paper. I am responsible for the final draft of this manuscript.
2 The research example presented in this manuscript is adopted from a paper I read before the ninth annual meeting of the Southern Anthropological Society, April 4-6, 1974, Blacksburg, Virginia.

References

Alland, Alexander, Jr.
1966 Medical Anthropology and the Study of Biological and Cultural Adaptation. American Anthropologist 68: 40-51.
1967 Evolution and Human Behavior. Garden City, New York: The Natural History Press.
Barg, Benjamin
1973 Nutrition and National Development. In Nutrition, National Development, and Planning. Proceedings of an International Conference, Massachusetts Institute of Technology, October 19-21, 1971. Alan Berg, Nevin S. Scrimshaw, and David L. Call, Eds. Cambridge, Mass.: The MIT Press. pp. 49-69.
Berg, Alan and Robert Muscat
1973 Nutrition Program Planning: An Approach. In Nutrition, National Development, and Planning. Proceedings of an International Conference, Massachusetts Institute of Technology, October 19-21, 1971. Alan Berg, Nevin S. Scrimshaw, and David L. Call, Eds. Cambridge, Mass.: The MIT Press. pp. 247-274.
Binford, Lewis R.
1972 An Archaeological Perspective. New York: Seminar Press.
Boyden, Stephen V. (Ed.)
1970 The Impact of Civilisation on the Biology of Man. Canberra: Australian National University Press.
Campbell, Robert D. and A. L. Roark
1974 Man-Environment Systems. Man-Environment Systems 4: 89-99.
Cohen, Yehudi A. (Ed.)
1968 Man in Adaptation: The Biosocial Background. Chicago: Aldine.
Dubin, Robert
1969 Contiguous Problem Analysis: An Approach to Systematic Theories About Social Organization. In Interdisciplinary Relationships in the Social Sciences. M. Sherif and C. W. Sherif, Eds. Chicago: Aldine. pp. 65-76.
Dubos, René
1965 Man Adapting. New York: Yale University Press.
Freeman, J. D.
1970 Discussion. In The Impact of Civilisation on the Biology of Man. S. V. Boyden, Ed. Canberra: Australian National University Press. p. 214.
György, P. and O. L. Kline (Eds.)
1970 Malnutrition is a Problem of Ecology. New York: S. Karger.
Handler, Philip (Ed.)
1970 Biology and the Future of Man. New York: Oxford University Press.
Jelliffe, Derrick B.
1973 General Discussion. In Nutrition, National Development, and Planning. Proceedings of an International Conference, Massachusetts Institute of Technology, October 19-21, 1971. Alan Berg, Nevin S. Scrimshaw, and David L. Call, Eds. Cambridge, Mass.: The MIT Press. p. 46.

Krebs, Charles J.
1972   Ecology. New York: Harper and Row.
Manners, Robert A. and David Kaplan (Eds.)
1968   Theory in Anthropology. Chicago: Aldine.
Nour, Mohamed A.
1973   Planning Priorities in Nutrition and Development. *In* Nutrition, National Development, and Planning. Proceedings of an International Conference, Massachusetts Institute of Technology, October 19-21, 1971. Alan Berg, Nevin S. Scrimshaw, and David L. Call, Eds. Cambridge, Mass.: The MIT Press. pp. 87-90.
Sahlins, Marshall
1968   Evolution: Specific and General. *In* Theory in Anthropology. Robert A. Manners and David Kaplan, Eds. Chicago: Aldine. pp. 229-241.
White, Leslie A.
1949   The Science of Culture. New York: Grove Press, Inc.
Young, J. Z.
1971   An Introduction to the Study of Man. Oxford: Oxford University Press.

Farming and Foraging in Prehistoric Greece: The Nutritional Ecology of Wild Resource Use

Mari H. Clark Forbes, Department of Anthropology, Duke University.

As social scientists we are concerned with order and clarity, devoting much time and discussion to specific definition and classification of our subject matter. In analyses of human modes of subsistence we generally speak in terms of technological stages such as gathering, horticulture, plow agriculture, hydraulic societies and the like. We must not lose sight of the continuities of subsistence activities that cross cut these divisions. The concern of this paper is the continuing importance of gathered wild resources in the human diet in Greece. Using an ecological framework, looking at nutrition as a system of exchange of material and energy, a working model is constructed for the ethnography of wild resource utilization by cultivators. Because the energy flow of the nutritional system, as with an ecosystem, can only be assessed by close quantified analysis of the particular conditions of a given community, this paper offers an outline and generates questions for future study rather than a final analysis in itself. The weight of the argument rests on ethnographic literature and ethnographic data gathered in a twenty-eight month period of field research on the peninsula of Methana in the eastern portion of the Greek Argolid.[1]

In approaching basic changes in the food-getting system, we should consider the larger picture of long-term or evolutionary changes, in this case the initial transition from food gathering to food getting as a primary mode of subsistence. Similarly, in viewing the long-term picture of subsistence change, detailed data on short-term contemporary *processes* of change must be collected and analyzed as a guide to the interpretation of the past, not in direct analogy, but using the dynamics of present systems as an indication of the way in which systems can function and might have functioned in the past.

The stimulating contributions to prehistoric economics in the work of Hole and Flannery on the Deh Luran Plain of the Iranian Plateau (Hole, Flannery 1969), Macneish in Mexico's Tehuacan Valley (Macneish 1967) are outstanding examples of the importance of combining sophisticated retrieval and analyses of prehistoric economic evidence with data on contemporary systems of subsistence.

In Greece, where archaeology was long dominated by a tradition of arts and letters scholarship, the economics of prehistoric subsistence has only recently become a topic of major archaeological concern (Theochares 1973). Though many archaeologists excavating sites in Greece do make a practice of familiarizing themselves with the basic environmental features of their site as well as talking with their workmen and local farmers and herders about subsistence practices specific to the area, the archaeologists are rarely in Greece through the entire period of major agricultural and gathering acitivity (October through June). The archaeologist cannot observe these subsistence processes in full seasonal cycle nor does he have access to such data in the perspective of its total context as does the ethnographer. Thus there is a need for ethnographic research addressed to the problems of the processes of food procurement and general nutritional ecology in Greece.

A Model for the Nutritional Ecology of Wild Resource Use

"Gathering" is approached here as a strategy that may be combined with other subsistence modes such as hunting, fishing, farming, or trading. The term "gathering" is used to indicate the exploitation of non-cultivated plant and undomesticated stationary animal resources. The exploitation of stationary animal resources such as limpets, sea urchins, and honey, involves neither the strategy nor the technology necessary for the pursuit of moving prey. Instead, their collection requires techniques quite similar to those used in harvesting edible wild plants.

The research of Lee and others has gone a long way toward dispelling the stereotype of a meat-based hunting economy dominating pre-agricultural times. Such a view was based on analogy from early ethnographic works. Recent dietary and energy-flow studies indicate the great importance of plant foods in contemporary hunter-gatherer diets (Lee 1968: 1973). Even the cold climatic extremes of the Eskimo environment allow more utilization of plant material than once realized (Nickerson et al 1973).

The inflexible view of a "stage" of gathering is similarly being modified by recent economic evidence. The continuity of wild resources in the diet of the Tehuacan Valley, Mexico, from 6,500 B.C. to 1580 A.D. is clearly documented in coprolites analyzed by Callen (Callen 1973). Hole and Flannery also indicate a continued use of a wide spectrum of wild plant resources in prehistoric Iran (Hole and Flannery and Neely 1969). Scudder's description of African Gwembe Tongan subsistence and Wilkin's discussion of Mexican farming ecology point out the continuing importance of gathered foods in the diets of farming peoples (Scudder 1971; Wilkins 1970).

As I have argued at greater length elsewhere (Forbes 1975), a comparison of the gathering activities of traditional hunter-gatherers and the gathering pursuits of cultivators suggests the shift in emphasis that accompanies the beginnings of food production is a change from gathered concentrated carbohydrate sources, such as the mongongo nut of the Kalahari Bushmen (Lee 1974), to gathered, vitamin-rich, flavorful, supplements to a basic cultivated staple. A classic example of such a supplement is the "leaf relish" that adds variety to the porridge diet of the Gwembe Tongan (Scudder 1971).

Farming and foraging in an agricultural community are parts of a single

47

subsistence system. These activities complement one another. They do not compete. For the farmers of Methana and elsewhere, gathered foods provide variety and nutritional supplement to a bland diet of bread, olive oil, and legumes. In terms of subsistence security, farmers who also gather wild resources are able to use a greater part of their natural environment. In the event of crop failure, thefts, or destruction in war, they are protected by the option of intensifying gathering pursuits.

What questions can we ask about prehistoric gathering activities in the Greek Argolid on the basis of data from the modern farmer-gatherer? Let us look at the material from the Franchthi Cave, the only excavated, Neolithic site in the area. The cave is located near the tip of a rocky, nonarable, headland, about fifteen meters above sea level. Stratified occupation levels extend from the Upper Paleolithic (roughly 20,000 B.C.) to the Late Neolithic (around 4,000 B.C.). The preliminary excavation has been well described by Jacobsen elsewhere (1969a; 1969b; 1973).

Our concern here is not to reconstruct the prehistoric economy of the Franchthi Cave but to consider the continuing role of gathering in that economy from the viewpoint of its satisfying basic human needs. We shall first consider the environmental potentials and limitations for human use of wild resources. Along with this we will look at the "scheduling," or the organization and timing of subsistence activities necessary to make the most of the given resources within their seasonal limits. From scheduling we will move to the discussion of the technology needed to produce and prepare the wild food energy for human consumption. Technology must be viewed both in the limited sense of tools used for foodgetting and in the broader sense of the shared knowledge about the environment and its exploitation. Finally we will assess the nutrients available in the gathered diet in terms of basic human nutrient requirements. For each of these points: 1. seasonality and scheduling; 2. technology; and 3. nutritional requirements, we shall look first to the modern data on wild resource use and then posit the potential conditions for the Franchthi man for Mesolithic and early Neolithic times.

Seasonality and Scheduling

Water is the primary limiting factor in the subsistence pursuits in Greece in general and in the Argolid in particular. Because the prevailing rainbearing winds are westerly, the Argolid, located on the eastern portion of the Peloponnese, is one of the areas of lowest rainfall in Greece (Kayser and Thompson 1964). The "Mediterranean" climate of the Argolid is characterized by hot, dry, rainless summers. In addition to the seasonal variability of rainfall the total rainfall fluctuates from year to year. For the peninsula of Methana, the total annual rainfall was 22.5" in 1972-73 and only 13.9" in 1973-74, a contrast of 9.4".

The agricultural and gathering cycles vary from year to year in response to the pattern of rainfall, reflecting not only the amount of rain per annum but timing and distribution (whether it falls in torrents or a gentle mist). Each wild or cultivated plant has its own response to fluctuating conditions according to its requirements and growth pattern. On Methana, the gathering of wild greens in 1972 began in late October. In 1973 the gathering of wild greens did not begin until December because the autumn rains were late, retarding the growth of the greens (cf. figure 1).

The villagers are well aware that the timing of the rains is a crucial factor in the growth of plants, particularly with cultigens. If the rain does not fall at the crucial periods in the plant cycle, the plant won't mature properly. This range of tolerance can be extended somewhat by the use of fertilizers to speed up tardy growth when the timing of the rains is not fortuitous. Fifty years ago the farmer on Methana did not have this safety margin. He had no chemical fertilizers at his disposal and only very limited quantities of livestock manure.

The scheduling of subsistence pursuits on Methana is shown in figure 1. Current gathering activities are scheduled together with agricultural activities. The farmer rarely does only a single task. Each trip to the fields serves several ends. Greens or bulbs are frequently gathered while taking the sheep to graze on fallow land. Gathering intentions often direct a woman's route in tending her sheep. In the spring and early summer, women take their sheep to the fields near the sea so that they can gather sea urchins and limpets, bathe in the sea, and pick the produce of the non-irrigated summer vegetable gardens that are grown in flat fields near the sea. A man going to inspect the state of his fields on a Sunday afternoon, since as a good Christian he "should do no work" on the Sabbath, is likely to return with a bag of greens, mushrooms, limpets, etc., depending on the location of his fields and the time of the year. Weeding grain crops provides fodder for animals, greens for the dinner table, as well as performing the necessary task of preventing weeds from taking valuable moisture and soil nutrients from the cultivated crops.

The seasonal gathering cycle begins in the fall as does the Greek religious calendar and farming year (Megas 1956). Autumn is the time when hunting of small game such as hare, quail, and partridge, is common. Young boys trap small songbirds with simple metal traps. In the late fall and winter, the birds move down from the higher parts of the peninsula of Methana (735m.) to the area of the village (200 m.) to sea level.

Wild olive fruit is not exploited on Methana today. In the past these olives were collected for oil to be used in soap making. Beaujour, the French Consul in Greece in the late 1700's, compares wild olives to domestic, concluding that the oil of wild olives is higher in taste quality but the domestic olive produces ten times as much oil[4] (Beaujour 1800: 119). This evaluation corresponds very closely with recent chemical analyses of wild olive oil. Thus we must consider the wild olive as a potential pre-historic food resource. Wild olives, like domesticated olives, bear fruit only on alternate years.

Wild greens grow with the moisture of the fall and winter rains and continue until late spring. As these edible plants begin to flower, the unopened buds and tender shoots are eaten until late April. The bulbs of the grape hyacinth are excavated in late February as soon as their distinctive leaves appear.

Capers grow on the rocky cliffs by the sea. When they ripen in May, the capers are gathered and pickled. The summer months from July through September offer the fewest wild plant resources. Summer is the time when the domestic legumes are harvested, threshed, or de-hulled by hand and stored. Wild legumes are only sporadically exploited today. A type of vetch is eaten green as a snack while in the fields. Summer is the most pleasant and the most practical time for marine gathering activities. Although practiced year-round, the most active time for marine gathering is the summer slack period in the agricultural cycle, following the grain harvest in early July through September. The summertime collection of figs, almonds, carobs, and the tending of summer vegetable gardens require little labor output. Village men often fish from the shore with cane poles at this time.

Late summer and fall bring the ripening of fruits and nuts. Wild fruits are not a major concern in the Methana gathering effort, as they are on the Adriatic island of Corfu (Sordinas 1971). On Methana, valonia and holm oak acorns are gathered for goats, sheep, and pigs in the late summer and autumn when they ripen. In times of hunger the valonia acorns and carob beans were eaten by humans as well.

Turning to the prehistoric environment of the Franchthi Cave, preliminary pollen analyses, corresponding with pollen analyses for Epirus in the north of Greece, indicate a steppe-like environment, colder than today, during the Early Paleolithic (approximately 20,000 B.C.; Jacobsen 1973) and a change to a wooded setting with a warmer, wetter climate toward the end of the Upper Paleolithic (approximately 8,000 B.C.). The environmental constraints on the Franchthi economy were probably similar to the present, though less restricting in terms of rainfall. We must wait for further reports of pollen core and other paleo-environmental analyses before any final statements can be made.

Given the coastal location of the Franchthi cave, marine gathering would have provided a ready resource requiring minimal effort. Given the likelihood of a lower sea level and the warmer and wetter climate in prehistoric times (Jacobsen 1973), it is quite possible that the present Koilada bay area in its inland parts may have been a marsh, providing another zone of exploitation, rich in marsh plants and wildlife.

The rocky hillsides around the cave could have provided other resources. Small mammals and snails are both evidenced in the archaeological record. Insects and their larvae might have been eaten. Birds may have followed a seasonal pattern similar to that on Methana, moving up Mt. Didyma in the summer and down to the Koilada lowlands near the cave in the winter. Reptiles, also evidenced in the archaeological record, may have been consumed even though they are not consumed in any form today (Payne 1973). Wild olives and perhaps grass seeds and legumes may have grown in the more favorable, less rocky, spots on the hillsides, along with mushrooms and wild fruit trees. Larger game, grasses, greens, and other plant resources are likely to have been available in the Fournoi Valley, that runs inland to the north of the headland, and on the Koilada Plain that extends inland to the south of the headland. Wild honey, a highly favored resource for gatherers in many parts of the world today, may have been gathered in the autumn and in early summer as is domestic honey today in Greece.

After the beginnings of agriculture and man's interference with the natural vegetation in his cultivation of crops and grazing of livestock, a new class of plant that we term "weeds" or "secondary domesticates" would have been available for exploitation for their leafy greens. Figure 2 offers a listing of the wild plant species now exploited on Methana today that may well have been exploited by Franchthi gatherers. The same species are collected in the Franchthi cave area today.

Gathering Technology

The tools used for the exploitation of stationary wild resources are few and simple. Farming tools are also foraging tools, reflecting the intermesh of agricultural and gathering pursuits. The primary implements for wild resource collection are the knife for cutting and prying, and the wooden pole for knocking off resources that are out of reach. Proper hunting and fishing require a more specialized technology which is beyond our concerns here. Grinding stones (saddle querns) or metates, used today only for grinding rock salt, and containers (fashioned from local clay, woven from straw or threads, or carved from hollow gourds) for carrying and cooking would be basic to food preparation along with the knife. Most meals today are stews cooked over the fire in a single earthenware pot. Meat, fish, and shell fish are often roasted in the coals or hot ashes of the fire or cooked on a spit. Pit roasting was practiced in the past. Seventy-five years ago on Methana, the home-made wooden spoon was the only utensil used for eating a stew shared by the entire family from a single large ceramic bowl.

Obviously this leaves little evidence of gathering technology for the archaeologist to retrieve. Only stone knives and grinders and ceramic cooking vessels might survive. None of these artifacts offers any clear distinction from the agricultural year of later cultivators. Reinforcing this rather dim picture for the reconstruction of gathering economics is Lee's statement that abandoned Bushmen camps in the Kalahari show no evidence of the vegetable matter that comprises over 60% of the diet (Lee 1968: 48,282).

Diet and Nutrition

Let us now consider the potential resources of the area of the Franchthi Cave with regard to basic human dietary requirements. Nutritional surveys conducted on mainland Greece and on Crete following World War II provide a general outline of the subsistence diet in rural Greece. Local nutritional data gathered on Methana and in Didyma in the Greek Argolid gives a general picture of the pattern of food consumption today in the region of the Franchthi Cave (Allbaugh 1953; Tsongas 1951; Koster and Koster 1975). Comparing the Greek rural diet with the American rural diet (Murray and Black 1959) we see a heavier emphasis on vegetable foods and a lower intake of animal protein and sugar in Greece. In Didyma and on Crete, where potatoes are a local cash crop of less than 100 years antiquity in the area, potato consumption replaces that of a fair amount of bread and vegetables in relation to the Methana diet. On Methana, bread and olive oil are the staples of the diet. Less meat and more legumes provided protein on Methana in pre-World War II days. Allbaugh's study concludes that diets of this nature do provide the minimum daily requirements of the basic nutrients (1953:119).

In one Greek Argolid, a sample farmer-shepherd family ate wild greens on the average of once a week during the period of availability. This provided a total of nine kilos of wild leafy greens per person during the six months of the year when they could be collected. In pre-World War II days, wild greens consumption on Methana was probably four times this amount. Sordinas estimates that gathering activities of greens and all other exploited wild resources on the Adriatic island of Corfu comprised 20.8% of the total subsistence effort during W.W. II, diminishing to 7.5% of the total food-getting effort during the post-war period (1971).

Turning to the prehistoric diet, it is important to note that we cannot make definite statements about the relative importance of plant and animal foods without the rough guide of coprolitic evidence. The poor preservation of pollen at the Franchthi Cave, as well as the improverished state of the vegetable remains, apparently due to soil acidity, tends to give a picture overemphasizing the meat portion of the prehistoric diet. We must also keep in mind that it is impossible to state the exact ratio of domestic to wild food consumption, given the differences in the nature of the evidence, and factors of error, as well as the extremely limited state of the investigation. We can only suggest trends. We can posit the potential of the environment for satisfying the needs of the Franchthi man but we cannot say what he actually selected to satisfy those needs.

Unlike the Kalahari bushmen, Franchthi man had no mongongo nuts to provide 40% of the daily calorie requirements as well as other vital nutrients (Lee 1973: 32). However, many of the foods evidenced in the botanical finds at the cave (Renfrew 1969; 1973) *are* good sources of concentrated energy and protein. Almonds, found in stratified Mesolithic levels, (Renfrew 1974) (in a 100 gm serving) satisfy the following portions of the daily food needs: 25% of the calories; 32% of the protein, 31% of the calcium, 44% of the iron, 37% of the riboflavin, 22% of the niacin, and 17% of the thiaming, as well as offering a source of fats (Leverton 1959). Pistachio nuts, also present in the Mesolithic offer a similar contribution to the diet. Similarly, as with nuts, legumes offer a concentrated source of calories and protein. Thus far, peas, lentils, and vetch have been identified in the Franchthi material (Renfrew 1974). One hundred gms of lentils provides 41% of the daily requirements of protein, if it is combined with meat or a complementary vegetable protein to balance out the lacking essential amino acids (Akroyd 1964: 71-79). Octopus and sea urchin, both available at the foot of the Franchthi cave, offer a good source of vitamins and minerals as well as proteins and energy. The olive provides minerals as well as a source of concentrated vegetable fat (Pellet and Shadireven, U.S. Dept. of Agriculture 1963). Any mixture of wild greens and fruits should complete the daily vitamin and mineral requirements.

The diet of stationary wild resources combined with the fishing and hunting activities indicated by the bone remains, could have easily provided the minimum of essential nutrients for most of the year. If the large vertebrae of fish found in the Franchthi archaeological record are those of tunny (blue fin tuna) they are evidence of a rich source of protein in a large package. Single fish can weigh up to 200 kilograms. Tunny move in large schools, going inshore on their way to spawn in the early summer and on their return in the autumn (Davidson 1972). Given 25 gms of protein per 100 grams of edible tunny, the daily protein and other needs could have been satisfied by a single fish. Wild game also provide high protein potential. A 100 gm portion of quail contains 25 gms protein. Both rabbit and venison offer 21 gms protein per 100 gms in contrast to domestic sheep with 16 gms of protein per 100 gm portion (Pellet and Shadireven 1970, U.S. Dept. of Agriculture 1963).

Assessing the seasonal availability of wild resources, it would seem that the winter months from January through March would have been a lean time in terms of concentrated plant protein and energy for man, unless seeds and nuts were stored for the winter. Almonds can be stored in the shell for up to five years. Olives can be preserved simply by placing the black ripe olives in a coarse cloth bag with ground salt. It is very likely that fishing, hunting, and trapping would have played a greater role during these winter months.

Despite this potential for a well balanced set of nutrients, good health is not evidenced in the Franchthi skeletal remains. Angel, who studied the human bone material for the Franchthi Cave, argues that there is a condition of porotic hyperostosis – a change in the bone structure caused by a genetically based hemoglobin variation associated with the anemia, Thalassemia. Like sickle cell in Africa, Thalassemia is considered likely to be adapitve to an environment of endemic faliciparum malaria (Angel 1966; Allande 1970: 97). In the recent past, prior to United National programs of drainage and pesticide sprays, malaria was a major cause of death in Greece (FAO 1957). Villagers in the Koilada Bay area can recall cases malaria in the area.

According to Angel, farming on flatlands near marshes and a change to a low meat, high cereal diet and sedentary living conditions of a farming as opposed to hunting life, contributed heavily to the incidence of malaria (1972). If the Koilada Bay area was a marsh during these warmer wetter times, of the Mesolithic and Neolithic, gathering activities and perhaps incipient cultivation in the marshlands may have carried the disease to the high rocky Franchthi headland, just as Methana farmers carried malaria from the low, damp, mosquito-ridden plain of Trizinia, back to the drier Methana environment where malaria was never endemic.

The dietary explanation is a less satisfactory one for the Franchthi Cave's apparent incidence of malaria. The limited evidence to date does not allow the assertion of a cereal dominated economy or diet for the Franchthi Neolithic. Cultivated forms of wheat and barley along with the bones of domesticated sheep and goat appear suddenly in the Franchthi archaeological record. Domesticated animal bones appear in considerable numbers. On the basis of this evidence, the investigators posit the introduction of agricultural techniques from elsewhere (Jacobsen 1973). Fish bones indicate a persistence of marine exploitation. Small mammal bones suggest continued trapping. It is unlikely that sources of concentrated protein and energy, such as wild nuts and seeds, would have been abandoned with the first sowing of cultivated grains. Octopus, limpets, and sea urchins, as well as land snails still gathered by local villagers today, undoubtedly continued to play a role in the diet.

With the presence of cereal grain crops, an increase in the use of wild greens as flavorful leaf "relishes" would be expected, particularly leafy crop "weeds". It is possible that the diet was rather similar to that on Methana within living memory. The Franchthi diet was probably higher in animal protein due to the proximity of the sea and its marine resources.

Wheat, barley, and legumes may have been mixed in the same field as is suggested by the paleobotanical material in Northern Greece (J. Renfrew 1969). Until fifty years ago on Methana, wheat and barley were sown together in the same field for more certainty in obtaining some yield every year despite the great variability of rainfall from year to year. In nutritional terms, according to Allbaugh's figures, a stremma of legumes will produce the same energy in calories and twice the protein as would the same area planted in wheat (Allbaugh 1953). If harvested and consumed together, the wheat and legumes would complement each other's deficiency in amino acids for fuller protein use by man (Aykroyd, Doughty 1964: 71-9).

Alternatively we might suggest that Franchthi man was never a farmer but always a gatherer, fisherman, trader, and later a shepherd. The location of the site is not near the best agricultural land in the area. The cave itself is used today as a winter stock enclosure by a local goatherd. The large fishbones in the archaeological record suggest that involvement with the sea extended beyond the shoreline. More intriguing still is the Mesolithic through Neolithic presence of obsidian that has been identified by spectrographic analysis to be from the island of Melos in the Cyclades (Jacobsen 1973; C.

Renfrew 1966). Some lines of communication are necessary to explain an abundance of Melian obsidian in stratified layers in the Franchthi Cave – a distance of 120 kilometers sail.

Conclusions: An Outline for Future Research

As promised at the outset, we have generated more questions than answers in the discussion of wild resource utilization by cultivators. Obviously the nutritional status of the Franchthi people and other transitional prehistoric economics cannot be adequately reconstructed without a solid base of data to build upon. An ethnography of the wild resource utilization of cultivators promises to offer a guide to the *processes* involved in man's utilization of his environment. Given the outlines of viable systems of present wild resource use, we may more satisfactorily extrapolate the ways in which such systems may have functioned in the past.

A systematic interdisciplinary effort is needed to approach the nutritional ecology of wild resource exploitation. Ideally this should be conducted on a long-term basis to realize seasonal variation and to reflect long-term trends. Following the model presented in this preliminary discussion of wild re- source utilization with regards to the Franchthi Cave, the following outline for future research focusses on: (1) environmental potentials and con- straints; (2) general technology of wild resource exploitation; (3) diet – the input/output analysis of the role of wild resources.

The Ethnography of Wild Resource Utilization by Cultivators

I.   Environmental Potentials and Constraints
   A.   Local Climatic Data
   B.   Survey of Wild Resource Potential
   (each of the following sections will include (a) species identified, and (b) human uses of all species).
      1.   Local Flora
      2.   Marine and Marsh resources
      3.   Small Fauna (small mammals, birds, reptiles, insects, etc.)
   C.   Synthesis: The Range of Exploitable Niches

II.   General Technology of Wild Resource Utilization
   A.   Informant Histories
   B.   Time and Motion Studies of Wild Resource Exploitation
   C.   Photographic Documentation
   D.   Synthesis: The Range of Techniques in Wild Resource Use

III.   Diet: The Input/Output Analysis of Wild Resource Use
   A.   Food Consumption Survey – the quantitative contribution of wild re- soures in the diet for autumn, winter, spring, summer

B. Food Composition Analyses – the basic nutrients in the local wild foods

C. Bio-medical Survey – assessment of the nutritional status of sample communities in the area
   1. Blood testing (haemoglobin variations) and other chemical tests
   2. Analysis of Local Health Records
   3. Informant Medical Histories

D. Synthesis: The Nutrient Potential for the Local Environment

Notes

1 This research was conducted in cooperation with the Argolid Exploration project (Jameson 1975). It was funded through a University of Pennsylvania Fellowship and a Department of Anthropology travel grant awarded Hamish Forbes (1975). A preminary version of this paper was presented at the conference on Greek Studies, February 1975, and will be published with the other conference papers in one *Annals* of the New York Academy of Sciences (Friedl and Schein 1975).

2 Supporting the past existence of a marsh in the Koilada Bay area, in 1971 Argolid Project botanists pointed out traces of marsh vegetation along the shoreline near the village of Koilada. That area has since been filled with soil and gravel.

3 K. Economidou, Department of Botany, University of Athens, identified the botanical samples.

Figure 1. A schedule for the seasonal availability of wild resources on Methana

SEPT.	OCT.	NOV.	DEC.	JAN.	FEB.	MAR.	APR.	MAY	JUN.	JUL.	AUG.	
0.08	6.76	1.25	1.15	5.17	2.63	2.93	0.98	0.40	0.06	1.01	0.06	1972-3
0.08	0.97	2.57	1.10	3.12	0.94	3.89	0.54	0.53	0.03	0.00	0.08	1973-4

————————————— Rainfall in inches —————————————

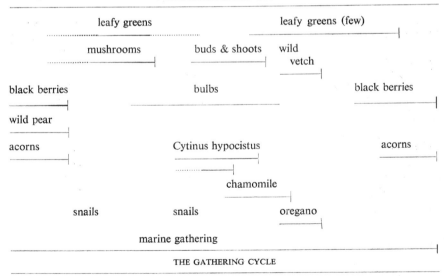

dry garden   winter garden   summer dry gardens

weeding grain

grapes   grain reaping & threshing
harvest pulses

pears   olive harvest

honey   green
almonds

figs & pears

honey

carobs, almonds
chick peas

THE AGRICULTURAL CYCLE

leafy greens   leafy greens (few)

mushrooms   buds & shoots   wild
vetch

black berries   bulbs   black berries

wild pear

acorns   Cytinus hypocistus   acorns

chamomile

snails   snails   oregano

marine gathering

THE GATHERING CYCLE

Figure 2. Edible wild plant species used on Methana.[3]

Latin Nomenclature	Common Name	Portion Eaten
1. *Agaricus* ssp.	field mushroom	whole
2. *Cytinus hypocistus*	rock rose parasite	juice
3. *Allium* ssp.	wild garlic	bulb
4. *Muscari comosum*	grape hyacinth	bulb
5. *Quercus aegilops*	valonia oak	nut
6. *Quercus ilex*	holm oak	nut (fodder)
7. *Amaranthus* ssp. (possibly *A. dellexus*, *A. retroflexus*, *A. blitum*)	pig weed	leaf, stem
8. *Silene vularis*	bladder campion	leaves, stem
9. *Papaver rhoeas*	red poppy	leaves, stem
10. *Capparis spinosa* & possibly *C. cirupestris*	caper	leaves, fruit
11. *Hirschfeldia incana*	charlock	leaves, buds, fruit
12. *Rubus*, ssp.	blackberry	fruit
13. *Pyrus amygdaliformis* Vill.	wild pear	fruit
14. *Vicia* ssp.	wild vetch	seed, pod
15. *Opuntia ficus indica* (New World introduction)	prickly pear cactus	fruit
16. *Myrtus communis*	myrtle	berry
17. *Tordylium apulum*	—	leaves
18. *Arbutus unedo*	strawberry tree	berry
19. *Olea europea* ssp. *oleaster* (Hoffn. & Link) Negodi	wild olive	fruit?
20. *Origanum onites*	pot marjoram	leaves
21. *Origanum heracleoticum*	oregano	leaves
22. *Satureia thymbra*	summer savory	leaves
23. *Thrymbra spicata*	spiked thyme	leaves
24. *Rosemarinus officinalis*	rosemary	leaves
25. *Solanum nigrum*	black nightshade	leaves, stem
26. *Sonchus* ssp.	sow thistle	leaves, stem buds, shoots
27. *Matricaria chamomilla*	chamomile	leaves, flowers
28. *Chorium* ssp.	chicory	leaves, stem
29. *Leontodon tuberosis*	dandelion	leaves
30. *Hypochoeris aetnensis*	dandelion	leaves
31. *Taraxacum officinale*	dandelion	leaves
32. *Sisybrium irio*	dandelion	leaves
33. *Chondilla juncea*	dandelion	leaves, buds, shoots
34. *Hypochoeris radicata*	dandelion	leaves
35. *Reichardia picroides*		leaves
36. *Centaurea mixta*		leaves
37. *Tamus communis*	black bryony	shoots
38. *Rumex pulcher*	dock	leaves

References

Alland, Alex.
1970 Adaptation in Cultural Evolution: An Approach to Medical Anthropology. pp. 68-79. New York: Columbia University Press

Allbaugh, L. G.
1953 Crete: A Case of an Underdeveloped Area. Princeton: Princeton University Press.

Angel, Lawrence
1966 Porotic Hyperstosis, Anemia, Malarias, and Marshes in the Prehistoric E. Mediterranean. Science 153: 760-3.
1969 Human Skeletal Remains From the Franchthi Cave. Hesperia 38: 380
1972 Ecology and Population in the Eastern Mediterranean. World Archaeology 4: (1) : 90-105.

Aykroyd, W. R. and Joyce Doughty
1964 Legumes in Human Nutrition. FAO Nutritional Study 19. Rome.

Beaujour, Felix
1800 View of the Commerce of Greece. London: J. Wallis (translated)

Callen, E. C.
1973 Dietary Patterns in Mexico Between 6500 B.C. and 1580 A.D. In Man and His Food: Studies in the Ethnobotany of Nutrition. C. Earle Smith Ed. University of Alabama Press

Davidson, Alan
1972 Catalogue of Fish, Crustaceans, Molluscs Etc. In Mediterranean Seafood. pp. 23-240. Hammondsworth: Penguin.

F.A.O.
1957 Greece: Mediterranean Development Project of the United Nations. Rome.

Flannery, Kent
1969 Origins and Ecological Effects of Early Domestication in Iran and the Near East. In Peter Ucko and G. Dimbleby Eds. pp. 73-100.

Forbes, Hamish
1975 We Have A Little Bit of Everything: The Ecological Basis of Some Subsistence Agricultural Practices in Methana Trizinia. In E. Friedl and Muriel Schein. In Press.

Forbes, Mari H. Clark
1975 Gathering in the Argolid: a Subsistence Subsystem in an Agricultural Community. In E. Friedl and M. Schein Eds. In Press.

Friedl, Ernestine and Muriel Schein Eds.
1975 Conference on Regional Variation in Modern Greece and Cyprus: Toward a Perspective on the Ethnography of Greece. Annals of the New York Academy of Sciences. In Press.

Harrison, G. A., J. S. Weiner, et al.
1964 Nutritional Ecology. In Human Biology: An Introduction to Human Evolution, Variation and Growth, pp. 413-440. Oxford: Oxford University Press.

Hole, Frank, Kent Flannery and J. Neely
1969 Prehistory and Human Ecology of the Deh Luran Plain: An Early Village Sequence form Khuzistan. Memoirs of the Museum of Anthropology 1. Ann Arbor: University of Michigan.

Iatridou, Marina
1974 Greek Ministry of Commerce. Personal Communication.

Jacobsen, Thomas
1969a The Franchthi Cave, Stone Age Site in Greece. Archaeology 22: 4-9.
1969b Excavations at Porto Cheli and Vicinity, Report II: The Franchthi Cave 1967-8. Hesperia 38: 343-81.
1973 Excavations in the Franchthi Cave 1969-71: Park II. Hesperia 42: 40-88.

Jameson, M.
1975   The Southern Argolid: the Setting for Historical and Cultural Studies. *In* E. Friedl and M. Schein. In Press.

Kayser, Bernard, Thompson, et al.
1964   Economic and Social Atlas of Greece. Athens: Center for Economic Research.

Koster, Harold and Joan Bouza Koster
1975   Personal Communication.

Lee, Richard
1968   What Hunters Do for a Living. *In* Man the Hunter. Lee and Irwin Devore Eds. pp. 30-48. Chicago: Aldone.
1969   Kung Bushman Subsistence: An Input-Output Analysis. *In* Environment and Cultural Behavior. pp. 47-79. Garden City: Natural History Press.
1973   Mongongo: The Ethnography of a Major Wild Food Resource. Ecology of Food and Nutrition 2: 307-313.

Leverton, Ruth
1959   Recommended Allowances. *In* Food. pp. 227-30. U.S. Dept. of Agriculture.

Macneish, Richard
1967   Introduction. *In* The Non Ceramic Artifacts. Douglas Byers general Ed. The prehistory of the Tesuacan Valley. Vol. 2. pp. 3-13, Austin: University of Texas Press.

McDonald, Wm., and George Rapp Eds.
1972   The Minnesota Messenia Expedition: Reconstructing a Bronze Age Regional Environment. Minneapolis: University of Minnesota Press.

Megas, George
1956   Greek Calendar Customs. Athens.

Murray, Janet and Ennis Black
1959   What Do We Eat? *In* Food: The Yearbook of Agriculture 1959. Washington, D.C.; U.S. Government Printing Office.

Nickerson, N. H., N. H. Rowe and E. A. Ricter
1973   Native Plants in the Diets of N. Alaskan Eskimos. *In* Man and His Food. C. Earle Smith Ed. pp. 3-28 University of Alabama Press.

Payne, Sebastian
1973   The Animal Bone. *In* Thos. Jacobsen 1973.

Pellet, P. L. and S. Shadirevan
1970   Food Composition Tables for Use in the Middle East. Beirut: American University.

Polunin, Anthony and A. Huxley
1965   Flowers of the Mediterranean. London: Chatto and Windus.

Renfrew, Colin, et al.
1966   Obsidian and Early Culture Contact in the Near East. Proceedings of the Prehistoric Society 32: 30-72.

Renfrew, Jane
1969   The Archaeological Evidence for Domestication of Plants: Methods and Problems. In Ucko and Dimbleby. pp. 149-172.
1974   Agriculture. *In* Neolithic Greece. D. Theocsares Ed., pp. 147-153. Athens: National Bank of Greece.

Scudder, Thayer
1971   Gathering among African Woodland Savannah Cultivators: A Case Study, the Gwembe Tonga. Zambian Papers 5. New York: Humanities Press.

Sordinas, Augustus
1971   Wild Plant Gathering for Subsistence on the island of Corfu Greece. Unpubblished Paper Presented at the 70th Annual Meetings of The American Anthropological Association. New York.

Theochares, Demetrios R.
1973   Neolithic Greece. Athens: National Bank of Greece.

Tsongas, A.
1951   Nutrition in Greece. F.A.O. Nutritional Study 7. Rome.
Ucko, Peter and G. W. Dimbleby
1969   The Domestication and Exploitation of Plants and Animals. Chicago: Aldine.
U.S. Department of Agriculture
1959   Food: The Yearbook of Agriculture 1959. Washington, D.C.: U.S. Government
       Printing Office.
1963   Composition of Foods. Agriculture Handbook 8. Washington, D.C.: U.S. Go-
       vernment Printing Office.
Wilkins, Gene
1970   The Ecology of Gathering in a Mexican Farming Region. Economic Botany 24:
       286-95.

Research Methods in Nutritional Anthropology: Approaches and Techniques

Christine S. Wilson, Department of International Health, University of California.

Theory and Practice

Nutritional anthropology, newer in recognition than in accomplishments, has resulted from the coming together of two disciplines in an area where their interests coincide, that of diet in the culture. Each of these fields alone encompasses a host of differing subject interests. Thus in theory the possible topics for exploration in a field combining nutrition and anthropology are almost limitless.

One might consider examining, for instance, how types of stoves or other food preparation equipment available to a group at a particular time have limited the kinds of foods that could be cooked and eaten and, postulating further, the effect of these restricted nutrients on growth of the children of this population, or on the ability of the people as a whole to withstand known environmental stresses, natural or man-made. Another might wish to study the alterations in diet of the poorer classes in Europe brought about by sumptuary laws in the Middle Ages and thereafter, or to explore cross-culturally the names of a rather widespread food plant in the places where it is found, in order to learn its relative importance in each locale. Still another nutritional anthropologist might want to search for the psychological meanings of food in different cultures, or to use food habits of descendants of immigrants from times long past to trace the regional or ethnic origins and subsequent peregrinations of these people.

In fact, much of the research which has been termed nutritional anthropology that has been done to date has been quite practical and capable of present-day application. Indeed, most of the examples cited in the preceding paragraph have practical components. Results of these studies have not, however, always been put to optimal use. As examples of this fact, repeated observations of effects of food beliefs on food choices of individuals and groups are still slow to be acted on by physicians, dietitians and other health professionals who give advice regarding needed diet changes. Information on indigenous cuisines would seem a desirable baseline to be determined before international planners attempt to improve nutritional intakes of malnourished populations by food donations, but even where such data have been available prior to initiation of food programs they have not always been consulted or used as guidelines for the types of food to be provided

(Brown and Pariser 1975: 589-593). Research on how to influence attitudes of other health professionals toward recognition of the importance of cultural components of food behavior is an area much in need of encouragement and expansion.

Nutritional anthropology, a discipline in its own right, is also one facet of medical anthropology, a profession which concerns itself with cultural aspects of health. Health is thus a core interest of both these types of anthropologists. Both also tend to use the epidemiological approach to research problems. However fascinated he may be with crosscultural comparisons of food practices and manipulations of food themselves, the nutritionist-anthropologist is bound by training and ethics to recognize also that what man does to food in his environment ultimately affects his nutritional status through the nutrients in this food. This is true even when the food is not consumed but offered at a shrine to some god, for these nutrients are not then available for people to eat, unless the religion permits its subsequent consumption.

Methods in Use

Anthropological techniques lend themselves well to the study of diet and food intake in a culture. Indeed, they appear to be more pertinent for learning true food use and nutrient intakes than the more structured standard approach of the trained dietitian. A great deal may be learned about nutrition in its social setting by one person, working alone, or at most with occasional collaboration of a physician colleague (for verification via examination of blood specimens from certain individuals of effects of observed food intakes and therefore of calculated nutrient intakes or deficiencies), or the help of a literate local assistant to collect household information desired.

Participant observation permits direct knowledge of food preparation procedures – what part of the animal or plant is used, as well as how, under what conditions and with what it is cooked. Through participant observation one can learn distribution of food within family groups: who eats first, last, and in-between, who gets the choicest (not necessarily the most nutritious) bits, and approximate amounts eaten by each person (Wilson 1970; 1971: 96-98).

Participant observation can be adapted to learn an entire day's food intake of one individual, by "following behind" him for that day, noting everything he eats or drinks in a pocket notebook. This variation in the participant observer technique is particularly useful among people who eat much of their food away from the home, or are given to frequent snacking, or are part of a society in which the rigid three-meal-a-day eating pattern of western people is at most casually adhered to. It gives the best approximation of a day's total food and nutrient intake that can be obtained on one person, providing the observer has trained himself previously to estimate amounts of foods that do not come prepackaged or in standard units.

This technique has been used to good effect by several workers (Williams 1973: 51-65; Wilson 1974; M. G. Whiting, personal communication). As indicated above, food intakes learned in this way, as is the case with family meals observed, can be quantitated by prior practice at measuring, by eye, usual-size servings of foods common in the community, and weighing these amounts for verification. A small scale calibrated in grams is the most useful equipment for this purpose. The nutrients in the food can then be calculated from data in a table of food composition values (nutrients). A local table is used if one is available, or one might seek the guidance or assistance of a nutritionist or dietitian in this matter.

Participant observation can inform the researcher what persons are invited to feasts, what the guests bring to the feast for what they get, and elucidate food exchange networks. It makes clear how or whether food taboos are practiced, as well as when they are circumvented, and can lead to understanding of why some potential edibles are chosen for consumption while others are not. It is probably the most desirable means for learning social roles associated with foods.

Use of a key informant, widely relied on for general ethnographic work, does not seem so satisfactory in a study of diet and food in the culture, if for no other reason than that food habits, while following a general pattern in each culture, can still be idiosyncratic and personal. Minimally, a sample of several informants should be sought if this technique is employed, depending upon the design and scope of the research, and on how much the study revolves around food.

Open-ended interviews and loosely structured questionnaires are other anthropological techniques helpful for learning about food beliefs, child feeding and weaning practices, expenditures for food and food-related necessities, crop practices, hunting, and other subsistence food-getting activities. Among traditional peoples who obtain part or all of their food through their own efforts, such as farming or fishing, observation of these activities at different seasons is advisable, as well as some study of input and yield, including subsequent consumption or other disposition of the food so got.

Some workers have been able to obtain collaboration of literate family members in a community to keep a daily diary of foods bought, raised, gathered, or exchanged. This method gives qualitative information on types of food eaten, although it is not so readily quantitated into nutrient intakes. Another means that has been used for learning what a family eats, once it is certain the investigator is sufficiently well acquainted to be welcome, is dropping in at mealtime, on some pretext, in order to note what is being dished up or eaten. A technique used by some is to make daily visits to selected families about the time of the evening meal, to inquire what has been prepared and eaten at home that day and what is planned for the evening meal. An assistant may be trained to make such inquiries and even to approximate the quantities of food reported.

In any society in which markets are part of the economy, a satisfactory technique for learning what food is available and selected for consumption is to make regular visits to those nearby. Not only the variety, quantity and quality of the food, but also its price and hence its potential ability to serve as part of the cuisine of the community under study, may be learned in this way.

This method may be used in societies of sophisticated technology such as our own. In this case, not the varieties of food available but the individual choices made among them are what is to be noted: One examines shopping carts in the supermarket, or notes what the purchaser passes through the cashier's checkout counter, to get a picture of customary food preferences. Knowledge of how these foods are used or combined of course requires other techniques such as some which have been discussed or referred to earlier.

Anthropologists particularly concerned with the effects of available food and diet, as well as other factors, on health and nutrient status of individuals in a community have sometimes made certain physical measurements of its inhabitants. Although these measures might be considered to be the domain of the physical anthropologist, they have been used in standard nutrition surveys for decades. These measurements include body weight and height. In addition, head and arm circumferences of children are sometimes measured. All these physical measurements are, of course, considered in relation to some pre-selected "standard," such as those developed for use of the United Nations agencies, for instance (Jelliffe 1966). With some previous training and minimal equipment, such as weighing scales and a steel measuring tape, the field worker has been able to perform these measurements as part of his protocol of study.

Other parameters of nutritional status sometimes employed by nutritional anthropologists include determination of hemoglobin or hematocrit levels of a portion of the group studied and biochemical analyses of key blood nutrients, such as vitamin A or protein, as preliminary findings warrant these confirmations of results of dietary observations. These last methods are best carried out through cooperation of medical professionals, if such are available and willing to help. Information on disease incidence is valuable background information. This can be learned from national or regional statistics and compared with reports from and observations within the community. The anthropologist can make visual diagnoses of certain obvious nutrition-related conditions such as goiter and rickets himself. More subtle indicators of nutrient inadequacies are best elicited through assistance of medical collaborators.

Head circumference measures have been related to brain size and by extrapolation to mental ability. Arm circumference has been used as an indicator of protein status in the young child. As with other observations suggested above, however, any correlations of these measures with nutritional status or aberrations thereof should be made with great caution.

Usually no one method is suitable for making a nutritional-anthropological study of a population or community unless, by design, only one aspect is to be explored. Most of those discussed above have been utilized in differing combinations by various workers. It should be apparent, especially to the seasoned field worker, that insights and discoveries resulting from use of "typical" study techniques often lead to adaptations of old and even development of entirely new methods of examination in order to explore further these outcomes of the "primary" research or intent.

Breaking New Ground

Most of the methods discussed above have been used in studies which deal directly with food intake. In this the bias of the writer appears, the nutritional component of the nutritional anthropologist having been inprinted first and longest. There are other ways of learning man's use of food than examination of diet preparation and consumption and measurement of its effects on physical status. A few have been alluded to earlier, such as the work of the ethnobotanist, which through local definitions of plants learns what of potentially edible foods will be eaten.

Several anthropologists have studied human energy needed for crop production and handling, in terms of food energy available (Gross and Underwood 1971: 1-16; Ruyle 1973), as well as the carrying potential of the area. Energy expended in these tasks has been estimated from standard tables of caloric expenditure. A refinement in these measurements has been introduced through use of portable physiological equipment worn by the worker which measures respiratory gas exchange, permitting more precise estimates of energy used during work (Montgomery 1973, personal communication). In addition to the equipment, chemicals are needed to measure the gases in the respired air.

Paleonutritionists examining partially digested plant foods in coprolites (fossilized feces) are shedding new light on the types of foods eaten by ancient man (Kliks 1975). Such studies, in conjunction with paleogeographic surveys, give clues to prehistoric diet and may, through archaeological findings, be related to effects of such diets on facial bone structure and body build. Other researchers examining traces of foodstuffs on potsherds to determine their nature through chemical analysis are adding further to the information on diets of earlier man. Both this work and paleodietary studies require reagents, laboratory skills, and equipment.

Examination of kitchen middens is not limited to those of our forebears. A group from the United States has recently used systematic sorting of household waste (garbage) to obtain information on food utilization, and particularly on food waste (Harrison, Rathje and Hughes 1975: 13-16). The technique does not involve the population studied either indirectly or in cooperation, and requires only permission from local sanitary officials and availability of personnel with the fortitude and willingness to sort the raw (pun not intended) material.

New problems call for new methods to study them, or modifications of older ones. Thus N. W. Jerome (personal communication) has examined the effects of television advertising on children's food choices, using combinations of interviewing and questionnaires of child and mother, plus psychological tests of the child. Other researchers in the United States are working with movement therapy classes to learn cultural attitudes of obese members of the group which are related to problems of weight control among middle-class Americans. These attitudes are not found among the wealthier classes (Mackenzie 1975).

The methods of the geographer have been utilized to study food use and avoidance. Simoons (1970: 695-710; 1973: 595-611), in an elegantly worked-out hypothesis, has been able to relate the prevalence of lactose intolerance among adults to earlier lack of the pastoral practice of keeping milk-producing animals. (Lactose intolerance is due to absence of lactase, an enzyme present in the intestine of human infants for approximately the first two years of life. It breaks down lactose, the principal milk sugar of mammals, in digestion. In many populations, this enzyme "turns off" after weaning. Individuals in whom this occurs are no longer able to drink milk without gastric distress.) Simoons (personal communication) has since applied this geographical technique to a study of celiac disease, a condition, like lactose intolerance, sometimes labeled an "inborn error of metabolism." Its sufferers are unable to consume wheat and rye, or their products. In this case the physiological problem is a defect in intestinal structure which inhibits absorption of the digestive breakdown products of gluten, the protein of wheat.

Conclusion

Nutritional anthropology, as a newly recognized subdiscipline, with increasing numbers of proponents and practitioners, seems to be suiting its methods and techniques to the problems it addresses and research in which it is applied. A variety of approaches has been essayed to date, as varied as the backgrounds from which these students of social aspects of nutrition have come. Little prejudice regarding tried and true methods of study exists, probably because no one way of making such a study has as yet been set down. This is all to the good. One hopes hard and fast rules for doing research in nutritional anthropology are far in the future, providing only that certain fundamental precepts of its constituent sciences are not flouted and the objectivity of the scientific approach prevails.

It is very rewarding to be taking part in the beginnings of a new scientific field. Discussions of methodology of such a field let through only a glimmer of the excitement of discovery and new insights which repay the practicing scientist. Method is the frame on which we hang our theory, a guide to the information we wish to gain, and the structure through which we present our results. Further research will no doubt lead to new methodologies, which we will share, along with our research outcomes, with colleagues and other interested readers.

References

Brown, N. L., and E. R. Pariser
1975   Food Science in Developing Countries. Science 188: 589-593.
Gross, Daniel R., and Barbara A. Underwood
1971   Technological Change and Caloric Costs: Sisal Agriculture in Northeastern Brazil. American Anthropologist 73: 1-16.
Harrison, Gail G., William L. Rathje and Wilson W. Hughes
1975   Food Waste Behavior in an Urban Population. Journal of Nutrition Education 7: 13-16.
Jelliffe, D. B.
1966   The Assessment of the Nutritional Status of the Community. Geneva: World Health Organization Monograph Series No. 53.
Kliks, Michael
1975   Paleoethnopharmacology: Anthelminthic Plant Substances in the Coprolites of Early Man in the New World. Paper presented at the Annual Meeting of the Kroeber Anthropological Society, University of California, Berkeley. Abstract.
Mackenzie, Margaret
1975   Anthropological Therapy: An Adjunct in Treatment for Obese People. Paper presented at the 74th Annual Meeting of the American Anthropological Association, San Francisco. Manuscript.
Montgomery, Edward
1973   Problems in the Study of Human Energy Utilization. Paper presented at the 72nd Annual Meeting of the American Anthropological Association, New Orleans. Manuscript.
Simoons, Frederick J.
1970   Primary Adult Lactose Intolerance and the Milking Habit: A Problem in Biological and Cultural Interrelations: II. A Culture Historical Hypothesis. American Journal of Digestive Diseases 15: 695-710.
1973   New Light on Ethnic Differences in Adult Lactose Intolerance American Journal of Digestive Diseases 18: 595-611.
Williams, A. W.
1973   Dietary Patterns in Three Mexican Villages. In Man and His Foods: Studies in the Ethnobotany of Nutrition – Contemporary, Primitive and Prehistoric Non-European Diets. C. E. Smith, Jr., Ed., University: University of Alabama Press, pp. 51-65.
Wilson, Christine S.
1970   Food Beliefs and Practices of Malay Fishermen: An Ethnographic Study of Diet on the East Coast of Malaya. PhD dissertation. Berkeley: University of California.
1971   Food Beliefs Affect Nutritional Status of Malay Fisherfolk. Journal of Nutrition Education 2: 96-98.
1974   Child Following: A Technique for Learning Food and Nutrient Intakes. Journal of Tropical Pediatrics and Environmental Child Health 20: 9-14.

Anthropological Approaches to the Study of Food Habits: Some Methodological Issues

Thomas K. Fitzgerald, Department of Anthropology, University of North Carolina at Greensboro.

Introduction

Far too little is known about food acceptance and rejection in individual community settings and the means by which people in these communities are reached through effective channels of communication. One of the challenges of "nutritional anthropology" is, precisely, to help effect some balance between the rapid growth of nutrition knowledge, on the one hand, and the much neglected understanding of the social and cultural significance of food behaviors, on the other (Freedman 1974:3). Appreciation of some of the anthropological methods used in studying food habits, then, could be most valuable to nutrition educators, as well as help to further the interchange already begun between nutritionists and anthropologists.

In this paper we outline briefly some of the anthropological methods that were employed in our two-year study[1] of changing nutritional patterns in a North Carolina community in transition, i.e., changing from a rural to an urban way of life. Focus will be on the strengths and weaknesses of some anthropological methods used in the investigation of food practices. We conclude our discussion with a fairly detailed description of a test instrument that we have developed for measuring food choices.

The Community

Anthropologists have turned their attentions from studying only primitive tribal groups to studying modern complex societies, including our own. Although the community study has been a prominent part of contemporary anthropology ever since the 1920's, the term "community" is often difficult to define. It is clearly much more than simple a geographical area or place. In essence, a community is a "process", i.e., an ongoing interaction of individuals and groups that has organizations and/or interests in common (Crane and Angrosino 1974:180).

The community we[2] have been studying is called Whitsett after William Thornton Whitsett, headmaster of the local boarding school established in 1888. Today it is a small suburban village of approximately 600 residents, sandwiched between the true rural hinterlands of Piedmont North Carolina and the urban sprawl so characteristic of this expanding area. Whitsett is a fairly typical community in North Carolina to the extent that it, like so many rural communities in the state, is rapidly moving away from farming toward more suburban ways of life. The community is racially mixed, thus providing a good opportunity to compare differences in food behaviors between blacks and whites. It also has the usual range of age, sex, occupation, education, religion, and other social variables important to consider in a community study. Yet the community is small enough in size that we could reach most of our informants in a relatively short period of time.

Perhaps one atypical characteristic of Whitsett is its class structure, especially between blacks and whites. So often blacks occupy a lower status position in a community, and their food habits may be incorrectly interpreted as being a reflection of racial affiliation rather than social status. In Whitsett, however, both blacks and whites belong to the middle class, with some slight slant toward lower-middle, working-class status for both groups.

Although a community of some antiquity – founded by German Lutheran and Reformed settlers around the 1750's – today Whitsett bears only nostalgic traces of the once intact, homogeneous community of the past. Now it is truly a community in transition, moving rapidly from its rural base toward a more suburban way of life. As these social and cultural bases change, food habits also are altered. Our long-term research goals, then, include an examination of the specific characteristics of, and changes in, food practices of special groups in this community in transition.

Some Methodological Issues

In our study of changing nutritional patterns, we have used both traditional and modern techniques of ethnographic fieldwork. These included methods such as participant observation, interviews, standardized questionnaire, and photography. In addition, most anthropologists pay at least some attention to kinship networks, formal organizations, and behavioral documents. In the following exposition we shall comment on these (and other) categories associated with the "anthropological approach" and point out where a particular field technique was found to be either "strong" or "weak" in terms of the goals of our research on food choices. Needless to say, a method that is adequate in one field situation may be less than suitable in another. We hope, nonetheless, to derive from our experiences a few generalizations about the kinds of anthropological approaches that may have meaning and application for nutritionists.

Fundamental to the anthropological approach is participant observation; it denotes first-hand experience in the field. Without going native, the anthropologist tries to be an active member of the community. Crane and Angrosino (1974:63) suggest that participant observation is actually less a research technique than a state of mind or a framework for guiding one's experiences in the field; however, the term implies more methodological coherence than is likely to be encountered in the actual field situation. A good deal of ethnographic research consists of quite informal interactions, e.g., rapping with the local storekeeper, attending a community council meeting, or just random conversations with people. Gradually, though, the fieldworker moves from pure observations to participant observation, from nondirective to directive questioning (Crane and Angrosino 1974:20). These experiences are, then, both progressive and cumulative. Direct experience is the core of the participant observation technique, and there is really no substitute for it. In the study of food behaviors, however, direct observation is not always possible nor always desirable. We did occasionally drop in on people while they were eating, unannounced as it were. We also attended church picnics and observed these ritual forays into the past. And, where possible, we attempted to check our indirect hunches with direct, though often casual, observations.

There are, though, potential biases that can arise out of the participation itself. Individuals, who are being formally interviewed about their food habits, will tend to select, distort, and even fabricate a more favorable image of themselves. It was just as well that we did not make any special effort to be invited to meals, since our very presence would have changed the dining atmosphere, not to mention the menu!

The anthropologist accumulates knowledge of the culture or community by asking essentially the same questions in a variety of ways. One method for asking about food practices is through formal nutrition surveys; another is to use various kinds of questionnaires. However, for the anthropologist, the standardized questionnaire should not be considered the sum total of one's field research (Crane and Angrosino 1974:135). Such data gathering methods are too apt to yield rather flat results unless interpreted in the context of very sensitive observations.

The bulk of an anthropologist's time in the field, then, is devoted to some form of interviewing, whether in casual conversation or through quite structured approaches. In our research on food habits, we used an oral questionnaire, i.e., we asked a number of standardized questions and recorded responses ourselves. Such a strategy leaves room for interpreting the informant's behavior. The interviewee, for example, may say "no" when asked "Can you name the four food groups?"; yet later in the interview, he or she may actually name the groups. This information must be noted. There were numerous examples of such discrepancies between what people said and what they actually understood.

An essential part of any field situation is establishing rapport with the members of one's community. Obviously, forced information is highly suspect, thus unreliable. The anthropological approach allows time for people to feel at ease and, equally important, time for the investigator to increase his self awareness and function as a potential research "instrument." This personal dimension is a major strength of the ethnographic approach. Ethnography is, after all, more complex and subtle than just manipulating tests and research tools.

The role of the door-to-door interviewer, therefore, is not too popular in anthropology, although some modifications of the ideal are often necessary in research on food choices. In order to save time (and money, getting to and from the field site), it often became necessary to do some spot interviewing, door-to-door fashion. One way to avoid this approach was in recognizing the kinship networks that exist in the community. Kin and family affiliations influence food practices. Thus, the traditional anthropological concern for genealogy and kinship becomes an invaluable tool for establishing rapport and for gaining pertinent dietary information.

Sometimes entry into the field is best secured by working with key informants like community leaders and such, but this approach also has its weaknesses. Though it is good practice to avoid the socially "undesirable", what is undesirable to the community may be desirable to the researcher. One of our key informants (intelligent, witty, seemingly an excellent resource person) turned out, for example, to be a reputed alcoholic. Too much association with this individual would have only hindered our project.

The sex of the investigator also must be considered in anthropological work. Traditionally female ethnographers may have had more acute problems in the field than their male counterparts. In food research, on the other hand, the male researcher has special problems of which he must be aware. Food is considered, by our culture at large, to be in the woman's domain. Although this stereotype is changing, few lower middle-class males wanted initially to participate in the interview sessions because, to quote one such individual, "Men don't know nothing about these things." Despite this sort of chauvinistic hang-up, we made every effort to include men in our sample and managed to do so frequently. We feigned a "don't-give-a-darn" attitude and instead deliberately created a potentially competitive situation between husband and wife. More often than not, the husband – off in his corner pretending not to be interested – eventually volunteered his opinions in this "game" that he had almost forsaken to his wife.

The single male interviewer encountered more serious obstacles. Women alone are reticent to invite an unaccompanied male into the house, even if the two had met just the day before at a church function. It is easier to conduct such interviews in male/female pairs. Even when I asked the questions, the informant tended to answer my female assistant!

Another potential problem in ethnographic studies is related to the difference between studying one's own culture as opposed to studying an exotic culture. Often it is hard to convince American informants that the researcher must ask questions about something it is believed he should already know! Studying one's own culture requires concentration on details that one unconsciously takes for granted. It becomes difficult to interest people in the obvious: "We eat just like everybody else, after all!" is a not atypical response.

Related to this problem is the actual/ideal dimension in field reporting. Anthropologists try to avoid sterile questionnaires that are mailed in bulk

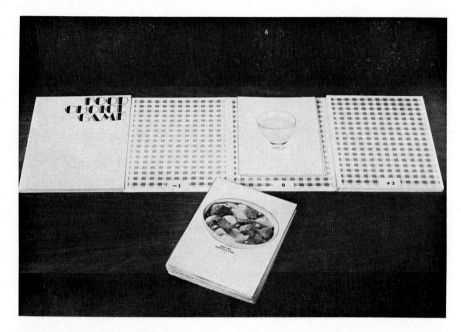

Figure I: Food Choice Game

Figure II: Food Choice Game

and focus on more real-life, face-to-face situations. Even when questionnaires are necessary (and they often are in food research), the items must be checked with contextual observations for accuracy and interpretation. There is no subsitute for good observation.

Anthropological investigators, usually focusing on relatively small groups, typically have been unconcerned with sampling methods. When studying food practices, on the other hand, one cannot afford to omit the statistical assumptions that accompany sampling. The inherent dangers, however, need only be potential ones. Although it was a common practice for the local inhabitants to introduce the field worker first only to the "nice people" (and blacks in our sample were slightly more likely to do this than whites), most anthropologists persist until they have seen as many people as will satisfy their criteria of acceptability. We started out, for instance, with what in sociology has been labelled the "snowball effect," a sort of referral system. As we became more and more familiar with the ramifications of the kinship network, we shifted to kin channels for referrals. Gradually we moved to a quota sample, making certain that various types of people were begin represented. If, for example, older people were becoming over-represented in our sample (as occurred initially), we made a conscious effort to redress this imbalance with the inclusion of more younger persons. Finally, in the second year of our investigation, we began to approximate a true cluster sample, having interviewed X number of families drawn from every street (cluster). Consequently, every part of the community was covered in two years' time!

A more formidable problem, not confined to either nutrition or anthropology, is the "we-they" feeling of some informants vis-a-vis the ethnographer and the linguistic barriers felt to exist between these two groups (cultures?). Some local people still identify strongly with a rural culture and, thus, anyone not rural is potentially a stranger or outsider. When one informant tried to introduce me to an elderly lady in the community, her reply was: "I don't want to talk to any nutritionist; I eat only country food, meat and potatoes."

Often associated with this attitude is a linguistic or semantic barrier. Anthropologists studying their own culture occasionally (and naively) think that everyone is speaking the same language. Actually most academicians communicate in the jargon of what Dr. Ralph Patrick calls "the culture of the educated technican."[3] This educated technician will speak of "carbohydrates"; the lay person, by contrast, talks of "fattening foods." Although our informants seldom used the word "cholesterol", they felt that "fatty foods" are somehow "bad for your heart." A number of our questionnaire items, then, had to be translated into the language of the non-technician. Many failures in communication in the field are essentially linguistic barriers of this sort.

In short, although most of the research strategies mentioned above were integral parts of our research design and quite invaluable, we discovered that such tools had their limitations when applied to the investigation of food habits. There are, then, some recognized potential weaknesses in several of the traditional ethnographic field methods. The anthropologist, for instance, normally manipulates no independent variables, is not experimental in the sense of control groups and the like, and hence is not able to achieve the same degree of precision as, say, the laboratory scientist. However, field studies have many positive advantages that tend to make up for these limitations: they are strong in realism (hence not artificial), strong in social significance, and at least potentially strong in theory orientation (Kerlinger 1964: 405-407).

Beyond the Ethnographic Approach

As we said above, there are advantages in using the ethnographic approach, especially due to its emphasis on total immersion into another culture and its awareness of extra-food facets, such as economics, family history, and social status. However, in any interdisciplinary endeavor, we need to go beyond what either discipline has to offer singly. Sharing insights, we can hope to develop newer and better models to guide our research questions. In the following section we shall outline one modest attempt to overcome some of the limitations of the ethnographic approach – at least for the study of food habits.

In our study of a North Carolina community and its changing nutritional patterns, we used many field techniques for eliciting from our informants data about food practices. Though invaluable as research strategies, many of these tools were unable to fully perform the tasks assigned to them. We had to devise some more indirect means of getting the same information. We combined the basic features of the projective test, which has an established prominence in anthropology, with the more quantitative measurement techniques from psychological and educational studies; likewise we were influenced by recent attempts to use pictorial representations as a strategy in nutrition education campaigns.

Borrowing ideas from these several sources, we devised a research instrument – essentially a type of projective test – that we call the "Food Choice Game", because it utilizes the notion of food preferences (choices) in a game context. As a research tool, the Food Choice Game is able to overcome one of the major and most frequently voiced complaints in research studies on food habits, viz., the tendency toward idealized reporting. Intellectualized responses stem from the human desire to "save face" in situations perceived as threatening. Hence, the research instrument described – being basically non-threatening – may be more reliable for gathering information on food habits than the traditional methods, such as the 24-hour recall or various verbal and written questionnaires.

It should be understood, however, that no test, game, questionnaire, or the like, should be substituted for ethnographic fieldwork; such techniques "go beyond the ethnographic approach" *only* in the sense of extending or adding to the original methodology. The intent is to render the ethnographic approach flexible enough to handle new research possibilities without, however, detracting from its basic contribution.

The Food Choice Game consists of a game board with seven boxes represented on the surface of the board. (The board is attractively designed so that it resembles a checkered tablecloth in appearance). The boxes form a scale, a sort of continuum between two extremes. In the center of the board is a neutral category (0); on the right the pole runs +1 through +3; on the left the pole is naturally −1 through −3. Either extreme can be defined using any number of separate scales. We have employed three, which will be described shortly.

Instead of using only verbal or written concepts to be sorted, visual symbols in the form of food cards are utilized.[4] Responses, then, can be recorded and are ultimately measurable. In fact, accompanying the Game is a score sheet for each informant with all the major categories typed on it. After taking the "test", the informant's answers (choices) can be quickly recorded and put aside for later analysis, interpretation, and comparison.

The major advantage of any game approach, in contrast to direct questioning about food practices, is fairly evident: such an approach does not put the informant in a defensive position; hence, it is less threatening. If, for example, informants are asked about their drinking habits, they are not likely to answer truthfully (especially in a church-dominated community). On the Game Board, however, informants seem to be able to project their feelings onto this more abstract cognitive space and hence, we assume, are able to make accurate choices without the threat of censure.

The food cards (laminated onto white pasteboard) include only those foods common to the community under study. Before making up such cards, however, one must compile a folk taxonomy of local foods to discern the foods with which the informants are truly familiar. It would make little sense to ask a Dutch or New Zealand informant to sort cards that portrayed only American foods. This is not – as is – a cross-cultural instrument although it could easily be modified for cross-cultural use. From this list of "folk foods", one then prepares the 100 cards for sorting onto the Game Board.

Each informant is asked to sort the total set of 100 cards (there could be as few as 60 cards if circumstances dictated) according to the rules of the Game. In this case, the rules correspond to three separate dimensions or scales: (1) foods the informant likes most or likes least, (2) foods the informant thinks most healthful or least healthful, and (3) foods used most frequently or least frequently. Non-scalable items are placed in the neutral category in the center of the board. When the individual places a card onto the board, he or she is, in essence, selecting a choice position on whatever dimension is being considered at that moment.

Schensul (1970:4), in making a rural/urban comparison, has used a similar three-dimensional cognitive model, but his scale is essentially linear, with similarities and differences in meaning of concepts expressed as a function of their distance in "semantic space" on a scale from "hospitable" to "inhospitable". He also employs the semantic differential technique for statistical analysis.

Because our sample is small, we used the Q-sort statistical technique for analyzing informant responses. The Q technique is a ranking procedure. One of its major advantages is that it lends itself to correlations between people or between different conditions for the same person (Wittenborn 1961:132). It is a practical technique for sorting out differences between groups, e.g., black/white, male/female, older/younger, and so on. Q only requires a conceptually structured set of statements – in this case, food choices – in order to interpret correlations between groups of people. The Q method also permits a study of a single individual by means of an analysis of variance of choice items. This alternative, however, leaves unanswered the question of the parent population from which the informant is drawn; one must assume, therefore, that somewhere there are more people like the one under scrutiny (Wittenborn 1961:132).

Q-sort typically has been used in therapeutic settings by psychologists. Nutritionists and anthropologists have made almost no use of this valuable statistical device, and unfortunately so, since Q-sort lends itself to small populations in a way that Osgood's (1957) semantic differential, for example, cannot. Because much anthropological research is concerned with small groups and comparisons of subgroups within this context, the Q-sort is a useful statistical technique with which anthropologists could well gain some familiarity.

One aspect of Q-sort that interested us was the comparison of subgroups along the stated dimensions (or three scales). For example, let us say that we want to know whether blacks and whites in this community actually eat differently. From the questionnaire data, we discovered that, when asked to list foods "used" or "liked", blacks made about the same kinds of food choices as whites. However, the Food Choice Game may be slightly more discriminating. It allows for selections along several dimensions, probing, in addition, the symbolic levels of food preference. It may be that blacks and whites, from the same social class, eat about the same foods, nevertheless evincing differences in food symbolism, perhaps food preparation techniques, folklore about food and health, or whatever other dimensions are being measured. Blacks and whites may list different foods along our "healthful/not healthful" dimension because these foods have different symbolic meanings for each group. The Food Choice Game is especially handy for this sort of comparison between subgroups.

While there are many advantages in using the Q-sort, there are also some controversies. For one thing, the question of reliability or the validity of the Q-sort is rarely raised. Stephenson (1953) feels confident of its ultimate contribution to methodology and believes that Q-sort can lead us to think more realistically about features which contribute to the degree of correlation between either subject or items. In addition, he feels that Q-sort is well grounded in theory construction, often a weakness of research designs in both anthropology and nutrition.

Another controversy surrounding Q concerns the shape that the distribution will take. Subjects can sort cards under either "free" sort or "forced" conditions. If free choice, subjects are at liberty to use as much of the range (or as little) as they please; this results in differences in means and standard deviations. The general tendency among investigators has been to require subjects to distribute their Q-sort in a quasi-normal fashion, i.e., forced choice. In both instances, Q-sorts are then typically correlated, using Pearson's product-moment r, and factor analyzed (Brown 1971:283).

In the literature on Q-sort, one finds little agreement on the issue of forced vs. unforced sorts. Some authors say one way, some another. One of our goals has been to use two boards – one with forced choices, one free – to see if we can discern any real differences. So far, the free choice alternative seems to be more advantageous. Food choices are fairly matter-of-fact selections; it is difficult to force a choice when one totally rejects a food! Probably distribution shape alone does not really matter, at least within the factor-analytic context (Brown 1971:284).

The Food Choice Game has some definite advantages over the questionnaire or the 24-hour recall technique so popular in nutritional studies. This approach is, as pointed out above, both natural and non-threatening. Subjects like to sort the cards (especially these cards, as they are so delicious looking); they also like to think of the exercise as a game. The procedure is relatively time consuming, although we hope eventually to use several assistants and several boards for simultaneous administration. There is no time limit in taking the "test", and this usually appeals to informants. The Game, in fact, is fairly easy to administer.

One other advantage of this instrument is its projective, non-quantitative possibilities. If the researcher wants to obtain information other than statistical or scaled comparisons, he can simply take the sorted cards and have the informant verbalize about his or her choices. Why did you reject these foods? Why do you feel these foods are healthful? And so on. The cards can be used to make up menus, to elicit further memory recall, and to suggest new combinations. It is easy to see how useful such a procedure might be in working with patients who have language difficulties or with elderly people who have problems of verbalization. The choices then can be discussed with a didactic purpose in mind, for such a "test" should be used by nutrition educators and dieticians, as well as anthropologists.

In summary, we have discussed various research techniques that we have been using in our field study; we have pointed out some of their strengths and weaknesses in relation to doing food research; and, finally, we have offered one compromise technique for gathering and interpreting data on food choices, namely, the Food Choice Game.

Notes

1 This study is based on fieldwork carried out in Whitsett, N.C., between January, 1973, and January, 1975, and was made possible by a Faculty Research Grant and a grant from the Penrose Fund (Grant No. 7130) of the American Philosophical Society.
2 The field data was gathered by myself, with the assistance of two undergraduate anthropology students, Jewel Butler and Fred Eberhart. We did not take up residence in Whitsett but visited the community about three days a week.
3 Personal communication.
4 Most of the foods for the food cards have been borrowed from the National Dairy Council "Food Models" but laminated onto a surface or card. One could just as easily cut out magazine pictures, but consistency would be a problem.

References

Brown, Steven R.
1971 The Forced-Free Distinction in Q Technique. Journal of Educational Measurement 8: 283-287.
Crane, Julia A. and Michael V. Angrosino
1974 Field Projects in Anthropology. Morristown, New Jersey: General Learning Press.
Fitzgerald, Thomas K.
1976 Ipomoea Batatas: The Sweet Potato Revisited. Ecology of Food and Nutrition 5: 107-114.
Freedman, Robert L.
1974 Nutrition and Anthropology: Each Can Help The Other. Community Nutrition Institute Newsletter 4: 3-4.
Kerlinger, Fred N.
1964 Foundations of Behavioral Research. 2nd Edition. New York: Holt, Rinehardt, and Winston, Inc.
Mead, Margaret
1970 Changing Significance of Food. Journal of Nutrition Education. Summer: 17-19.
Osgood, Charles E., et al.
1957 The Measurement of Meaning. Urbana: University of Illinois Press.
Pelto, Pertti J.
1970 Anthropological Research: The Structure of Inquiry. New York: Harper and Row.
Schensul, Stephen L.
1970 The Anthropologist vs. The Villagers: The Cognitive Models of Marginal Rural Residents. Paper presented at the Central States Anthropological Society meeting, Bloomington, Illinois.
Whisett, William Thronton.
1926 A Brief History of Alamance County. Whitsett Historical Monographs. 4.
Wittenborn, J. R.
1961 Contributions and Current Status of Q Methodology. Psychological Bulletin 58: 132-142.

Food Use and Household Ecology in a Mexican Community

Kathleen M. Dewalt and Gretel H. Pelto, Department of Anthropology and Department of Community Medicine, University of Connecticut.

The purpose of this paper is to describe food use in a group of families in a community of central Mexico and to explore some of the factors that influence their food use patterns. In conjunction with a study of modernization in the valley of Nopalcingo,[1] data on household food use were collected from families in the major town in the valley. These patterns will be examined in relation to other aspects of household ecology: factors such as family composition, economic situation, and beliefs about the nutritional value of various foods. Before we turn to this analysis, we will discuss the theoretical and applied issues to which our research relates.

Homogeneity and Diversity of Mesoamerican Foods

The classic trilogy of the Mesoamerican diet – maize, beans and squash – is a well-known ethnographic fact. Many anthropologists with limited nutritional knowledge understand the significance of the protein complementarity of maize and beans. When lysine-deficient maize is eaten together with typtophane-deficient beans, the limiting amino acids in each are "complemented," making the combination a more nutritionally complete protein (FAO 1953; 1964). The ancient method of preparing corn by soaking it in a lime solution adds another important component, calcium, and in addition it also makes a greater amount of niacin available (FAO 1953). It has been argued that the maize-beans complex (supplemented with vitamin-rich squash, chilis, and wild greens) provided the basis for a stable agricultural economy (Kaplan 1973; Callen 1973). Thus, this dietary complex can be seen as one of the major factors that enabled the growth of population and cultural complexity in prehispanic Mesoamerica.

Although ethnographers have not been particularly interested in collecting dietary data, many monographs on Mesoamerican communities include some description or listing of commonly eaten foods (e.g., Colby and Van den Berghe 1969; Lewis 1963; Foster 1967 and others). Cultural beliefs concerning the role of food in the etiology and management of disease also capture the ethnographer's attention, and some mention of the "hot-cold" system of Mesoamerican medicine is a common feature in contemporary monographs. As is true of other aspects of behavior, description of diet tends to emphasize the normative or "typical" diet, creating an impression of gener-

79

al homogeneity. This familiar peasant diet consists of the consumption of large quantities of tortillas, with a *salsa* of chilis and beans. Stews made of tomatoes, squash, and/or greens are relatively frequent in all but the poorest of households. But festival foods, of which turkey *mole* (turkey in a thick chili sauce) is perhaps the best known, are reserved for only the most special occasions. Sometimes, however, the ethnographer will mention differences in diet within the community. Oscar Lewis documented some variation in the complexity of diet and amount of food consumed by two Tepoztecan families, one wealthy, the other poor. He concluded, however, that there is "an underlying homogeneity in types of foods eaten" (Lewis 1963: 189).

A visit to the outdoor market in any Mexican town or village with all the great variety of foodstuffs on display, is a visually and gustatorily exciting event. In central Mexico one typically finds oranges, limes, bananas, melons, mangoes and other products from "the hot country." Tomatoes, chilis, potatoes, squash, many kinds of greens, berries, apples, pears, figs, avocadoes, nuts, and many other fruits and vegetables appear in season. It is not unusual to find sellers of fish (fresh or salted); the butcher's booth is standard; sellers of eggs, cheese and milk are usual; and many markets house sellers of fancy breads and sweet meats. A survey of a large market in the administrative center of the area in which we did research revealed no less than 45 different food products. In Nopalcingo (the focus in this paper) we found that, on the average, 99 food vendors sell their products in the weekly market.

While the weekly, outdoor market is the most commanding evidence of the great variety of dietary possibilities, the local stores and the increasing presence of the "supermercado" make many foods available for purchase on a daily basis. In addition to such exotic items as corn flakes and peanut butter, a great variety of canned fruits, vegetables, sardines, macaroni products, rice and prepared mixes are typically to be found on the shelves, along with toilet paper, light bulbs and soap powders. Between the markets and the stores, then, there are possibilities for a nutritionally sound and highly varied diet. A description of the food system from the perspective of the food market, rather than the food consumer, reveals a highly adequate, complex and interesting system.

We are faced, then, with an interesting problem: on one hand ethnographers report a simple, quite homogeneous food consumption pattern; and, on the other hand, the richness and variety in the market suggest that some people must be eating diets that are quite different from the picture painted by ethnographers. Who buys all that food? Is it a small minority of the well-to-do? What variations in diet are to be found within a community? The answers to these questions require a research strategy that is somewhat different from the typical anthropological approach, for it involves the documentation of the range of variation, rather than a focus on what is presumed to be standard or normative (cf. Pelto and Pelto 1975).

Clearly, food availability is one thing and food consumption another. Some people are regularly buying those products for sale in the local markets and stores; but many people are not, as we know from health statistics and observation. Malnutrition is a very serious health problem in Mexico and Guatemala, and a great deal of research has gone into the documentation and analysis of its extent.

In attempting to understand the dynamics of malnutrition and its causes, anthropologists and nutritionists influenced by anthropological ideas have focussed on the role of cultural beliefs. For example, Cravioto (1958) has suggested that an important factor in infant malnutrition is the cultural belief that certain foods are bad for children. Jelliffe, in a survey of infant feeding in underdeveloped tropical regions, wrote: "Recently there has developed a belated realization of the great significance in human nutrition of the complex of local habits, attitudes and prejudices making up the cultural food pattern. A knowledge of this aspect of the subject is vital, especially in relation to public health progrtms aimed at improving methods of infant feeding" (1962: 19-20).

Beginning in the post-war years, one of the hallmarks of applied anthropology has been the assumption that one major factor in changing the health and nutritional status of particular populations is education. If people can be *taught* to practice good hygiene and to make better use of available resources, nutrition and health can be improved. Writing for a Mexican readership, Foster suggested that "it appears as if important categories of culture that should be more or less completely understood to carry out successful health and hygiene programs are local ideas about health, welfare, illness, their causes and treatment" (1955: 20; translation by DeWalt). Cassel (1955) also reports that the main focus of a health program among South African Zulu people was in educational modification of locally held beliefs concerning food items. Cravioto (1958), in an evaluation of infant malnutrition in Mexico, suggests that two steps are necessary to improve infant diet: there must be an improvement of sanitation to reduce dysentery, and there has to be re-education of mothers. There are many examples of applied programs in which a major emphasis has been to change beliefs about foods and to educate people in the fundamentals of good nutrition.

The theoretical position reflected in the quotations from Cassel, Foster and Cravioto, and in the writing of many applied anthropologists, has been sharply criticized. A number of writers, most notably Harris (1968) have discussed the theoretical and empirical weaknesses of the "cultural-ideological" approach. The political and pragmatic implications of various theoretical positions have become the subject of serious, and sometimes acrimonious debate. In a thoughtful discussion of the problem, Bonfil Batalla (1966) noted that many anthropological studies of health and nutrition " ... refer to subjects such as ideas and beliefs on health and illness; concepts and rationalizations about nutrition; stereotypes carried by the community about the personnel in charge of sanitation programs; communication problems derived from differences in cultural traditions, and other subjects. The need and value of such studies is unquestionable; but it is more important still to point out the fact that greater attention has been paid to these subjects than to the basic causes of public health and malnutrition problems in our countries. In general, the problems studied have secondary importance as causal elements; that is, they are not primary factors in the alarming state of chronic malnutrition and poor health which affects most of the people in Latin America" (pp. 247-248).

During the 1960s an alternative theoretical position developed, a position that is articulated in both the research and theoretical writing of anthropologists and others. Rather than focussing on beliefs and values, the emphasis is on economic, political and structural features. In research on malnutrition many writers have begun to stress the importance of variables other than local beliefs and ideas. For example, Oshima (1967) examined the role of economic and structural variables in malnutrition in Asia. He emphasized the importance of increasing income and caloric production, rather than changing cultural beliefs. Sai in a review of nutrition in underdeveloped countries, wrote, "Although this paper deals with health and nutrition problems, it has been made abundantly clear that many of these problems cannot be solved by health agencies" (1963: 231). He then suggests that the answer lies in programs of integrated economic development. Kupferer (1962), in research among the Eastern band of Cherokee, found that differences among people in matters of health were not only attributable to differences in acculturation, but that social class seemed to figure prominently in behavioral differences.

We see, then, two quite different approaches expressed in research in nutritional anthropology. The first is characterized by a focus on idea systems and the role of cultural beliefs in nutritionally relevant behavior. The second places emphasis on economic, political, and social structural factors as keys to understanding food intake patterns. The differences in these two approaches are of more than theoretical importance for they have profound policy implications. If beliefs about the qualities or values of particular foods are essentially irrelevant in food consumption behavior, then education programs that attempt to change beliefs are a waste of time and money and may even be harmful. If, on the other hand, they have important effects on eating, then education aimed at giving people information about food values might bring about desirable changes in eating habits.

We believe that anthropologists have a part to play in illuminating this and other difficult questions, but there are certainly no simple answers. While there are broad principles that probably apply everywhere, the determinants of nutritional status take on different dimensions in different parts of the world. In this study we have attempted to examine some of the factors that affect food use among a small sample of Mexican families. We were interested in finding out to what extent differences in beliefs about food were related to differences in food consumption, and to what extent other factors seemed to play important roles.

The Research in Nopalcingo

Nopalcingo is a community of about 3,000 people. It is the *cabecera* (administrative center) of a *municipio* in the northwest part of the state of Mexico. Located on the Rio Lerma, at the opening of a long valley with a mixed agricultural economy, the town serves as an economic, political, medical and religious center for a population of about 33,000 mestizos, Mazahua and Otomi Indians. Although outlying neighborhoods of the town are Indian-speaking, the town residents are almost entirely identified as Mexican and disclaim Indian-identified customs.

People in Nopalcingo make their living in a great variety of ways. Among the elite there are physicians and dentists (migrants to the town from other areas), local large-scale entrepreneurs who deal in corn and other products, and owners of prosperous stores and dealerships. Many families make a living from operating small shops and services; others derive their main income from the wages of family members who commute to Mexico City to work, returning home on weekends. In the towns there are also many families whose major source of income is farming. Some of these households have land in the *ejido* system and family members go out to work their fields during the day. While some families claim access to sizeable holdings, others have very small plots that are less than adequate to support them. There are also families with no land at all who eke out a bare subsistence through work at odd jobs, raising some food in their small garden plots and collecting wild foods.

During 1970 and in subsequent years a team of researchers from the University of Connecticut carried out research on the effects of a large-scale development project in the communities in the valley. A government program of flood control, irrigation, and various agricultural and manufacturing projects had been established in the valley in a concerted effort to improve conditions in this poor but potentially productive part of the state. Although our research was concerned mainly with the outlying villages and hamlets, we collected basic ethnographic information in Nopalcingo and carried out structured interviews with 52 informants. Each informant was asked a series of questions about household composition, economic situation, educational attainment of family members, and some other items. Food use data were obtained by asking the frequency (in times per week) of consumption of particular types of food, as well as recording the composition of the main meal (the *comida*) on the day of the interview. Food beliefs and attitudes were collected with a modified form of the Semantic Differential test (described below).

83

Food Use and Diet in Nopalcingo

Based on the survey of 52 households, the diets of families in Nopalcingo show a wide range from varied and nutritionally sound meals to inadequate and monotonous dependence or two or three staple foods. Practically all families report the daily consumption of tortillas, and a considerable number also consume bread on a daily basis. About half of the families interviewed eat fruit and vegetables regularly, but many do not. A few families eat animal proteins daily; most, however, do not. There are some who practically never do. Table I shows the frequency of consumption of various types of foods.

Table I. Frequency Distribution of Consumption of Types of Food

Food Type	(Reported) Number of Times Eaten Per Week								
	0	1	2	3	4	5	6	7	8*
Beef	4	4	6	13	3	1	–	3	18
Pork	31	14	5	2	–	–	–	–	–
Fish	45	7	–	–	–	–	–	–	–
Chicken	17	28	5	2	–	–	–	–	–
Milk	10	1	–	–	–	–	–	–	–
Cheese	16	23	5	4	1	–	–	–	3
Eggs	12	6	4	10	2	–	–	–	18
Fruit	8	11	1	4	2	–	–	–	26
Vegetables	9	18	8	6	2	–	–	–	9
Beans	–	4	4	8	1	–	–	–	35
Bread	4	2	1	1	–	–	–	–	44
Tortillas	–	1	–	–	–	–	–	–	51

* Since our informants conceptualized a week as having eight days, and reported consumption on that basis, we have maintained their convention in this and subsequent analysis.

For ease of analysis we grouped foods into six categories, representing a modified form of the "basic food groups." These six groups – 1) meat and fish, 2) milk and cheese, 3) vegetables, 4) fruits, 5) eggs and 6) beans – were then used to construct an index of Diet Complexity (the D.C. index). Although we cannot assess nutritional adequacy directly with the available data, there is evidence (cf. Chassy, et al. 1967) that a more complex diet is more likely to be nutritionally adequate than a less complex one. In addition, we have chosen our categories to reflect groups of foods that contribute nutrients important to a balanced and adequate diet. By assigning a score of one for each day (of an "eight day week") in which a food from each group is eaten, we have an index that ranges from a hypothetical zero to 48. Table II gives the distribution of scores for the 52 households on the D.C. index. The median score for the group is 33, with a range from 7 to 48. It should be noted that many families have less than adequate diets, even when we interpret the scale quite broadly.

Table II. Distribution of Scores on Index of Dietary Complexity

D.C. Score	No. of Households
45-48	3
40-44	8
35-39	10
30-34	7
25-29	8
20-24	6
15-19	3
7-14	7

Conceptions of Flavor and Healthfulness of Foods

Many anthropologists have had the uncomfortable experience of observing people consuming worms, grubs, snakes and other exotica with apparent gusto, a feature of field work that is frequently used to illustrate "cultural relativism" back home. The idea that food preferences are culturally conditioned is generally accepted, and there is ample proof of this principle in ethnographic writing. On the other hand, there has been very little documentation of *intra*-group differences in food preference outside of our own society. If beliefs about the healthfulness and flavorfulness of foods influence their consumption, we could hypothesize that the differences in food consumption illustrated in Tables I and II might be related to such beliefs. For example, perhaps many people don't consume vegetables because they don't like them or don't drink milk because they consider it to be somewhat unhealthy.

In order to get a picture of food beliefs in Nopalcingo, as well as to test this hypothesis, we devised a version of the Osgood Semantic Differential test. People were handed a board with seven slots and a stack of cards with pictures of various foods. They were told that one end of the board represented the highly desirable quality of "best flavor," while the other represented "poor taste" or "least flavor." They were then asked to place each of the food cards in the slot that best represented the characteristics of that food. The task was repeated with the ends of the board representing the continuum from "most healthful" to "least healthful." We found that people readily understood the "game" and enjoyed playing it.

The results of this research procedure suggest that conceptions about food qualities in Nopalcingo are nearly as varied and heterogenous as is food consumption itself. One would be hard-pressed to describe a *shared* cultural pattern of evaluations about the healthfulness and flavorfulness of particular foods. On the other hand, there is also evidence of cultural influence in these data – interestingly, showing up in the form of polarization of opinion, rather than replicated uniformity. Some foods – especially beans and pork – show a sharp division of opinion, with about half the people rating them very high in flavor and half very low. Although we cannot establish it on the basis of our data, it seems possible that people who rate beans as very low are expressing an attitude of rejection of "Indian" or "poor people's" food, while those who rate it highly are more emotionally accepting of traditional elements. The low rating some women assign to pork may be a reflection of "modern" attitudes about disease causation, for some people told us that pork is bad to eat because it contains little "animalitos" that cause people to become sick.

While these responses do require interpretation in terms of the food habits and patterns of rural Mexico, it is also clear from the size of the standard deviations in Table III that there are differences of opinion about the characteristics of all of the foods tested. In every case the range of scores covered the full range of slots on the semantic differential board.

Table III. Health and Flavor Ratings

| Type of Food | Flavor | | Healthfulness | | Correlation of |
	Mean	S.D.	Mean	S.D.	Health & Flavor
Beef	5.7	1.5	5.7	1.5	.17
Pork	3.9	2.4	2.4	1.7	.32
Chicken	6.0	1.5	6.2	1.4	.25
Fish	4.5	2.6	4.3	2.5	.59
Cheese	5.0	1.8	4.5	2.0	.28
Milk	6.1	1.7	6.1	1.5	.10
Eggs	4.8	2.1	5.5	2.0	.49
Vegetables	5.1	2.1	5.8	1.6	.41
Beans	4.3	2.2	4.4	1.9	.41
Fruit	6.1	1.5	6.2	1.2	.60
Tortillas	5.6	1.8	5.6	1.7	.48
Bread	5.5	1.9	5.2	1.9	.35

Although there are wide individual differences in beliefs about the flavor and healthfulness of foods, there are also interesting, if expectable consistencies in individual food conceptions. Thus, there is a tendency for ratings of health and flavor to be correlated (see column 5 Table III). Furthermore people apparently perceive groups or categories of foods which share similar ratings of health or flavor. We discovered this feature through a factor analysis, which was intended as a methodological tool to reduce the data to more manageable proportions. The factor analysis of the "healthfulness" ratings identified five factors.

We see from these factors that ratings of, for example, fish or eggs are essentially uncorrelated with ratings of beef, pork, chicken and cheese; whereas people who give high ratings to beef or chicken are also likely to rate bread and tortillas as high in healthful qualities.

Table IV. Factor Analysis of Healthfulness Ratings

Food	Factors				
	1	2	3	4	5
Beef	.73	.14	—.07	.05	.11
Chicken	.55	.48	—.07	—.39	—.28
Pork	.42	—.22	—.08	—.01	—.01
Cheese	.52	.00	—.07	.35	.25
Bread	.63	.18	.32	—.12	.30
Tortillas	.62	.01	.24	—.07	—.28
Fruits	—.01	.87	.21	.25	.05
Vegetables	.08	.67	—.02	.22	.02
Milk	—.02	.62	—.07	—.08	.10
Beans	.02	—.04	.99	—.05	—.12
Fish	—.01	.23	—.06	.71	.03
Eggs	.06	.10	—.09	.05	.66

We interpret these factors as follows:
Factor 1 – "the protein factor" (includes beef, pork, chicken, cheese, and also bread and tortillas)
Factor 2 – "the fruit and vegetable factor"
Factor 3 – "beans"
Factor 4 – "fish"
Factor 5 – "eggs"

Do Ideas about Food Qualities Influence Their Consumption?

Returning to the hypothesis suggested above – that conceptions about (e.g., the healthfulness of) particular foods influences the frequency of consumption – we examined the food belief factors from the semantic differential task in relation to the reported food use data.[2] A correlational analysis reveals that in *only two cases* – that of beans and tortillas – is there a relationship between belief and consumption. People who believe that beans and tortillas are very healthful report eating them more times per week than people who rate these foods as lower in healthfulness. The direction of causality, however, can be argued either way. Perhaps people eat these foods often because they think of them as highly nutritious. On the other hand, it is possible that people who rely heavily on tortillas and beans out of necessity adjust their perceptions to accord with or to justify their eating habits.

As can be seen in Tables V and VI, with the exception of tortillas and beans, *people do not eat more of foods that they consider to be highly nutritious.* Thus, there is virtually *no relationship* between the food beliefs of the female household head and the nutritional adequacy of her family's food patterns, whether measured in terms of the consumption of particular types of food or the overall richness of their diet, as reflected in the D.C. scale.

Table V. Correlation of Food Belief Factors with Number of Times These Foods are eaten in a week

Factor	Food	Correlation
1	Beef	+.04
	Pork	—.01
	Chicken	—.04
	Cheese	—.14
	Bread	—.14
	Tortillas	+.32*
2	Fruit	+.15
	Vegetables	+.16
	Milk	+.23
3	Beans	+.31*
4	Fish	+.13
5	Eggs	+.04

* $p < .05$

Table VI. Dietary Complexity and Food Belief Factors

Factor	Correlation with D.C. Index
1	—.10
2	+.26
3	+.15
4	.00
5	—.15

None of these correlations are significant at $p < .05$

Determinants of Food Intake in Nopalcingo

If a woman's food beliefs apparently have very little effect on her family's food intake, then what factors are important in explaining the large differences revealed in the survey? To answer this question we must go back to look at aspects of household ecology. As mentioned above, there are obvious differences in wealth and income, differences in the number of wage earners, differences in access to land and in the ownership of animals. All of these characteristics might be expected to influence the amount and kinds of foods coming into a household.

In addition to differences in the material characteristics there are also differences among Nopalcingo's inhabitants in access to information. Some people have direct contact with urban affairs and have travelled to other parts of the country; others have never travelled outside the valley. Woods and Graves (1973), in their study of illness management behavior in Guatemala, found that exposure to new ideas had an important, although indirect, influence on people's use of modern medical practitioners. It could be argued that exposure to urban ideas and alternative life styles might also influence a family's behavior and the allocation of resources for food.

Theoretically, any or all of these aspects of household ecology and experience could play a role in determining dietary complexity and other aspects of family nutrition. Rather than individually examining the relationship of each theoretically interesting variable (such as health, occupation, exposure to new ideas) to dietary complexity, in the form of two variable correlations, we wanted to examine their multiple, additive effects and relative importance. To do this we used a multiple regression analysis, a statistical tool in which a series of variables are entered into a predictive equation with the most powerful predictors entered first. The effect of previously entered variables is controlled for in each subsequent step, and new variables are added until the significance level of remaining variables falls below an acceptable level. At this point the computations are terminated. In setting up the multiple regression analysis, we used the full sample of 52 households.

We measured wealth with a number of variables, rather than as cash income. Cash income is often very difficult to assess, in part because of people's reluctance to reveal this information. In addition, cash income is less meaningful and more difficult to estimate in a peasant economy. Wealth, then, was measured with several variables, including "number of wage earners in the households" and the "occupation of the household head." The latter was divided into three categories: upper level (professional and entrepreneurial), middle level (white collar, service and ejido farmers), and lowest level (unskilled labor, including farm laborers.) Another measure of wealth is the "material-style-of-life" index, a Guttman scale composed of material items (size and construction of house, ownership of applicances, types of furniture, etc.) that reflect the accumulated cash expenditures of a household over time.

The economic variables were entered into a regression analysis, along with measures of animal ownership, education of the male household head, measures of exposure to outside influence (e.g., birthplace, location of siblings) and variables of household composition. Table VII shows the results of this analysis:

Table VII

Variable	Cumulative Multiple R	% of Variance Accounted for %
1. Material-Style-of-Life (High)	.54	29
2. Kill Animals for Food (Yes)	.64	40
3. Occupation of Household Head (High)	.70	49
4. Years of Education (male) (High)	.73	53
5. No. of people in Household (High)	.74	54
6. No. of Women in Household (Low)	.75	56
7. Birthplace (female) (City)	.77	59
8. No. of Large Animals Owned (High)	.78	61
9. Have Siblings in Other Cities (Yes)	.79	62
10. No. of Males in Household (Low)	.90	63
11. No. of Wage Earners in Household (High)	.81	65

In this table, the most important variables are listed first, and the remaining variables are listed in decreasing order of importance in terms of the amount of predictive power they add to the regression equation (this can be seem from the incremental change in the multiple R produced by each variable when the variables entered before it are controlled for).

The most powerful predictor of nutritional adequacy of Nopalcingo families is material lifestyle or general economic well being. This variable accounts for nearly 30% of the variance in our D.C. index. People who enjoy a higher standard of living in housing and furnishings also enjoy a more varied and nutritionally adequate diet. From Table VII we see that ownership of animals that are killed for household consumption is also very important. This indicates that families who put time and money into raising animals for their own table enjoy a better diet, *independent of wealth*. Variables 3 and 5 are both further indicators of the importance of socioeconomic status on food consumption. Men with more education and better jobs earn more, and some of that money is used to buy food.

Household composition is also relevant for nutritional adequacy. Our interpretation of the effect of the household composition variables is that families with able-bodied, productive children enjoy better nutrition, for the working junior members of the family contribute their earnings to the family pot. On the other hand, those families that are enlarged by the presence of dependent elderly do not seem to fare as well, as can be seen by the effect of variables 6 and 10. Thus, it is nutritionally "smart" for Nopalcingo couples to have large families, provided their children become wage earners at an early age, a situation that has been quite possible in the expanding economy of the town.

Exposure to urban ideas also appears to influence family eating, though to a lesser degree. The fact that urban birthplace of the woman and having siblings in other parts of the country (usually urban) is positively *correlated* with the D.C. index suggests some effect of new ideas about eating. On the other hand, it is noteworthy that the education of the female household head does *not* correlate with nutritional status. Although it was entered into the regression analysis, it did not reach a level of significance high enough to be included in the equation. In further exploration of this finding, we discovered that the woman's level of education does not correlate with any of the sub-sections of the D.C. scale (the six food groups). Furthermore, her educational level does not influence her perception of the healthfulness of particular foods, with the exception of pork. There is a low, but significant correlation, in which women with more education tend to rate pork as low in healthfulness: ($r = -.28$; $p < .05$).

The results of the preceding analysis suggest that the major determinant of dietary flexibility and variety in Nopalcingo is socio-economic status. It has been demonstrated that households with better jobs and more wage earners enjoy a higher dietary standard of living, along with other amenities. Raising animals for food also contributes to improved diet. The role of "modern" or "urban ideas" is much more equivocal and difficult to assess, particularly since a woman's educational level does not appear to influence family eating patterns. Her beliefs about the nutritional value of specific foods is apparatly also irrelevant to family food consumption.

Implications of the Findings for Nutritional Change Programs

The survey of food use in Nopalcingo, as well as the clinical impressions of local physicians and health workers, shows that many families have less than adequate nutrition. While there are relatively few children within the town who show evidence of frank malnutrition, we judge the subclinical level to be fairly high. In many families where caloric intake is sufficient to maintain normal growth, the lack of fully nutritionally balanced meals probably has a more subtle effect, measured indirectly in disease frequency and reduction of energy. There is, undoubtedly, room for improvement in family nutrition.

Reasoning from the cultural-determinist point of view, many applied anthropologists and public health workers would argue that a well-planned program of education – especially if it were coupled with a program to start gardens and encourage animal keeping – would be one way of improving family nutrition. The conditions for testing the usefulness of an education program are present in the community in the form of already existing differences in educational level and food beliefs. From our examination of the relationships between these variables and dietary adequacy, we would suggest that the introduction of an education program is unlikely to achieve the desired goals. Preliminary data from another community in which a number of women participated in a series of nutrition classes and garden projects reinforces this view. When the diets of women who attended the classes were compared with those who had not attended, no differences could be found (DeWalt 1971).

From the research results in Nopalcingo, it appears that, in this community, people are already oriented to the value of good nutrition. That is, when they have financial means they use them to improve their nutrition. In contrast to some popular images, the anachronism of a poor household with half-starved children listening to a stereo or watching T.V. does not occur in this community. The problem, then, is not education or unwise allocation of resources but financial means.

One problem with results of this kind is that it leaves the applied health worker in a very difficult position. The development and implementation of an education program is an activity that can be carried out by a dedicated and intelligent worker, with minimal expense and minimal cooperation from governmental agencies. Changing the economic structure of the community in such a way as to provide everyone with the means to maintain an adequate diet is something else again!

We are not suggesting, on the basis of this study, that educating people in Nopalcingo (and other such communities) about good nutrition would be completely ineffective in terms of changing eating patterns. A well-designed program that included all family members, and especially the male household heads, might bring about some significant changes in the allocation of household resources, including the directing of more resources into food buying or production. But, there is also compelling evidence to show that increasing the resources that families have to work with is likely to have a dramatic effect on nutritional adequacy. It is to the larger picture, then – of household ecology in relation to the economic and political structure of the community and the region – that health workers or change agents must turn their attention in their efforts to improve health and nutritional status, at least in Nopalcingo.

Notes

1 To protect the privacy of the people in the valley, we have used pseudonyms to identify the communities.
2 Twelve of the fifty-two interviews were with males, and these were deleted from the correlational analysis of beliefs and eating patterns. While the preferences of male household members probably do have some effect of food choices, we felt we did not have enough information about possible male/female differences in food beliefs to justify considering them as a single group. Since women in Nopalcingo are almost solely responsible for buying and preparing food, we felt that their attitudes might more directly influence food consumption than those of their spouses. However, since the data on income, family size, etc., represent the collective situation of households, rather than individuals, we return to the full sample when examining these variables.

References

Abramson, J. H., H. C. Slome, and C. Kosovsky
1963 Food Frequency Interview as an Epidemiological Tool. American Journal Public Health 53: 1093-1101.
Callen, E. O.
1973 Dietary Patterns in Mexico Between 6500 and 1580 A.D. Man and His Tools. (C. Smith, C. Earle, eds.), Birmingham: University of Alabama Press.
Cassel, John
1955 A Comprehensive Health Program Among South African Zulus. In Benjamin Paul, ed., Health, Culture and Community. N.Y.: Russell Sage Publ.
Chassy, J. P., A. G. van Veen, and F. W. Young
1967 The Application of Social Science Research Methods to the Study of Food Habits and Food Consumption in an Industrializing Duo. American Journal of Clinical Nutrition 20: 56-64.
Cravioto, Jouguins
1958 Consideaciores Epidemiologilos of Basos Parala Formulation de un Programma de Pneuencion de la Wes Nutricion.
DeWalt, K. M.
1971 Preliminary Investigation in the Effects of a Home Improvement and Nutritional Change Program. Paper read at Northeastern Anthropological Association Meetings April, 1971.

92

FAO (Food and Agriculture Org of U.N.)
1953   Maize and Maize Diets. *FAO*, Nutritional Studies 9, Rome.
FAO
1964   Legumes in Human Nutrition. FAO Nutritional Studies #19, Rome: FAO.
Foster, George M.
1955   Analisis Anthropologico Intercultural de un Programma de Ayuda Tecnico. Instituto Nacional Indigenista: Mexico.
Foster, George M.
1969   Tzintzuntzan: Mexican Peasants in a Changing World. Little, Brown and Co.: Boston.
Harris, Marvin
1968   The Rise of Anthropological Theory. New York: Crowell.
Jelliffe. D. B.
1962   Culture, Social Change and Infant Feeding-Trends in Tropical Regions. American Journal Clinical Nutrition 10: 19-45.
Kaplan, Lawrence
1973   Ethnobotanical and Nutritional Factors in the Domestication of American Beans. Earle Smith (ed.) Man and His Foods. Birmingham: University of Alabama Press.
Kupferer, Harriet J.
1962   Health Practices and Educational Aspirations as Indicators of Acculturation and Social Class Among the Eastern Cherokee. Social Forces 41(2), 154-163.
Lewis, Oscar
1963   (Orig. 1951) Life in a Mexican Village: Tepotzlan Restudied. Urbana: University of Illinois Press.
Marr, J. W., J. A. Heady, J. N. Morris
1961   Towards a Method for Large-scale Individual Diet Surveys. Proc. 3rd Intern. Congre. Dietetics. London: Newman Books.
Oshima, Harry T.
1967   Food Consumption, Nutrition and Economic Development in Asian Countries. Economic Development and Culture Change 15: 397.
Pelto, Pertti J., and Gretel H. Pelto
1975   Intracultural Diversity: Some Theoretical Issues. American Ethnologist 2(1): 1-18.
Sai, F. T.
1963   The Health and Nutrition Problems of Less Developed Areas. Impact of Science on Society 111-3: 213-232.
Woods, Clyde and Theodore Graves
1973   Process of Medical Change in a Highland Guatemalan Town. Latin American Studies Center, University of California, Los Angeles.

Sociological Aspects
of Nutrition Education in Jamaica

Han Bantje, Mwanza Program of Public Health, Tanzania.

Introduction

Anthropometric surveys to determine the nutritional status of Jamaican children (under five) in the rural areas have shown that just over $1^0/_0$ of them are seriously malnourished (below $60^0/_0$ of standard-weight for age), about 10% suffer from moderately severe malnutrition (60% - 75% of standard-weight for age), whereas some 40% are mildly malnourished (75% - 90% of standard-weight for age). Data from poor urban areas show a slightly lower prevalence of infant malnutrition (Gurney, Fox, Neill 1972; Bantje 1974). The type of malnutrition commonly found in Jamaica is protein-calorie malnutrition, a syndrome consisting of a deficiency of proteins and calories in the diet in combination with gastro-enteric and respiratory infections.

There are indications that a shift in the pattern of infant malnutrition has taken place over the past decades. Because of changes in feeding habits, the age at which protein-calorie malnutrition occurs has been lowered, and the kwashiorkor type of nutritional disease (caused primarily by protein deficiency) has made place for marasmic and mixed types (cased primarily by caloric deficiency). The peak of infant malnutrition now falls between 6 and 18 months, the slow recovery normally being completed by the end of the fifth year.

Under the influence of theories about the implications of malnutrition for the physical and intellectual development of the child, concern has been expressed of late in government circles about the fact that half of the children of the low-income groups show signs of malnutrition. Also one has become aware of the cost to the country in terms of the expense of hospital treatment of children suffering from malnutrition and related diseases and in terms of reduced labor output of inadequately nourished adults (Cook 1968).

Studies of malnutrition in Jamaica have been done mainly from the medical and nutritional viewpoints, such as dietary surveys, studies of mortality and growth development, and studies of clinical and metabolic changes related to malnutrition (Ahsworth, Waterlow n.d.). In fact, much biochemical data concerned with malnutrition of the young are derived from research in

Jamaica. Until recently, little study had been done on the social and economic factors which induce malnutrition. It is true that these factors have been taken into account in a general way, but no attempts had been made to assess their importance in relation to specific cases, target groups or programs. Intervention programs have been based on the spread of information about dietetics and proper feeding practices by way of training programs for middle-level personnel. Besides, in the last few years, there have been several field projects in the rural areas to test the effectiveness of nutrition education.

The core of the present paper is a discussion of such field projects. In order to prevent malnutrition, it's cause has to be understood not only in terms of feeding practices but in terms of the social and economic conditions that produce them. At first sight the conditions in Jamaica appear quite favorable: a relatively high per capita national income ($\pm$ \$ 600), a favorable climate and fertile soils, absence of tropical diseases like malaria or bilharzia, and a relatively well-developed public health system. One may wonder then, first of all, why malnutrition persists under these conditions. The answer to this question can be given by examining the economic structure of the country.

The Economy

Jamaica's economy displays a markedly dualistic character. The modern, industrial, capital-intensive, urban level; and the archaic, labor-intensive rural level bear little relation to each other. The national economy depends mainly on the mining of bauxite, the exports from plantation agriculture (sugar and bananas), and tourism. These sectors are all highly dependent on foreign capital, foreign control, and world market prices – therefore, sensitive to world inflation. The foreign exchange income from these sectors is not transformed into production assets which might benefit the population as a whole, such as food production, manufacture, or the creation of jobs but is largely spent on consumption goods. This enables a small section of the population to live comfortably by Western standards. The great demand for imported goods thus actually hampers the development of the internal economy. In the way of food, for example, Jamaica imports 50% of her caloric requirements and 70% of her protein requirements. This entails not only a heavy drain on capital resources but indicates the poor state of the rural economy, which is basically agrarian and involves some 60% of the population.

The rural level has not only been left behind but actually set back by a combination of soaring food prices and stationary incomes. The plight of the national economy has not been accompanied by any significant improvements of the rural economy. Following rapid urbanization, in particular the exodus of young adults from the rural areas, the focus of the society has shifted to the towns, while the rural area was reduced to an unviable slum. The government admits to a 25% unemployment rate, for which the rural area is the largest representative. The per capita rural income is less than one tenth of the average national income. Living conditions are often appalling and perspectives virtually nil.

This imbalance also entails effects in the cultural and psychological spheres. Because of the small size of the island and the frequency of rural-urban communications – as well as through the influence of the mass media – urban standards have invaded the rural area. The influence of migrants returning from abroad also plays a part in this. Every year some 10,000 agricultural laborers work in the U.S.A. on a seasonal contract. The expectations and ambitions which are derived from the familiarity with these urban standards clash with the actual conditions and low prospects of rural life at home. This clash gives rise to strong feelings of relative deprivation, resentment, frustration, and mental withdrawal. According to a local saying these people "dream of heaven, but they live in hell." There is an "I don't belong here" mentality that finds symbolic expression in the purchase of luxury goods – sometimes at great effort – to create the illusion of a better life. The purchase of expensive commercial baby foods, to be discussed in the next paragraph, should also be seen in this light.

Patterns of Infant Feeding

In the wake of the change from breastfeeding to artificial feeding in the U.S.A., Jamaica is now undergoing a similar development. Initially an urban phenomenon, artificial feeding is spreading rapidly into the rural area and is still on the increase. Urban mothers breastfeed less than rural mothers, younger mothers are found to nurse their babies shorter than older mothers, and later children often get less breastfeeding than earlier children of the same mother.

The attractiveness of artificial feeding lies in its convenience and connotation of sophistication. It enables the young mother to move around, to have another boyfriend, or try and find a job. But it should also be realized that, in spite of the present official policy of "back to the breast," artificial feeding has been taught through the health services and is still informally encouraged at various levels. Especially to be blamed is the fact that glucose is commonly prescribed as a treatment for intestinal troubles in babies because it introduces the mother – and the child – to the practice of bottle feeding at a very early age. The false glamour of the propaganda by the commercial milk companies also plays a part but would not be so effective if it were not given tacit support in hospitals and health centers. Perhaps as a result of somewhat misinterpreted nutrition education, few mothers now believe that breastmilk alone is enough for their baby. Additional bottle feeding has become a must. Mothers are even heard to remark: "We don't get anything for it. It takes too much out of us."

In the rural districts of Western Jamaica, where these observations were made, the following pattern prevails: breastfeeding is supplemented by glucose almost from birth; from the second month the glucose is replaced by commercial powdered milk, sweetened condensed milk or, more rarely, diluted cow's milk. The period of breastfeeding itself varies greatly, depending on whether the baby continues to accept the breats once it is familiar with the bottle. "Self-weaning" was mentioned most often by the mothers as the reason why they stopped breastfeeding. Some 75% of the children are breastfed for more than 3 months, whereas 10% are still breastfed at the age of 1 year. The age at which more solid foods are introduced also varies from case to case. Some mothers do so from about 6 months, but one also finds children in their 3rd year still mostly being fed on thin cornmeal or oats porridge, alternated with biscuits and tea.

The ills of this pattern mostly result from its application in the poorer homes. All too often the milk that is fed to infants is too diluted, given too infrequently; or otherwise undesirable subsitutes are used such as bushtea, condensed milk, or sugar water. Moreover, because of poor hygiene, gastric infections are common. Their cause is not understood and the remedy is to feed the child on glucose, or bushtea, or not at all. Breastfeeding is usually stopped in case of gastric or respiratory infections on the assumption that the milk is too heavy.

A shortened period of breastfeeding is frequently viewed as a direct cause of infant malnutrition, and therefore longer periods of breastfeeding are strongly emphasized in nutrition education. There are indications that such a view does not hold true for all cases. In a rural district of Western Jamaica, I found that short breastfeeding (up to 3 months) was more common in households where no malnutrition occurred (26%) than in households where malnutrition was found (8%). The young women who are most likely to stop breastfeeding early are often among the more dynamic and ambitious. They tend to be more interested in child care and have higher standards of hygiene, and to be in a better position to secure financial support, either from their boyfriends or by working themselves. The real danger lies in the adoption of these practices in the poorest households. There infants may be found under the care of slightly older sisters, while the mother works in the field all day. Their only comfort is likely to be a bottle of "tea" (diluted condensed milk) of which the older children may also take their share.

Poverty and Ignorance

It is generally recognized that the causative factors of malnutrition may be seen as a complex of poverty and ignorance, but there is no unanimity as to their relative importance and underlying causes. The dominant interpretation in Jamaica – now being challenged more and more by progressive elements in the society – is that poverty is caused by ignorance and a poorly developed work ethos rather than by structural features of the society. As a result the "ignorance" component is emphasized, whereas the "poverty" component is underplayed. This attitude is reflected in a profusion of pro-

97

grams that are focused on the concept of education, without being matched by any serious attacks on poverty. It is true – as is sometimes said in defense of this state of affairs – that it is not within the competence of health educators or nutritionists to combat poverty as such. Nevertheless, one wonders if a more effective approach would not be possible by founding education projects on the hard realities of lower-class life, rather than on pre-established ideas.

Formal teaching of the principles of nutrition takes place through a number of high and middle-level schools and training colleges, as well as by way of special courses for middle-level government personnel. The importance of nutrition education for the improvement of feeding habits at the middle and working-class levels is incontestable. But the question is whether this knowledge effectively reaches the lower levels and thus contributes to the reduction of the incidence of infant malnutrition. We shall discuss the social barriers that hamper the spread of knowledge and the conditions of poverty which prevent people at the lowest economic level (the target population) from taking advantage of nutrition education.

This emphasis on nutrition education does not imply that nothing at all has been done to fight the symptoms of poverty. Over the years there have been various programs to distribute food supplements (especially powdered milk) by way of the schools and clinics. These programs have some drawbacks in that they often function intermittently, that the food is not always put to proper use, and that they induce people to become dependent on them – sometimes to the point where they show no interest in any project unless they are given free food at the same time. While one may defend food aid on the ground that it brings relief in desperate situations, it does not in any way tackle the actual causes of poverty.

Other relevant approaches to combating poverty include the government price-controls on essential food items and the subsidizing of school meals. Plans and experiments to produce a low-cost infant food to replace the expensive commercial feeds have been going on for years. In 1974 this project seemed in an advanced stage. Important results can be expected from the establishment of minimum wage rates (which were announced by the Prime Minister in 1974 and were to come into effect in 1975), but only for those who are able to secure jobs.

The Social Organization of Nutrition Education

Some basic points have to be made regarding nutrition education as it applies to the grassroot level. The first concerns what might be called the social organization of the education system. This involves three categories of people:
1 The nutrition educators with an urban middle-class background who design the content and strategy of the projects. This group consists of local university graduates, backed up by international experts.

98

2 The middle-level cadre, especially nurses and other health staff, who are expected to transmit the knowledge emanating from the top level. They are recruited mainly from the rural middle class.
3 The beneficiaries, supposedly including all levels of the lower class.
This transmission of education "from the top to the bottom" rests on the assumption of a free flow of information through these various levels. In reality, however, there are a number of factors that prevent this free flow of information. Among these are:
1 The strong class feelings that prevail in Jamaican society preventing the development of a true national commitment. The absence of a sense of responsibility for, and identification with, the state of affairs in the country as a whole is a major political problem and an ongoing concern of progressive intellectuals.
2 The vast difference in life style, wealth, and degree of security and protection between people from different status levels, which insures that they live in different worlds and therefore find it hard to identify with each other's world view. These differences are consciously and unconsciously expressed in details such as speech, way of dressing, and social habits.
3 The established patterns of interaction and communication between people of different classes, which are highly restricted and stereotyped, always tending to re-enact status differences rather than trying to bridge them. Classes in Jamaica are to be taken as broad strata of the population without unifying solidarity. Class behavior is positional: the same person may assume a superior or inferior role according to the circumstances.

Class Perception

Class behavior is a reflexion of culturally defined patterns of identification and perception. In the West Indies these are linked on the one hand to the "middle-class myth," the body of ideas and assumptions about the lower-class that prevails among the middle class. On the other hand, they are linked to the adaptations of the lower class to their subordinate position in the society.

It should be pointed out that, in general, the urban middle-class is not familiar with the extremes of poverty that govern the daily life of the poorest section of the society. They do not come in contact with these people and make no attempt to do so. Their perception of problems is conditioned by a number of myths that stem from the past and are still reiterated in different forms. There is now a tendency to supplant the cruder qualifications of the lower class by pseudo-scientific arguments. Daily one may hear the opinions expressed that there can be no shortage on the land, because "people can just pick from the trees" (referring to the rather plentiful supply of fruit-bearing trees); that people are poor because they don't want to work (supported with the argument that some farmers cannot find field laborers – which is true, but rather as a result of the extremely low wages those farmers offer); that middle-class leadership is indispensable, because the lower-class has no organizational abilities. The atmosphere is one of strong paternalism, sometimes corresponding to near-feudal relationships.

The essence of these myths is that they support the dominant position of the middle class while misjuding the realities of lower-class life. The condition of the poor is viewed as the result of inherent characteristics (coming very close to genetic inferiority) and not as a result of the society that prevents economic and social equality. This is not to say that certain middle-class individuals are not sincerely interested in improving the lot of the common man. In fact, many are but on a strictly individual basis, and this concern is expressed in terms of charity – a regular concomitant of rigid class societies. Far from attacking their structural features, it underlines the dependence of the poor and the dominant position of the rich, while providing the latter as it were with an alibi.

In many cases lower-class attitudes can be shown to be perfectly rational. But in other cases the cultural and psychological patterns that have been developed by the lower class in response to its subordinate status are evidently characterized by suspicion, cunningness, stubborn refusal to cooperate, overt agressiveness; and at the same time by a syndrome of dependency, self-hate, fatalism and withdrawal. These are the attitudes shown by Allport (1954) to be typical of the oppressed. They are dysfunctional in that they strive towards emotional satisfaction rather than the search for rational solutions. It can be said with some reason, therefore, that lower-class people do not always make the necessary efforts themselves and do not take full advantage of the facilities that are available to them. But the irrational response of some individuals at certain occasions should not be seen as unavoidable and representative of the whole group.

Madelin Kerr (1952) had dealt with the problems of self-identification of individuals that are torn between the respectability of official (middle-class) norms and the convenience of tactitly accepted lower-class alternatives. This is particularly true for those who have recently risen from the masses. In their striving for acceptance by a higher social level, they make every effort to distanciate themselves from the lower level, thereby incurring the jealousy and malice of the latter. Obviously these patterns of class perception affect the relations between individuals from different classes. We shall discuss their impact on education projects that precisely depend on the interaction of people from different social backgrounds.

The Contents of Nutrition Education

Nutrition education for the lower classes is based on the promotion of breastfeeding, the use of mixtures of locally available foods (so-called multimixes) as weaning foods, and general concepts of nutrition, hygiene, and infant care. These principles are excellent in themselves but not sufficiently adapted to the actual life conditions of the lower class and the adjustments to poverty they have made for themselves. We have already referred to the prevailing ideas about breastfeeding and the considerations of fashion and convenience which deter the young mothers from adopting it. The propagation of multi-mixes hardly takes into account the lack of differentiation in the diet, the irregularity of meals, the lack of time available to poor mothers, and the lack of storage facilities – not to forget the problem of social and cultural acceptability. To get across the principle of multi-mixes, mothers are taught the basic food groups and their nutritive value by means of visual aids and sometimes demonstrations of meal preparation. It was found that regular attendants at the group meetings were able to memorize what they had been taught but that very few people made attempts to put it into practice. This was commonly attributed to lack of motivation but more likely resulted from the fact that people considered this kind of knowledge irrelevant to their situation. For nutrition education to be effective, it has to base itself on the actual life conditions of those it is trying to reach and provide realistic solutions to felt problems and needs. In fact the assumptions behind nutrition education are too academic and often quite alien to the actual needs as experienced by the target population.

The Characteristics of Rural Nutrition Education Projects

Nutrition education projects show a number of common traits which directly result from what we have called the social organization of nutrition education and the underlying middle-class assumptions:
1 An *urban bias* is introduced by the mental makeup of the project directors and the simple fact that they reside in the capital. A few times a month they drive or fly to the project area for a day or two (a day meaning only a few hours because of the long trip.) As a result they spend very little time on the project, and that time is more taken up by discussions with rural middle-class friends and colleagues than by direct contact with the population. Therefore they do not become familiar enough with the local population to gain their confidence or to understand their reactions. At the same time they are often reluctant to delegate responsibilities, especially where decision-making powers and spending of funds are concerned, and thus fail to make use of information provided by field officers.
2 Associated with this idea is the *attitude toward data-collection*. If someone happens to be available for the job, social and economic surveys are conducted, sometimes on a fairly large scale. Lip service is paid to the importance of the collection of "baseline data" and they are usually added as neatly tabled appendices to final reports. But little attempt is made to interpret such data realistically, i.e., to base the strategy of the project on conclusions drawn from them. More often than not, all major decisions have already been taken before the collection of base-line data even starts.

Unfamiliarity with the vital importance of socio-economic data may play a part here.

3 Instead of concentrating on practical and concrete matters, such as the availability and accessability of food items and services, the projects are focused on the promotion of knowledge and the attack of social-psychological aspects such as *motivations and attitudes.* As the mechanisms of causation and change at this level of reality are still largely unknown, the design of strategies and the assessment of results are arrived at by intuition rather than by scientific method. It is the author's conviction that attitudes and motivations develop by and large in reaction to the socio-cultural reality and in particular to it's power structure. Assuming this is true, little can be expected from attacks on attitudes without corresponding changes in the social structure and the living conditions of the target population.

4 In practice the outcome is that nutrition education projects mainly consist of *trying to talk people into changing* their attitudes and practices. Some individuals may try to follow the advice that is given, mostly because of good personal relations with one of the field officers. But the general picture is that the attendance at meetings drops rapidly once people have satisfied themselves that the project is not likely to bring them any direct material benefits. Those who keep coming back usually know in the long run what they have been taught, but they rarely understand the reasons behind this knowledge and do not integrate it with their established feeding practices because there is little connection between the two. A common observation is that regular attendants come from the group that is not desperately poor and has some potential for social mobility. To them attendance is status promoting, and their feeding habits already conform more closely to what is desirable than those of the target population. The lack of effectiveness of such projects is illustrated by the example of a project that was closely observed by the author. In the district concerned, half of the mothers whose children were found to be underweight never attended the project at all.

5 In the course of a project the nutritional status of some children may improve at the cost of much persuasion and personal attention. It is questionable if such improvements justify the amount of time and money that is invested in the project. Also, one may wonder how exactly the improvement has been arrived at. It may mean that a larger share of the household's resources and the mother's time are spent on a particular infant for the time being, but there is no guarantee that the same line of action will be followed with a next child when there is nobody to persuade the mother.

Ritualization

Apart from the odd expatriate, field officers are recruited from the rural lower-middle class, either on an employment or voluntary basis. They are expected to carry out the instructions from the urban level without having much say in the matter. They have to try and convert somewhat vague and unwieldy concepts into practical action. Work at the grassroot level is not any more popular with them than it is with the urban class; and, if they accept to do it at all, it is out of need rather than conviction. Employment opportunities are very few, and this kind of a job may be a stepping stone to get a better job in town or abroad. This kind of worker does not identify with the lower class. Their greatest fear is to get "mixed up", to be associated with a level to which they are still very close but with which they emphatically deny any connections. To emphasize their status they tend to voice middle-class prejudices, which is likely to make them unpopular with the target group. In their defense it should be said that the envy and antagonism of the common people on the one hand, and their lack of decision-making power on the other, make their work very difficult. They are expected to propagate practices in which they only half believe themselves and of which they can only see too clearly that their applicability for the target group is very limited.

Even if they start their work with a certain enthusiasm, the lack of results and the lack of effective support from the urban level causes it to die out soon. The teaching becomes empty routine. The project reaches the stage of ritualization. Interaction and communication only take place with a small group that has shown interest in the project and are very limited and stereotyped outside this group. The primary function (education) has been largely replaced by secondary functions, such as entertainment, or a baby show for the somewhat more fortunate. No education is given because "nobody comes," and nobody comes because "nothing is done." The real target group has dropped out well before this stage is reached, because of the irrelevance of the project to their immediate problems, its class-degrading implications to them, and the little time and energy they can afford. Instead of having accomplished something the project may have reinforced class antagonism and deepened frustrations.

What Can Anthropologists Do?

The anthropologist who is associated with this kind of project faces the dilemma that the data he considers most valuable for an understanding of the problems at stake are disregarded by those who are in charge of the projects. Middle-class bureaucrats welcome all data that are consistent with their view of society (i.e., data on food habits, food taboos, prejudices, wrong beliefs – in short, all data about cultural and psychological aspects). They have a firm belief that a vast body of quaint beliefs and practices exists with the rural folk, and that this is responsible for a great deal of the problems of the lower class. It is true that some of these folk beliefs may still be found locally, but it has not been shown that they have more than marginal significance. On the other hand, data on the implications of the social structure, class prejudice, and the impact of poverty are very much resented by the same officers. The problem that arises is therefore this: What real contribution can anthropologists make in the field of nutrition education under these circumstances?

Two approaches have emerged that seem to be valuable and to which anthropologists can make a contribution: First, there is a great need to make the type of nutrition intervention, or the content of the message, relevant to the specific circumstances of each case so as to break away from the stereotyped application of standard techniques. To this end much more research will have to be done on the relative impact of various socio-economic variables and the success of various types of intervention. This can be done along two lines:

1 by *epidemiological analysis* – the study of the distribution of infant malnutrition over various regions and population groups and its correlation with various socio-economic variables.
2 by the *in-depth study of specific cases* of malnutrition and their etiology, which permits differentiation of causative factors and makes possible specific help and advice.

Second, apart from specific education projects, the relevant social field for nutrition education consists of various service institutions, such as clinics, hospitals, and health-aid programs. The study of such institutions shows certain specific shortcomings and discrepancies between theory and practice which deter clients from them and reduce their effectiveness. Along this line, Marchione (1973) has done a study of the Community Health Aid Program in St. James parish. The same author has done a follow-up study of the results of the treatment of infant malnutrition in a rural hospital in Hanover parish (Bantje 1974). It is perhaps significant that a proposal to have the results of the latter study published in Jamaica was categorically refused.

Both studies showed that many of the stated objectives are either irrelevant to the real problems or not carried through in the field. The hospital study, for example, revealed that many of the recommendations by international and government experts are disregarded in practice. There is hardly any emphasis on proper feeding and weight increase during the treatment; no weight charts are used; mothers are not involved in the treatment and are not given any instruction; nurses and wards privately recommend practices which they are expected officially to discourage; and records are inadequately kept – thus hiding the long duration of treatment, the high fatality rate, and the poor results. The high incidence of readmissions seemed to imply that mothers failed to keep their children in good health after they had been treated in the hospital. A closer look at the matter revealed that many children had been discharged while they were still seriously underweight (below 75% or even below 60% of standard weight for age), so that the slightest infection brought them back to the hospital.

104

Conclusion

This paper has developed along two distinct lines: that of the message of nutrition education and its relevance to the problem of infant malnutrition, and that of the social context in which this message is transmitted. Its main thesis is that these two levels are interdependent, as the content of the message is a function of an élitist interpretation of lower-class problems. The real issue lies not with food habits and cultural beliefs, but with the structure of the society and the semantics of nutrition education. What is needed is not so much sociology *in* nutrition education but a sociology *of* nutrition education. There is abundant evidence that the lack of motivation of the rural population can be largely attributed to the ineffectiveness of the health services themselves. Middle-class attitudes and lack of commitment of the staff may be largely responsible for this ineffectiveness. Rather than to pursue misguided education programs, one should set out to re-examine the functioning of the health services and to take steps to gear them to the needs and ways of life of the lower class.

References

Allport, Gordon W.
1954   The Nature of Prejudice. New York: Addison Wesley.
Ashworth, Ann and J. C. Waterlow
        n.d. Nutrition in Jamaica 1969-70. Dept. of Extra-mural Studies, u.w.i., Kingston, Jamaica.
Bantje, H. F. W.
1974   A Follow-up Study of Cases of Infant Malnutrition and Gastroenteritis in the Noel Holmes Hospital, Lucea, 1972-73 c.f.n.i./Ministry of Health (duplicated report).
Cook, R.
1968   The Financial Cost of Malnutrition in the Commonwealth Caribbean. Journal of Tropical Pediatrics, No. 2, 14: 60-65.
Gurney, J. M., Helen Fox and J. Neill
1972   A Rapid Survey to Assess the Nutrition of Jamaican Infants and Young Children in 1970. Trans. Royal Society of Tropical Medicine, 66:653-68.
Kerr, Madelin
1952   Personality and Conflict in Jamaica. London: Collins.
Marchione, T. J.
1973   An Evaluation of the Nutrition and Family-planning Components of the Community Health Aid Program in the Parish of St. James, Jamaica (a preliminary report). c.f.n.i. (duplicated report).

Endemic Cretinism Among the Maring:
A By-product of Culture Contact

Georgeda Buchbinder, Department of Anthropology, Queens College.

Introduction

It is well known that culture contact between members of a technologically advanced, politically dominant population and members of a technologically simple and politically subordinate culture can have serious consequences for the health and nutritional status of the latter population. Frequently these adverse effects are the result of direct and deliberate intervention by representatives of the dominant culture, as, for instance, in the after-effects of wars of conquest, slave raiding, the alienation of lands formerly used for subsistence, the imposition of taxes and a cash economy. However, it is likely that just as often the adverse effects on the subordinate population are unintended and inadvertent by-products of the contact situation. Examples of these include: the introduction of infectious disease or agricultural pests; the disruption of traditional trade networks; the substitution of bottle for breast feeding of infants, with all its hazards; vitamin D deficiency caused by the forced wearing of clothes which reduce bodily exposure to the sun; and a host of other deficiency diseases caused by the substitution of low nutrient "prestige foods" (e.g., white bread and Coca Cola) for high nutrient indigenous foods.

In this paper I shall demonstrate that iodine deficiency resulting in endemic goiters and in endemic cretinism among the Maring, a recently contacted New Guinea highland population, may also be considered an example of an unforeseen and harmful by-produce of culture contact.

To do this I will demonstrate that iodine deficiency among this population was both a recent and transient phenomenon lasting approximately a decade, from ca. 1960 to ca. 1970. Further, I will show that this deficiency was an unexpected result of the substitution of introduced non-iodized trade salt for locally manufactured salt which happened to be rich in iodine.

The Maring of New Guinea

The Maring are swidden horticulturalists who occupy a territory of about 100 square miles in the central Simbai and Jimi Valleys in the Bismarck Mountains on the nothern fringe of the central New Guinea highlands. Their total population numbers about 7,000, with about 5,000 living in the higher

106

and more open Jimi and about 2,000 in the lower, steeper and more heavily forested Simbai. The Maring are divided into 20 or more autonomous local groups, which range in size from slightly less than 100 to about 900 members. The composition of these groups is somewhat variable. Generally each group consists of two or more putatively patrilineal exogamous clans, but in a few instances the entire local population claims descent from a common patrilineal ancestor. Although clan exogamy is the rule, local-group endogamy is strongly favored and as many as 50% of spouses may come from within the local group. The remainder come from adjacent non-enemy groups on the same side of the range or from friendly groups across the range. These latter marriages were important in facilitating the trade of Simbai salt for Jimi stone axes, for affines were frequently trading partners. Some marriages were also contracted with non-Maring speakers to the north across the Simbai and to the south across the Jimi, thus extending the trade network.

Linguistic and cultural evidence suggests that the Maring are most closely related to peoples to the south in the Central Highlands, and it is likely that they entered their territory from the south, or southeast, occupying the Jimi Valley first and later spilling over into the Simbai. It is not known how long they have been in their present territory, but the high degree of genetic and linguistic variation which exists among local populations suggests an occupation of at least several centuries (Buchbinder 1973). To the north and west of Maring territory are distantly related Gainj and Karam speakers. To the east and northeast Maring territory borders on a vast tract of uninhabited virgin forest.

The Maring region differs from the highlands proper in being somewhat lower, steeper and more heavily forested. Perhaps because of this, the Maring engage in a classic form of bush fallowing horticulture rather than in a variant of the more intensive gardening regimes followed by the more centrally located highlands groups. Thus, new gardens are cut each year in the secondary forest that covers the slopes between the altitudes of 2,000 and 5,500 feet above sea level. These gardens yield crops for from 14 to 26 months and are then abandoned to fallow, which may last from about 8 to over 40 years. Tuberous staples include taro, sweet potato, yams and manioc. Taro is the most important crop in the Simbai Valley, but sweet potatoes may be more dominant in some of the higher Jimi Valley locations. Other significant crops include sugar cane, bananas, marita pandanus, and a large variety of greens. Pigs, chickens and some hunting dogs are raised, and a few cassowaries and occasional hornbills and cockatoos are kept. Hunting and gathering are also practiced, both in secondary forest and in the primary forest above and below the range of cultivation. The numerous, swift flowing streams in Maring territory yield eels in the dry season, and on occasion catfish are taken from the much larger Simbai or Jimi Rivers. Nonetheless, the Maring diet comprises well over 95% vegetable matter. Game is scarce, and pigs and chickens are killed and eaten only on ceremonial occasions.

Because of their large vegetarian diet, the Maring are particularly vulnerable to deficiencies in iodine and other trace elements. It is a well-known ecological fact that such substances tend to be concentrated in living tissues and that the higher up in the food chain that an organism is the greater the concentration in that organism. Thus carnivores are much more likely to obtain an adequate supply of these nutrients from their normal food sources than are herbivores.

The Maring were first contacted by Australian administration patrols between 1956 and 1960. The government considered them pacified by 1962, when it opened their territory to outsiders such as missionaries and anthropologists. Indirect contact, primarily in the form of trade, occurred earlier. Thus, the first steel tools entered the area in the late 1930's, and by the time of direct contact steel tools had replaced the indigenous stone tools. Commercially manufactured trade salt had also entered the area along traditional trade routes, and by the time of contact it had begun to replace locally made salt.

Prior to contact there had been an important trade of native salt for stone axes. The Maring as well as their Karam neighbors produced salt by evaporating the water obtained from mineral springs on the north side of the Simbai Valley. The stone axes came from the south where they were manufactured from stone quarried in the Jimi Valley. This exchange of stone axes for salt has been described in detail by Rappaport (1968). I will return later in this paper to a discussion of the importance of local salt to the Maring.

Studies of the ecological and biological adaptations of the Maring began in 1962 and still continue. These studies have involved anthropologists, geographers, and various kinds of health workers. By 1966 public health doctors and mission nurses working in the Jimi Valley began to realize that this population suffered from endemic goiter and endemic cretinism, which they attributed to iodine deficiency, a condition that is fairly common in the inland mountainous regions of New Guinea.

Endemic Goiter

Endemic goiter is believed to be caused by a deficiency of available iodine in the diet. The condition is characterized by enlargement of the thyroid gland in a large proportion of the affected population and is associated with a condition known as endemic cretinism, which is also thought to be caused by iodine deficiency (Greene 1973). The enlargement of the thyroid gland may be a compensatory response of the gland to increase its iodine trapping capacity, so as to maximize the use of whatever iodine is available and thus maintain the production of thyroid hormones within normal levels. An adequate supply of these hormones is necessary for the regulation of body temperature and metabolism, for normal physical and neurological growth and development, and for muscle contraction and nerve conduction (Means, De Groot, and Stanbury 1963).

The size and activity of the thyroid gland are controlled by a negative feedback mechanism involving both pituitary and hypothalmic hormones as well as thyroid hormones. The amount of circulating thyroid hormone depends both on the dietary intake of iodine and upon the ability of the thyroid gland to trap iodine and to synthesize its hormones. The concentration of thyroid hormone circulating in the blood stream has an inverse effect on the amount of thyrotropic hormone releasing factor (TRF) released by the hypothalmus and on the amount of thyroid stimulating hormone (TSH) released from the adenohypothesis. Low levels of iodine intake are paralleled by low levels of circulating thyroid hormones, which in turn stimulate an increase in the secretion of TSH by the adenohypothesis. The increased secretion of TSH stimulates the hyperplastic growth of the thyroid gland, with a concomitant increase in the secretion and release of thyroid hormones, in an attempt to maintain the normal euthyroid state (Dumont, Neve, and Otten 1969).

Thus, a deficiency in the dietary intake of iodine is the major etiological factor in endemic goiter, and contrariwise the ingestion of adequate amounts of iodine causes an involution of almost any enlarged thyroid gland (Greene 1973:121). The individual's demand for iodine is greatest during adolessense for both sexes and during the reproductive years for women. These categories of people tend to have a higher incidence of goiters than do adult males in the same population.

In addition to causing enlarged thyroid glands, iodine deficiency may also result in the production of children known as endemic cretins. Such children characteristically have multiple neurological defects, including deaf mutism, lack of muscular coordination, spasticity, crossed eyes and various degrees of menal and physical retardation (Querido 1969:85; Dumont, Delange, and Ermans 1969: 91-96).

The prevailing opinion is that endemic cretinism is caused either by hypothyroidism in the mother due to her deficient intake of iodine or by the insufficient intake of iodine by the infant in its first months of life. However, Pharoah, Buttfield, and Hetzel (1971:310) suggest that "it is possible that elemental iodine is necessary for the embryological development of the nervous system, quite apart from its role in the synthesis of the thyroid hormones." It is likely that both mechanisms were operating among the Maring, because both hypothyroid and neurological cretins were present in the population.

Van Rhijn (1969), as cited by R. M. Garruto, D. C. Gajdusek and J. Ten Brink (1974) suggests that goiter regions in New Guinea occur in specific geological settings. He notes in particular that areas consisting of soft Mesozoic sedimentary rock which has been heavily eroded into narrow V-shaped valleys tend to contain populations suffering from a high incidence of endemic goiterous cretinism. Contrariwise, populations living in wider valleys of harder Tertiary limestones are uniformly goiter free.

Although the geology of the Maring area is similar to that of other goiter areas in New Guinea, the discovery of iodine deficiency among the Maring had certain puzzling aspects. In other parts of New Guinea where there is iodine deficiency, goiters tend to be spectacularly large (R. M. Garruto, et al., op. cit., and McCullagh [1963]), whereas among the Maring, goiters tended to be small, perhaps suggesting their recent origin. In addition, the earliest evidence suggested that goiters were confined to those Maring inhabiting the Jimi Valley; before 1966 none had been detected by anthropologists or by public health workers among the Simbai Valley Maring. It is possible that no goiters were seen among the Simbai Valley Maring prior to 1966 because no one was looking for them at that time, or because they were present but hidden under the massive chokers of beads that were then a popular form of ornamentation among the Maring. However, it is equally possible that no goiters were seen then because there were none to see.

Another curious fact was that all of the cretins diagnosed by the Anglican Mission's Maternal and Child Health workers and by Public Health Department doctors among the Jimi Valley Maring in 1966 were young children, the eldest of whom were only about 6 years old. All older children and adults were judged to be normal. The explanation given by the public health workers for this age distribution of cretins was that of a very low survival rate for such individuals in this environment (Buttfield and Hetzel 1971:67). It was also suggested by some that, as the cretins aged, particularly those who were only mildly affected, their condition somehow improved and they became, at least on casual observation, indistinguishable from normal adults (Pharoah 1971:115). The latter explanation seemed particularly unsatisfactory, because adult cretins had been reported from other parts of New Guinea (Buttfield and Hetzel 1969).

My own research among the Simbai Valley Maring began in July 1966. At that time a few young cretins were known to exist in some of the local groups within this population. These had been detected by the Maternal and Child Health Service workers of the Anglican Mission at Simbai. The actual incidence of goiters among the Simbai Maring at this time was unknown but was generally thought to be low. Neither I nor any of the mission workers had seen a Simbai Maring with a goiter. Perhaps this was because we had never looked under their necklaces.

However, by January, 1968, I began to notice goiters on a few Simbai Maring women and girls. In two cases the goiter was relatively large and appeared to be growing. It also seemed to me that the number of cretins in the population was increasing. In June 1968, Dr. John Stanhope, an epidemiologist then with the Public Health Department, examined the entire Simbai Maring population of over 2,000 individuals. By looking under the beads he discovered that the overall goiter rate for this population was 25%. The incidence of goiters varied with age and sex, the highest rates occurring, as might be expected in terms of a biological need for iodine, among adolescents of both sexes and among women over the age of 20. The overall goiter rate for males was 15.8%, for females 34.2%. Of the boys aged ten to nineteen, 34% had goiters, as did 54% of the girls of the same age. Forty-four percent of the women over the age of 20 were also affected. In some of the local Simbai Valley Maring populations the goiter rates for girls and women approached 100%.

In addition to the high goiter rates, we discovered at least 24 typical cretins in this population, all under the age of eight years. A number of other young infants were considered to be suspect, although at the time we could not make a definite diagnosis. All these findings, comparable with those of Pharoah, Buttfield and Hetzel (1971) for the Jimi Valley, indicated that the level of iodine deficiency in the Simbai Valley was one of the highest to be found in New Guinea.

As a result of this study, in August 1968 all women of childbearing age in the Simbai Maring population were given injections of iodized oil by the Department of Public Health, a measure designed to protect against iodine deficiency for a period of up to 5 years. Some time after 1970 all commercial salt in New Guinea was iodized. In addition, by 1974 tinned mackerel, a food rich in iodine, had become a common, if minor element in the diet of the Maring.

In July 1974, I returned to the Simbai and recensused and resurveyed the Maring population. I detected no visible goiters at this time; as the Maring had by then abandoned the custom of wearing bead chokers, I am confident that my observations are accurate. Not only were there no goiters but also, with one possible exception, there had been no cretins born into the population after 1968. This one exception was born in 1971, to a mother who had escaped treatment with iodized oil in 1968 because she was secluded in mourning for a recently deceased husband. She had one prerious child who was also a cretin, which indicates that her iodine reserves were depleted. It thus appeared that the problem of iodine deficiency in this popolation, a problem which had been reaching serious epidemic proportions, had been overcome.

However, it was also becoming apparent that the problem of iodine deficiency for the Maring was of fairly recent origin. For, although no cretins had been born after 1971, a very high percentage of those born earlier had survived and the oldest cretins in the population were now 13 years of age. Thus, 30 of the 37 cretins diagnosed among the Simbai Maring were still alive in 1974, and all of these had been born after 1960. This survival rate of 81% compares favorably with the survival rate of 85% for all 836 Simbai children known to have been born during that time period. Furthermore, rather than blending in with the rest of the population, these older cretins were highly visible both to the anthropologist and to the Maring. Many were so retarded that they were still crawling, others walked only with assistance and frequently fell. All were deaf mutes. It appears likely, then, that the reason no older cretins had ever been found previously in the population was not that they had all died young, but rather that none had been born before 1960. In 1974, when questioned about this, many Maring informants said that this was true, that before the coming of Europeans, they had no such children. This absence may explain why the Maring have no name for cretins, other than the Melanesian pidgin term *long long*, whch means both "deaf" and "crazy". Their own term *pulum*, which occupies roughly the same semantic space as *long long*, was rarely used for cretins. It may also explain why Maring were slow to recognize that such children were defective. It should be noted that the Maring destroy any known defective children at birth.

During the 1968 epidemiological survey, Stanhope and I noted that there seemed to be a correlation between the size of the goiter and the amount of beads worn by an individual. I had also noticed an increase in the size of bead necklaces from 1966 to 1969. Moreover, C. Lowman (personal communication) has stated that in the early 1960's few Maring wore beads, and those who did wore them only in a few strands and not as heavy chokers. By 1974 the use of beads had declined markedly, and those who still wore them, wore them in longer strands which did not conceal the base of the throat.

I believe that the changing style in neckwear may also be related to the recency of the emergency of goiters among the Maring. In the early 1960's few Maring wore beads, possibly because few could afford them. However, between 1966 and 1969 the demand for beads was high both from me and from the trade store at Simbai. This change in style may have been facilitated by the greater affluence of the Maring at that time. However, although they had access to even more cash in 1974, their use of beads had declined. Thus, although I have no direct statements from Maring informants on this matter, it does appear that beads were used consciously or unconsciously to conceal goiters.

While all of the above data supported the view that iodine deficiency, with its resultant goiters and cretins, was a recent phenomenon among the Maring, it was still necessary to discover the traditional source of iodine in the Maring diet and to demonstrate that this was no longer available to them. An analysis of locally produced salt provided answers to these questions. Because Simbai salt was traded widely into the Jimi Valley and beyond, Dr. Peter Pharoah, who was investigating the problem of iodine deficiency in the Jimi Valley, decided to analyze this salt for its iodine content. To this end he followed the old trade routes to the salt springs located at Miami on the nothern side of the Simbai Valley and obtained samples of the spring water and of the salt manufactured from this water in the traditional manner. Both were rich in iodine; indeed, the salt contained twice the iodine content of any commercially iodized salt (Pharoah, personal communication).

Thus the traditional source of iodine in the Maring diet has been identified, a source that is known to have been abandoned before the onset of the symptoms of iodine deficiency. It seems clear, therefore, that as long as the Maring used salt from the Miami springs, they had an adequate iodine supply and were protected from endemic goiters and from endemic cretinism. Only when they abandoned this salt supply, in favor of commercial trade salt, did they become deficient in iodine.

Several questions remain to be answered. How much of this iodized salt actually entered the Maring diet? When and why did the local manufacture of salt stop? How long after this did it take for the Maring to exhibit signs of iodine deficiency?

The first question is difficult to answer with any degree of precision, but a number of facts about Maring salt consumption and availability are known. The Maring are exceedingly fond of salt, and if it is available they will consume it in large quantities. I have seen Maring children, and adults too, consume salt by the handful; and women make a kind of pacifier of salt-saturated cloth or bark cloth for infants to suck and chew on when they are teething. Salt also figures prominently in a number of Maring rituals, where it is consumed along with pig fat, generally by men. Finally, salt is esteemed as a condiment for the seasoning of vegetable foods, particularly of greens and of the sauce made from marita pandanus. Nonetheless, salt was probably always a rare and valuable commodity, and much of the salt on hand was set aside for ritual use or for exchanging for equally valuable stone axes. Another likely indication of a low level of everyday salt consumption among the Maring is that they exhibit very low blood pressures and that their blood pressure decreases with age. This is not a rare phenomenon in New Guinea highland populations, and it has been attributed to a low sodium intake (Maddocks and Rovin 1965).

The Miami salt springs do not yield large quantities of salt water at a time, and the preparation of salt is a long and arduous task. Many gallons of water have to be boiled down in specially constructed evaporating ovens to make even a few ounces of salt, and the process takes several days. The Maring had two ways, apart from trade, of obtaining local salt. They could either camp near the spring, on foreign soil, to prepare the salt; or they could carry the water home and process it there. Both alternatives were used, but neither had much to recommend it. In the first case there was the danger of meeting and having to fight enemies who were also making salt; in the second, people had to transport large amounts of water in bamboo tubes over very difficult terrain for long distances. Moreover, in the days before European contact when warfare was endemic in the area, the absence of men on salt expeditions might have left those remaining at home vulnerable to a surprise attack.

Once, early in the course of my field work, in order to demonstrate their amity and their willingness to assist in my research, a small group of Maring men went to Miami and brought back over 20 gallons of spring water which they processed into about eight ounces of salt. This salt, they asserted, was far superior in flavor to commercial trade salt. To judge from its smell, it had a high sulfur content and may also have been rich in other minerals. When I asked why, if they preferred this salt, they had ceased to manufacture it, the men simple replied that the work involved was too onerous. In short, although it is doubtful that large quantities of native salt were ever available to Simbai Maring, there was probably a steady, if limited supply, sufficient to prevent the occurrence of goiters and cretins.

Discussion and Conclusions

Throughout the New Guinea Highlands, trade salt has been used as a form of currency by Europeans (administrators, missionaries, explorers and anthropologists) to pay newly contacted New Guineans for local produce and for services, such as the carrying of cargo. We do not know precisely when trade salt first appeared in the Maring area. It certainly came in no later than the first administration patrols in the late 1950's, and it may have entered the area several years earlier along trade routes. At any rate, by 1962 there was enough trade salt in the area to satisfy the people's demand, and the manufacture of local salt had ceased. My informants told me that they had stopped making salt before the arrival of the white man, but just how much before is unclear. Nevertheless, as late as 1966 all adult Maring were still familiar with the location of the salt springs and with the techniques of salt manufacture, so that salt production probably continued at least through the middle 1950's, if not later.

Moreover, even though the production of local salt had generally ceased by 1962, C. Lowman (personal communication) reports that at least one local Simbai group still hoarded quantities of it. This group, which is one of the most distant from the Patrol Post, and hence from the source of supply of trade salt, had in 1968 one of the lowest goiter and cretin rates in the Valley. This suggests that enough local salt remained in circulation and in use to inhibit the occurrence of goiters and of cretins until the early 1960's, and that those populations most distant from the source of commercial trade salt were protected longer. Such a conclusion fits well with the known distribution of endemic goiters and endemic cretinism among the Simbai Valley Maring.

Now, one can hardly criticize the early, widespread use of trade salt as currency in New Guinea, for in those days nobody could be expected to know that, as in the case of the Maring, it would replace an indigenous salt rich in iodine and thus precipitate the occurrence of endemic goiterous cretinism. Nevertheless, one may wonder why the Australian administration was so slow to adopt the use of iodized salt for trade, particularly since the presence of iodine deficiency in parts of New Guinea was known at least as long ago as 1957 (McCullagh 1963).

The two explicit, albeit opposed, rationales that I have encountered for the failure to encourage the use of iodized salt are: (1) the distribution of such salt would have limited value in preventing iodine deficiency because

114

the salt would not reach the remote valleys where endemic goiters are most prevalent; (2) the ingestion of iodine by individuals who already had goiters would have an adverse effect on them, because their hypertrophied thyroid gland would produce an excess of thyroid hormone and throw them into a state of toxic hyperthyroidism.

Let us briefly assess the validity of these arguments. In the light of our present knowledge, the first makes little sense; it is now known that extensive trade networks ramify throughout New Guinea (Hughes 1973) and that many commodities travel great distances along these routes, even into the most remote areas. Thus, both steel and salt entered the Simbai Valley well before the coming of the white man. In fairness, however, it should be noted that the significance, even the existence of these trade networks, may not have been suspected by outside observers in the 50's. Their extent is only now being fully recognized.

Whereas the second argument for the continued use of non-iodized salt may have some medical validity, it appears from the point of view of public health maintenance that the benefits of the substitution of iodized salt far outweigh the disadvantages. It is true that ingestion of a substantial amount of iodine will cause the involution of almost any enlarged thyroid gland, while thyrotoxis occurs in only a very small minority of such cases. More important, an adequate supply of iodine in the diet of a population will prevent the occurrence of endemic cretinism. Hypothyroid cretins, if detected early enough, may sometimes be successfully treated; but the damage done to the nervous system of neurological cretins is permanent, and this type of cretinism is by far the most common encountered in New Guinea. So it remains surprising that it took about 15 years for the Australian administration in New Guinea to adopt a simple public health measure, one that has long proved successful in other regions of the world where there has been endemic goiter.

Notes

1 The research on which this paper is based was supported by grants from the National Institute of Mental Health, Columbia University, The City University of New York Faculty Research Foundation, and the Wenner-Gren Foundation.
2 A shorter version of this paper was read at the 1975 annual meeting of the American Association of Physical Anthropologists in Denver.

References

Buchbinder, G.
1973 Maring Micro-Adaptation: A study of Demographic, Nutritional, Genetic and Phenotypic Variation in a Highland New Guinea Population. Unpublished, Columbia University Ph.D. dissertation.

Buttfield, I. H. and B. S. Hetzel
1971 Endemic Cretinism in Eastern New Guinea, its Relation to Goiter and Iodine Deficiency. *In* Endemic Cretinism, B. S. Hetzel and P. O. D. Pharoah eds. Institute of Human Biology, Papua-New Guinea Monograph Series No. 2 Goroka.

Buttfield, I. H. & B. S. Hetzel
1969 Endemic Cretinism in Eastern New Guinea. Australasian Annals of Medicine 18:217.

Dumont, J. E. F. Delange & A. M. Ermans
1969 Endemic Cretinism. *In* Endemic Goiter. J. B. Stanbury Ed. Washington, D.C. Pan Am Health Organization Publication No. 193.

Dumont, J. E., P. Neve & J. Otten
1969 Recent Advances in the knowledge of the Control of Thyroid Growth and Function. In Endemic Goiter. J. B. Stanbury, Ed., Washington, D.C.; Pan American Health Organization Scientific Publication No. 193.

Garruto, R.M.; D. C. Gajudsek & J. Ten Brink
1974 Congenital Defects of the Central Nervous System Associated with Hyper-endemic Goiter in a Neolithic Highland Society of Western New Guinea. Human Biology 46: 311-329.

Green, L. S.
1973 Physical Growth and Development, Neurological Maturation and Behavioral Functioning in Two Ecuadorian Andean Communities in Which Goiter is Endemic. American Journal of Physical Anthropology 38:119-134.

Hughes, I.
1973 Stone-Age Track in the New Guinea Inland: Historical Geography without History. *In* The Pacific in Transition. H. Brookfield, ed., New York: St. Martin's Press.

Maddocks, I. & L. Rovin
1965 A New Guinea Population in which Blood Pressure Appears to Fall as Age Advances. Papua and New Guinea Medical Journal. 8.

McCullagh, S. F.
1963 The Huon Peninsula Endemic. *In* Endemic Goiter and Congenital Defect. Medical Journal of Australia 1:884.

Means, J. J., L. J. De Groot & J. B. Stanbury
1963 The Thyroid and Its Disease, Third Edition, New York: McGraw-Hill, The Blakiston Division.

Pharoah, P. O. D.
1971 Epidemiological Studies of Endemic Cretinism in the Jimi River Valley in New Guinea. *In* Endemic Cretinism. B. S. Hetzel and P. O. D. Pharoah, ed. Institute of Human Biology, Papua-New Guinea, Monograph Series No. 2 Goroka.

Pharoah, P. O. D., I. H. Buttfield and B. S Hetzel
1971 Neurological Damage to the Fetus Resulting from Severe Iodine Deficiency During Pregnancy. The Lancet: 308-310.

Querido, A.
1969 Endemic Cretinism: A Search for a Tenable Definition. *In* Endemic Goiter. J. B. Stanbury, Ed. Washington D.C.: Pan American Health Organization Scientific Publication No. 193.

Rappaport, R.
1968 Pigs for the Ancestors. New Haven: Yale University Press.

Van Rhijn, M.
1969 Een Endemic Van Struma en Cretinism in Het Centrale Bergland van West Nieuw-Guinea. Avanti-Zaltbommel, Utrecht, The Netherlands, pp. 198.

The Ecology of Vegetarian Diet in a Modernizing Mexican Community

Ellen Messer, Department of Anthropology, Yale University.

In the current history of food production, there is an ecological trend toward large-scale specialization. Whereas traditional agriculture in most areas was characterized by multiple cropping, crop rotation, differential exploitation of plant parts during plant life cycles, and also some plant gathering along with agriculture,[1] new agricultural strategies are directed toward highly mechanized monocrop cereal production. Through the efforts of the international grain development centers, many temperate-zone field systems are now dominated by single, high-yield cereal grains. There have also been attempts to convert non-temperate zones, such as African and South American tropical rain forests, into large-scale agriculture on the temperate-zone model (Meggers, Ayensu, and Duckworth 1973).

Though there have been spectacular increases in cereal production and increased cereal consumption by the producing populations, the "new agriculture" has had some unforeseen environmental and dietary consequences. Some tropical zones have suffered almost complete breakdown of traditional food production and consumption systems, along with the destruction of the ecosystem itself (Fosberg 1973). Many areas where the "Green Revolution" has had its greatest impact have also suffered some negative agricultural and nutritional consequences of specialized food production. In both India and Pakistan, where rice and wheat production have increased, legume production has dropped dramatically and deprived people of pulses, which have a protein value twice that of wheat and three times that of milled rice (Berg 1973:58-9). In Mexico, where the traditional field system and diet includes a combination of maize, beans, and squash, which taken together provide good quality vegetable protein (F.A.O. 1953), monocrop maize systems have eliminated the traditional local field and dietary diversity. While new varieties of maize have not affected the traditional mode of maize preparation – an alkali processing which increases the nutritional value of maize (Katz et al. 1974) – the strict chemical regimen under which new grains must be grown eliminates all other products from the field system. These non-maize field products include lysine-rich beans to supplement the lysine-deficient maize; squash leaves, flowers, and oil-rich seeds; and unsown herbs, the nutritional values of which are discussed below.

Rapid modernization in addition to agricultural mechanization is affecting traditional diets throughout Mexico. In the following sections, I will consid-

er some of the dietary changes and nutritional consequences of both specialization in agriculture and the general economic demise of the subsistence
farmer. Most of the data will be drawn from a Zapotec Indian community,
with an economically mobile population. Though the community has not received any "Green Revolution" miracle grains, their dietary response closely
parallels those of communities which are technologizing rather than elim-
inating agriculture in their recent economic strategies. Comparisons are
based primarily on Diaz Cisneros (1974), who discusses changes in a "Green
Revolution" agriculture community in Puebla, Mexico.

Ethnographic and Environmental Setting

Data was collected as part of an ethnobotanical project in Mitla, Oaxaca, in
the eastern arm of the Valley of Oaxaca, Mexico, over a twelve month period from 1972-1975.[2] The town is located in the southern highlands of
Mexico, approximately 16°N latitude and relatively frost-free, with ele-
vations ranging from 1600-1850 meters. The climate is marked by a pro-
nounced dry season, roughly November through March, during which the
mean monthly rainfall is less than 10mm. Rains are extremely variable, both
temporally and spatially. This results in highly unpredictable agricultural
yields for local farmers. The yearly timing and quantity of rainfall, as well
as the particular topographical locations of individual fields determines
whether or not dry farming strategies pay off in any given year.

Mitla's current population is approximately 4600. Most residents are bi-
lingual, speaking Zapotec in the home as a first language; later Spanish.
Though many adults never finished primary school, most men are marginal-
ly literate; and most children of both sexes now complete the first six grades.
Approximately half of the town households still farm *milpa* (maize field)
lands, but few are subsistence farmers. Most have alternative sources of income – either trade or domestic manufacture of textiles for tourists. These
part-time or non-farmers buy some or all of their food staples. In addition,
all households raise some domestic animals or fowl for home consumption,
ritual reciprocity, or cash sale.

Diet

The Mitla diet is largely vegetarian. Maize is the staple cereal, taken in the
form of tortillas or maize gruel (*atole*). People eat mainly the local (*criollo*)
large-grain white maize, which they prefer because it "looks clean," "tastes
better," and "makes a softer tortilla." Second in popularity is the local yellow *criollo* maize, which also has a large grain, tastes good, but makes a
slightly harder tortilla. People know from schoolbooks that yellow maize is
more nutritious, but they still prefer white maize and will eat it when it is
available.

Beans are the staple pulse. Local farmers, who have beans as income in

118

kind, eat beans almost daily. Those who do not have their own local supplies of beans do not eat beans as regularly but substitute macaroni, rice, and potatoes, each of which competes economically with beans in the market basket. All of these basic meal elements are prepared with a variety of condiments, including chile peppers, garlic, onions, tomatoes, groundcherries, and herbs, both wild and domestic. Greens – cultivated squash leaves and unsown herbs from the fields – or green vegetables from the marketplace also form basic elements of meals. Meat is eaten at least once a week, usually on Sundays. During the week, small quantities of dry meat, eggs, avocados, and cheese supplement the primarily vegetarian meals. There are four meals per day: "Coffee" in the morning and evening, with main meals anywhere between 9 and 11 A.M. and again between 2:30 and 6 P.M. "Coffee" is usually highly sweetened Mexican coffee, with one or two sweet rolls. More expensive substitutes are maize gruel or chocolate.

People also "snack" on fruits, crackers, and pastries. Fruits may be picked wild in season, but are more commonly purchased in the marketplace. Crackers, breads, and pastries are purchased in small shops, as are soft drinks. One note-worthy "modern" influence in local diets is the highly preferred status assigned to packaged cakes, crackers, and chips. These are expensive relative to more nutritious snack substitutes, yet are a regular expenditure in even poorer households' food budgets.

Potential Food Sources Within The Ecosystem

People distinguish several different vegetation zones, each of which yields some edible products. In addition to the *milpa* fields, which include beans, squash, unsown herbs, and sometimes chickpeas in addition to maize, there are uncultivated hillside lands, mountain zones, and uncultivated field and roadside borders. Hillsides are sometimes, though not annually, sown in maize. Their stony soils may also be sown in maguey (*Agave*), a cash crop, which yields a return in approximately seven years. Wild magueys provided edible hearts, a high carbohydrate source in prehistoric and historic times (Flannery 1970). Today, the inflorescences of both wild and cultivated magueys are still eaten. In addition, wild cactus fruits are collected in season.

Mountain zones provide a variety of fruits and vegetables, though in recent times they are rarely visited by Mitleños who rely on the markets for the products of these zones. More highly exploited are the uncultivated field and roadside borders, which supply a variety of fruits, vegetable herbs, and spices. The succulent *Opuntia* spp. provide both fruits (*tunas*) and succulent stems (*nopales*), the latter eaten as a green vegetable. There are also wild hackberries (*Celtis* sp.) *nanches* (*Malpighia* sp.), and cactus fruits (*Lemaireocereus* sp., *Myrtillocactus* sp.). These may be gathered by shepherds watching their flocks, men on route to their fields, or women collecting firewood and medicinal herbs. Certain spices used in the local cuisine also grow outside the fields. Two species of *Chenopodium* (*epazote blanco* and *epazote de*

119

elotes) – spices used with beans and green maize gruel respectively, *Tridax coronopifolia* (*yerba de conejo*) – a spice used with beans, and *Lycopersicon* sp. (*miltomate*) – a general spice used to make green sauces, are just a few of the edibles produced in field borders and roadsides.

In addition there are edible pot herbs produced within the agricultural field systems. These include *Amaranthus* spp. (*quintoniles*), *Anoda parviflora* (*violeta*), *Crotalaria pumila* (*chipiles*), *Galinsoga parviflora* (*beldobes*), and *Portulaca oleracea* (*verdolaga*) – all products of "disturbed" soils, conditions ideally provided by agriculture. *Quintoniles,* eaten in the young, tender stage of growth, provide the first greens of the season. All provide essential nutrients for the local diet (cf. Cravioto *et al.* 1945, Munsell *et al.* 1949, 1950a). They are a free source of vegetable proteins, vitamins, and minerals within the field system.[3]

In summary, traditional Mitla diet contains a variety of local products from their immediate surroundings. People know the wild plant foods potentially available in the uncultivated ecological zones, and seasonally exploit them to diversify their staple diet. They also recognize that agricultural practices create a field environment which produces edible herbs as well as cultivated seed crops. Fruits, vegetables, and spices are gathered in addition to the cultivated maize, beans, and squash. There is some evidence, however, that these "wild" food sources are being exploited less for food in recent years than in the past. People engaged in home industries, who rarely ventured into the fields, said that they wanted to eat wild greens but did not know where to find them. Others weaving in their homes, said that they no longer liked to eat wild greens but preferred the lettuce and cauliflower of the market if they could afford them. In the words of one young man: "When I have money, we won't eat *quintonil* anymore." Similarly, though certain wild fruits, such as *manzanitas* (*Arctostaphylos pungens*) are still delicacies in season, others are classified as "not edible" by the majority of the population. In a typical example, a middle-aged woman described hackberries and cactus fruits as "inedible" but then admitted that they could be eaten, but only by little boys ("People do not eat them, but little boys will eat anything!"). Thus, there was a social stigma attached to eating such "marginal" foods. Not only are they becoming less available in real environmental terms, but they are also becoming less socially acceptable as items of diet.

Food Customs, Nutrition Rules, And Prospects For Change

Current economic trends away from agriculture and technological advance within agriculture affect not only food production but dietary patterns. As highly technologized field systems become more specialized, people move from self-sufficiency or relative self-sufficiency to dependence on the market system and the state. Independent subsistence systems are often permanently broken. In place of the broad adaptation to the local ecosystem, people adapt to the larger regional state system, which includes redistribution by the state and market. Instead of local adaptation, people substitute their linkages with the market system and the state. There is a tradeoff in uncertainty – reliance on nature and traditional knowledge is replaced by reliance on the state and technological information.

Changes in subsistence knowledge and dependency abruptly change the role of traditional knowledge within a culture. In agriculture this means that the traditional productive factors of seeds, soil, sun, and rainfall, which were combined in set ways, no longer apply to seeds supplied by a laboratory, soil altered by pesticides, herbicides, fertilizers, and water applied by irrigation. In nutrition, this means that there are new food choices, other than what is produced in the home garden, local fields, and to a small extent within the market system.

In "Green Revolution" monocrop fields, there are no longer high lysine-content beans, squash, or herbs, since these have been eliminated by herbicides. They are similarly excluded as a relatively "free good" in the diets of non-farmers. Freed from the limited choice of their own production, people need nutrition education to help them select the right foods for adequate nutrition. People combine their old rules with new ideas in several ways: extending traditional categories of classification to cover new foods and adopting new categories of classification to further classify traditional dietary-items.

In Mitla, as in most of Mesoamerica, people classify foods according to their "heating" or "cooling" properties (cf. Foster 1953 for discussion). Every food has its traditional quality. Though two Mitleños might not agree on the nature or the degree of the quality in any given food, the hot/cold classification system, as a general system for classifying all items of the edible world, persists in the thoughts of the people, and affects eating and curing behavior during times of illness. Though in the past people referred to each food as "hot," "cold" or "neutral", they have now added the category "*puro alimento*" to their traditional discussions of "heating" versus "cooling" qualities of foods. Thus, maize in now said to be "*puro alimento*," rather than "cooling" in the local quality classification; and many classified potatoes and rice the same way. People continue to follow traditional eating patterns, but add a modern nutritional rationale.

People also talked about "*vitaminas*" in tomatoes, potato skins, and fruits, though they could not say which "*vitaminas*." They had heard that all of these items contained that element which made them particularly good for the health. In addition, most people ate carrots since they were "good for the eyes." In most cases, people cited the authority of the local primary school for their nutritional information. Even where individuals had not attended school themselves, they had listened to the reports of children in their homes, or the homes in which they were employed as domestic servants. People listened to the mass media (principally radio) and to local government workers for their nutritional information. Though neither the category *"puro alimento"* nor the category *"vitaminas"* has as yet had an effect on traditional food habits or nutrition, they do represent an enthusiastic (even if poorly understood) acceptance of "modern" nutritional vocabulary and ideas. Such conditioning should facilitate learning and comprehension of more specific nutritional information, which the population constantly seeks from many sources (including visiting anthropologists).

Women paid attention to government workers distributing information on infant nutrition and health care. Government extension workers visited homes and demonstrated how to prepare foods for infants three months and older. In addition, they listened to the doctor's recommendations on infant diet and care.

Medical advice has also had its effect on adult diets. Here it is interesting to see how people have combined traditional reasoning with modern medical consultations. For example, the doctor often recommended a bland diet of well-cooked greens with absolutely no fats, pork meat, chocolate or chiles for the patient under medication. People were delighted to point out that the greens were "cooling" and therefore good for most "hot" illnesses. The proscribed foods, on the other hand, were traditionally classified as "heating" foods, so people were able to combine their traditional classificatory system with the doctor's advice. Thus, they could adjust their eating behavior according to both traditional and modern medical wisdom.

Where modern and traditional food categories overlap, it is easy for people to behave accordingly. Other food customs change less easily. Though food habits centering around high and low prestige foods change rapidly, traditional tastes are less malleable. Probably the best example of traditional food preferences resisting modern nutritional wisdom is the standing preference for white over yellow maize. Though people know that yellow is "good for you," food scientists in Mitla and much of Mexico have been unable to entice people to choose yellow over white maize. Here, texture and color, not nutrition, are the most important qualities. Similarly, people will eat only large-grain maize, and feed thin-grain (non-*criollo*) maize to their animals. Any nutritional improvement will have to take into consideration preferences such as taste, color, and texture. Otherwise, increased nutrients from maize will be fed into human populations only through animal "converters" such as pigs and chickens. This has also been the experience in "Green Revolution" agricultural changes, such as the Puebla project, where increased maize yields were not consumed by people but used to feed more livestock (Diaz Cisneros 1974).

In the long run, new agricultural strategies with adequate nutritional information may improve the security of life in Mexican towns such as Mitla. Regional and national food production and distribution systems will provide better buffers against the vagaries of local agricultural yields than local wild food resources. When there were bad agricultural seasons in the past, people had to revert to food gathering in the uncultivated fields, hillsides, and mountain zones. As recently as 1915, when the crop failure following the drought, locust plagues, and disruptions of the Mexican Revolution decimated agricultural yields, people returned to *Agave,* various Cactaceae, and other wild plants for survival. Today, people turn to government assistance programs and market distribution to overcome the failings of local agriculture. While in the early part of this century people still got their foods, mainly vegetarian, from a full knowledge of the local environment, improved transportation and the market mechanism now give variety and a measure of stability to the diet. Social, psychological, and economic advantage can be the beneficial results of agricultural specializations which relieve some members of the population from the food quest. However, it is also instructive to learn from traditional agricultural strategies and nutritional patterns how people produced, classified, and consumed the potentially diverse "food" products of their environment. From this vantage point, one can assess how these food customs affected 1) the long-run stability and quality of the environment and 2) the nutritional status of the local population. In the future, planners can combine agricultural *and* nutritional objectives in directing culture change.

Notes

1 See, for example, Miracle (1966, 1967) for African examples of diversity in field systems and differential explotation of the environment. For Mexican examples of patterns of environmental exploitation which include more than agriculture, see Wilken (1970) and Messer (1972).
2 The author received financial support as a Junior Fellow of the University of Michigan Society of Fellows during this three-year period.
3 Obviously a fruitful area for future nutritional research will be to assess the quantity and quality of nutrients provided by such biproducts of agriculture as the edible green stages of certain seed crops as well as unsown herbs. Some attempt to assess the amino acid composition of *Amaranthus hybridus* and *Crotalaria pumila* was made by Lora Goldenberg, an undergraduate Senior Honors anthropology major at the University of Michigan. Using sun-dried plant materials collected by the author, she analyzed the two species for differential amino acid content. Though she was unable to derive a reasonable tryptophan value – the value most sought because of the tryptophan deficiency in the maize diet – she did isolate other protein values by chromotographic ion exchange amino acid analysis. She found that neither plant has extraordinary amounts of any amino acids, but that they supply small amounts of essential amino acids which may fill in some protein deficiencies in a diet which is predominantly maize. In particular, she found that the isoleucine-leucine ratio in both herbs is close to 1:1 (Goldenberg 1974:45) and therefore could fill one important nutritional gap in the maize diet.

References

Berg, Alan
1973   The Nutrition Factor. Washington, D.C.: The Brookings Institution.
Cravioto, B. R., E. E. Lockhart, R. K. Anderson, R. Miranda de P., and R. R. Harris
1945   Composition of Typical Mexican Foods. Journal of Nutrition 29:317-29.

Diaz Cisneros, H.
1974 An Institutional Analysis of a Rural Development Project: The Case of the Puebla Project in Mexico. Ph.D. Dissertation, University of Wisconsin, Madison.
Flannery Kent V., Editor
1970 Preliminary Archaeological Investigations in the Valley of Oaxaca, Mexico, 1966-69. A Report to the National Science Foundation and the Instituto Nacional de Antropología e Historia. Mimeo.
Food and Agriculture Organization of the United Nations
1953 Maize and Maize Diets. Rome, Italy.
Fosberg, F. R.
1973 Temperate Zone Influence on Tropical Forest Land Use. *In* Tropical Forest Ecosystems in Africa and South America: A Comparative Review. B. Meggers, E. S. Ayensu, and W. D. Duckworth, Eds. Washington, D.C.: The Smithsonian Institution.
Foster, George
1953 Relationships between Spanish and Spanish-American Folk Medicine. Journal of American Folklore 66:201-17.
Goldenberg, Lora
1974 Wild Plant Consumption in Mexico: Anthropology and Nutrition. Unpublished Honors Thesis in Anthropology. University of Michigan, Ann Arbor.
Katz, S. H., M. L. Hediger, and L. A. Valleroy
1974 Traditional Maize Processing Techniques in the New World. Science 184:765-773.
Meggers, B., E. S. Ayensu, and W. D. Duckworth, Editors
1973 Tropical Forest Ecosystems in Africa and South America: A Comparative Review. Washington, D.C.: The Smithsonian Institution.
Messer, Ellen
1972 Patterns of "Wild" Plant Consumption in Oaxaca, Mexico. Ecology of Food and Nutrition 1:324-332.
Miracle, Marvin P.
1966 Maize in Tropical Africa. Madison: University of Wisconsin Press.
1967 Agriculture in the Congo Basin: Tradition and Change in African Rural Economies. Madison: University of Wisconsin Press.
Munsell, Hazel E., L. O. Williams, L. P. Guild, C. B. Troescher, G. Nightgale, and R. Harris
1949 Composition of Food Plants of Central America I. Food Research 14:144-64.
1950a Composition of Food Plants of Central America II. Food Research 15:16-33.
1950b Composition of Food Plants of Central America III. Food Research 15:34-57.
Wilken, Gene C.
1970 The Ecology of Gathering in a Mexican Farming Region. Economic Botany 24:286-95.

Human versus Animal Nutrition: A "Development" Project Among Fulani Cattlekeepers of The Sahel of Senegal

Joel Mathless Teitelbaum, Department of Nutrition, School of Public Health, University of North Carolina at Chapel Hill.

Introduction

This paper addresses problems of transforming a subsistence society into a "cashcrop" system with the nutritional risks that agricultural development entails in an African context. The argument focusses on two key points made by Dr. Jacques May.[1] "Any transformation of the geographical environment may be pregnant with unsuspected consequences that can and will affect nutrition ... No shift from food crops to cash crops should go unnoticed."

"Changes in traditions and cultural habits, especially those pertaining to agriculture, can be indicators of impending nutritional improvement or disaster. These factors are all-pervasive and range from techniques people use to grow their food, to what they grow, how they harvest it, how they store it, how they market it, and how they prepare it for consumption ..." (J. M. May 1974).

In this light it is instructive to analyze the Sahelian policy pursued by the Government of Senegal and international donor agencies in response to the recent drought. Pre-drought plans were made to supply urban areas with beef grown in the Sahel. During the 1968 West African Conference on Nutrition and Child Feeding held in Dakar, the Minister of Plan stated, "Large livestock operations must be (created) based on, among other factors, an 80,000 hectare ranch and the formation of feed reserves, slaughterhouses, and cold storage facilities (N'Doye 1968). Between 1968 and 1974 (the drought years) little was done to implement this plan. Then, as a result of world-wide publicity about the disaster, several international agencies opted for massive technical assistance in range management and livestock development to transform the Sahel.[2]

The first development scheme was proposed for the Bakel District of Eastern Senegal where a "Range/Livestock Development Perimeter" is intended to use from 80,000 to 130,000 hectares of bush and grasslands for the market-raising of beef calves. A project agreement has been signed between the Government of Senegal and the U.S. Agency for International Development with funding of approximately $ 2.35 million over a period of three years. The main objectives stated in the agreement are: to improve the living standards and health of the poor, small-scale stockraising people of the Sahel by improving animal production, and to preserve their environment against further deterioration. However, in fact, the project is oriented toward a national livestock plan which designates Eastern Senegal as a breeding area for calves to supply urbanized coastal markets with meat. Herein lies the essential conflict.

Population Ecology

Having worked on the human populations of the Bakel district, the author was selected to act as an anthropological consultant with a team of experts sent to observe the region and design the range project for rapid implementation. This paper represents his analysis of human needs and nutritional factors associated with a shift from food crops to cash cropping of cattle. Field investigation took place during a two-month period at the end of the dry season and beginning of the wet season in the summer of 1975. It showed that the human population of the proposed perimeter consists of approximately 2,500 Fulani-seaking cattlekeepers. They live in the region traditionally known as the *Diery* – the dry, rainfed lands to the west of the Senegal River on both sides of a ridge of rocky high ground known as the Continental Terminal.

The inhabitants claim a dual ethnicity. Historically, a few Peul nomads were the original users of the Diery. However, the majority today identify themselves as *Torobe* (nobles of sedentary Toucouleur society) although many are mixtures of Peul nomads and various castes in the Toucouleur social hierarchy. Immigrants from the Toucouleur kingdom to the north in the last few generations have strongly influenced local institutions, since Peul and Toucouleur share a common language, *Al-Pular,* and the two groups have inter-married for centuries. The Peul faction easily integrates itself into the wider Toucouleur caste and class social system, while adjusting it in the direction of nomadism as a way of life adapted to Diery ecological constraints. Peul are the most recently Islamized people of the Sahel who retain many pre-Islamic beliefs and are considered to be "natural-born graziers."

For purposes of analysis, the Peul and Toucouleur of the Diery will be referred to collectively as Fulani cattlekeepers or husbandmen, as this is their linguistic grouping. The Fulani of the Diery possess about twelve thousand cattle and a few thousand goats. They see their major animal and human survival problem as lack of regular   water supply. With the end of a five-year drought in 1974 their pressing concern is to obtain deep-bore wells in their villages to permit the watering of animals (and people) year round. In the meantime, the major health problem of man and beast has become sheer undernutrition, accompanied by the various endemic forms of communicable disease.

The demographic result is increased mortality and emigration, a decrease of one-third of the cattle numbers and ten percent of the human population in the past eight years. Infant death rates have risen to epidemic propor-

126

tions. Fewer than fifty percent of children survive to the age of five years, and average human life span from birth is well below forty years. With an estimated rate of natural increase of close to 2.5 percent per year, the current 2,500 people would have increased to nearly 3,100 between 1968 and 1975 were it not for the drought.

Samples of administrative records and an anthropological census of the affected communities indicate a classic case of rural underdevelopment: high birth and death rates; an extremely youthful population profile; intense nuptiality; comparatively large cohorts of fertile younger women. These data raise questions concerning population pressure, i.e., the impact of the planned range project on demographic growth by natural increase should the project goals of raising living standards succeed. There is also the possibility of in-migration by previously displaced emigrants and others. However, as we shall see, the range/livestock plan may well reduce human food and water resources in the short run rather than improve them, possibly contributing to further depopulation and nutritional deprivation.

Ethnographic Analysis

Observations and analysis suggest a set of interlocked nutritional and social customs which may block the implementation of radical technological change in the Diery, indeed make it counter-productive. This configuration is termed the 'nutri-structure' (Teitelbaum 1973). Culturally, Diery husbandmen do not operate a livestock industry; rather they keep cattle and smaller ruminants as a way of life, mainly for subsistence purposes. Diery Fulani are divided into two distinct types of communities, geographically and ecologically:
a) larger stable villages of 80-300 persons with permanent wells, located near the bottom of drainages away from the Continental Terminal ridge. These villages are dominated by Toucouleur institutions and are sedentary in normal times.
b) Smaller unstable hamlets of 30-75 inhabitants which lack permanent wells and depend primarily on wet season surface water resources. These settlements are located further up the drainages and depend for survival on transhumance to permanent villages for five-six months per year during the dry season. The major ethnic element is Peul, and the populations are semi-normadic, i.e., transhumant.

The perimeter periphery includes some thirty-five communities, ten of which are stable villages with relatively adequate water resources, containing sixty percent of the total population of 2500. When rainfall is good the smaller hamlets enlarge due to a shift from the larger communities, but in times of drought the stabler settlements draw off population from the hamlets. In short, the two patterns of human settlement are based on water resources and the needs of the livestock, forming an ecologically interdependent system.

127

Extended Family Compounds

The Fulani extended family household is usually small and mobile to suit the tendency toward transhumance with cattle herd during the long dry season. The family labor supply is traditionally divided according to the needs of the animals, such that each category of person is assigned a task involving herd management: Children care for the calves near the village; women milk the cows morning and evening and prepare the milk products for consumption; old men braid ropes and do ancillary, often mystical tasks to protect the herds; adult and adolescent males drive the animals to pasture, take them to water, guard them at night, and control the herd movements during transhumance. Although usually pre-literate, Fulani are reputed for their knowledge of traditional cures for cattle disease; today they also accept some modern veterinary vaccination and treatment.

The headman is in charge of the sale and purchase of animals belonging to his family herd. He may be the grandfather of a group of brothers and their children, the paternal uncle of a set of patrilateral first cousins, a father of married sons or the eldest brother of a kingroup forming a core patrilineal genealogy. This group lives in an ellipse of mud huts around a central courtyard known as the compound. Within the extended family compound each married man heads his own family composed of wives (polygamy is the norm) and unmarried children. Members of each such household own personal property – notably cattle, goats or other beasts; each wife inhabits a separate hut. However, the compound shares food supplies. Wives and unmarried daughters pound grain, draw water and prepare meals together; the entire group shares food at mealtimes, the men dining at one end of the compound as a group and the women and small children at the other end. Adolescent boys and girls sometimes separate off from the others, especially for dining.

Clearly, the compound is the major production and consumption unit of daily life, and it is the human group for cattle herding *sine qua non*. Extended family cattle are kept together at night near the settlement; goats are sheltered in huts made of sticks. The cattle herd trails to pasture during the day and returns in the evening to be watered, milked and guarded. While near the community the cattle are used to manure the cultivation plots. Both men and women plant and harvest food crops for the group and share the stored supply of grains. Although women and children may own livestock, men manage the beasts in this patriarchal society.

Family Solidarity and Herd Size

It is traditional that the Fulani family herd involves individual ownership exercised by virtually all members of the compound. However, the herd also represents the extended family group by its size. The bigger the herd, the more prestigious its owners and, usually, the larger the family. Maximum herd size does not usually exceed more than two hundred cattle. Large herd are more difficult to manage. When male members of an extended kin group cannot agree on collective herding of their beasts, the extended family compound undergoes fission. One or more married men go off to form a new compound, often in another community. Since genealogical solidarity does not extend beyond the third generation, few cousins live for long together after the death of a common grandfather. They split company, and the social cleavage divides the herd into smaller herds; then the process of rebuilding numbers of cattle and people begins again.

This tendency accounts, in part, for the relatively small average size of compounds in Diery settlements (9-10 persons) compared to those of nearby agricultural river communities which average over 20 persons per compound. Herd size is also limited, with a mean of approximately sixty head of cattle per extended family group and ranging from less than ten beasts among the poorest to over two hundred in well-off, larger compounds. Herd size responds to the environmental vagaries, particularly extremes of drought and epizootic disease. During rainless periods compounds tend to remain closely knit for mutual aid. However, as water conditions improve, the grazing and food supply increases and cattle numbers are allowed to grow. Distant kin ties loosen and extended family compounds split into smaller human groups. Thus, food supply, water resources and cattle are key elements in community organization.

Customary Food Patterns

Diery Fulani subsist mainly on a diet of subsistence-grown grains, i.e., millet, maize and some sorghum or rice. Cooked grains are eaten with milk either fresh or fermented, as milk is the most sought-after consumption product derived from the herd. Milk and cream are mixed with hot cereal dishes such as porridge, or vapor-cooked semolina called couscous. Fulani do not bake bread and eat very few pre-prepared foods, but they do cook leaves, fruits, stems and roots of various Sahelian plants as vegetable sauces to be eaten with cereals. They use a variety of locally gathered or market-bought spices, but consider such refined products as tea, salt, peanut oil, sugar or sweets and biscuits to be luxuries. When available in trade, dried fish meal from river villages is added as relish to cooked dishes.

Meat is eaten irregularly. Poultry consumed is mainly chicken or guinea fowl, but due to low production there are few eggs. The goat is the most frequently consumed beast, slaughtered for guests or for small festivals. On important religious occasions the few available sheep may be sacrificed. More rarely a steer or old cow is killed, as the husbandmen prefer to accumulate beasts. Fulani do not raise animals for market, but they will sell older beasts to cattle buyers for cash or credit from time to time rather than literally consume their capital by eating it.

If sacrificed for an important ceremony, such as a wedding, a beef animal is consumed quickly to avoid spoilage; the meat is distributed to neighbors and kinsmen attending the feast. Although permitted by Islamic law, the slaughter and consumption of a sick or dying animal is rare. Fulani husbandmen have high hopes that such animals will recover, and many cures are attempted. However, once dead, animal flesh is ritually taboo and treated as carrion. In short, although Fulani are pastoralists their dietary staple is based on the cultivation of cereal grains and the gathering of wild plants, supplemented by milk and some meat from the herds.

Cattle Movements

To save cattle lives in the dry season, December to May, herds are driven eastwards to the Senegal River (or its tributary, the Faleme River) where the Fulani enter a new ecological and ethno-linguistic zone called Soninkeland. Diery Fulani graziers trade with the sedentary Soninke, exchanging animal products for access to river water and grazing rights on riverside field stubble during the long dry season. They barter milk for millet and arrange to manure the Soninke fields in exchange for grazing privileges. They also sell their cattle for slaughter to Soninke. Recently, Soninke men have been buying up numerous head of Diery cattle for investment purposes. They confine these beasts to Fulani herders for transhumant grazing on the Diery pastures in the wet season and riverside field stubble in the dry season.[3]

CROP CALENDAR

SEASON	DRY	RAINY	HARVEST
MONTHS	DEC.-MAY	JUNE-SEPT.	OCT.-NOV.
Movements	"Big" transhumance to permanent watering areas outside Diery	Return to Diery settlements with cattle	'Small' Transhumance to bushlands of Diery
Activities	Moving cattle; grazing field stubble; trading for food	Trailing daily of cattle to water holes; slash & burn and hoe-cultivation; manuring fields.	Herding cattle away from planted fields. Harvesting & threshing grains, poaching game. Cattle sales; weddings;
Staple Foods	Bartered grains; trade foods; a little milk & meat	Bush foods; stored and/or donated grains; some new milk, occ. small game	Bush fruits; milk & butter, fresh vegetables & fowl, occ. meats, trade foods.
Major Illnesses & Nutritional Problems	Dehydration and Communicable diseases	Insect Vector-born & parasitic diseases; contagious illness & dysentery	Least of nutritional problems & best health conditions of year
Major Problems	Lack of water, forage, food	Unsafe water; unbalanced food supply	Protection of crops and herds from wild animals.

130

Unlike the riverine system of private land tenure on irrigated plots, there is no individual landholding in the Diery. Its drylands are viewed as a commons available to all Fulani for grazing and for shifting cultivation. Even settlements change location from time to time. Water points such as ponds, pools, swamps and drainages are not owned by anyone, but some communities have dug shallow wells to which they control access. Due to the limited flow in these wells, outsiders are restrained from drawing water for their livestock during the dry season. However, residents and visitors may draw water for human consumption at any source.

Forage is also considered a free good, although cattle herds are usually spread out due to the dispersed location of their home communities. Nevertheless, accumulations of cattle by Fulani compounds lead to overstocked ranges in dry years, and cattle are often underfed. From the Western point of view, this collective pressure on pasture and water by cattle represents an ecological abuse. The project team planned to correct this "tragedy of the commons" by strictly limiting access to Diery pastures by livestock. As we shall see, this attitude has far-reaching social, economic and nutritional consequences for the Fulani way of life (G. Hardin 1958).

Hunger Months

The transhumant cycle draws Fulani herds back to the Diery when the rains begin in June or July. The rainy season from June through September is known as the 'hunger months'. During this period people clear new land by burning the bush and cultivate millet and maize patches, fertilizing old plots with manure. Cultivation is initiated at the most nutritionally precarious point in the year when grain stores are depleted and the animals are weak and starved. Surface water from new rains is often polluted, contributing to intestinal problems of dysentery, parasitism, as well as water-borne disease vectors which affect man and beast. Hoe-cultivation must be performed by male and female adults just when total caloric intake is at its lowest point in the year and malnutrition and debilitating illnesses are reaching their peak. Yet this is the time when the greatest output of work energy is required to prepare the land and plant the annual grain supply necessary for subsistence.

Since the drought, the Government of Senegal has distributed relief supplies of whole grains during the hunger months donated by European and American agencies. Fulani receive fifty kilos of maize and sorghum for each taxpaying adult (i.e., male adults) in a compound. Although these grains alone cannot provide a balanced ration, to some extent this relief has aided Diery people in surviving through the worst part of the year. In October-November they harvest their crops, store grain for the next dry season, and their dietary intake is improved by consumption of abundant milk and meat products as well as various leaves and bush fruits.

Some men hunt in the wet season but are restricted by government enfor-

131

cement of national poaching laws to preserve wildlife. The most ubiquitous source of wild animal meat in the Diery, the warthog, is ritually taboo to the Islamic Fulani as it is a member of the pig family. Gazelle and other small mammals are hunted for food, but they are rarer; and larger mammals have moved south since the onset of the drought. Even in good years wild animals are problematic. Monkeys and birds raid the cultivations of food crops and hyenas and jackals kill livestock, as does the occasional lion.

However, the wild plants of the Sahel have long been a major nutritional supplement used by Fulani especially during the hunger season. The women specialize in the gathering of the leaves, fruits, seeds, roots and stems of over two dozen species of plants, using their "prescientific" wisdom to select non-toxic foods. Food gathering provides energy and some vegetable proteins as well as necessary vitamins and minerals at a time when domesticated foods are in short supply (N'Doye 1968).

Weaning and Malnutrition

The hunger season cycle also coincides with two critical events in the nutrition of the young: the birth and suckling of many calves, and the weaning of children who have been breast-fed up to three years of age. Since able-bodied women work the fields and gather plants from the bush, they leave their babies in the village; thus, infants are often weaned after the return from transhumance at the beginning of the rainy season. Weaning is an abrupt transition to the adult diet of millet and corn gruels and steamed grains, to which is added fresh milk from new cows. The substitution of polluted water and cereal roughages provokes diarrhea and dysentery among young children. This leads to dehydration, increased susceptibility to internal parasites, and vulnerability to infectious disease. Measles and malarial fever kill many of the weakened children during the cultivation period. It is also the epidemic season for kwashiorkor; if an undernourished child survives, gross protein-energy deficits may develop into marasmus (N. Scrimshaw 1968).

The literature on states of malnutrition among Fulani children begins in the 1950's with observations of very low rates of deficiency due to the heavy emphasis on a regular milk diet to supplement cereals and fresh vegetable sources gathered in the bush. By the middle 1960's Cantrelle and N'Doye observed "mild increases" in kwashiorkor and pre-kwashiorkor rates among Toucouleur children of the Middle Senegal valley. N'Doye noted marked nutrient deficiencies caused by seasonal drop in food production and the cyclical hazards of drought, especially among vulnerable segments of the population. For pregnant and nursing women and young children he found, "carbohydrates dominate the Fulani diet and represent seventy-five percent of the total energy intake. Clinical nutrition data based on longitudinal surveys in depth and food consumption studies ... registered a three percent serious kwashiorkor rate, a twenty-five percent pre-kwashiorkor rate, and overall thirty percent mortality before age one, increasing with age and peaking at two years" (N'Doye 1968). Thus, even before the drought Senegalese nutritionists had become concerned about Fulani nutritional status. Attempts were made to develop a cheap, high protein product easily digested by infants and young children to prevent protein-energy malnutrition. However, to date these efforts have not resulted in an easily distributed weaning food acceptable to Sahelian peoples.

The recent epidemic of protein-energy malnutrition in the Diery appears to have resulted from the drought-induced loss of two major sources of protective foods traditionally consumed by the Fulani: cow's milk and wild plants. In times of severe drought these sources as well as wild game "dry up", exposing vulnerable groups in the population to excessive nutritional stress. This may account in part for the increased prevalence of protein-energy deficiency and higher rates of child mortality despite relief food donations. With the return of the rains during the last two years, local food sources are gradually being reconstituted, but malnutrition and disease remain a legacy of the prolonged famine. This makes it imperative to prevent diversion of critical protective foods, such as milk and wild plants, to other purposes.

In order to survive as cattlekeepers under marginal conditions, Diery Fulani must compromise between the needs of calves for maternal milk and the human use of cow's milk, especially for children. Customarily, the milk supply is divided with the calves allowed to suckle only at night after handmilking the cows each evening. The result has been shown to be inadequate nutrition of calves leading to heavy death losses and low production of meat and milk by stunted adult animals (Denis 1973). Only when there are large numbers of fresh cows per extended family can the share of milk for calf growth be increased significantly. Hence, the greatest stress falls on the majority of small grazier compounds. The people need milk for human consumption during the hunger months, but they are simultaneously trying to reconstitute their decimated herds. Losses incurred during the long drought period exacerbate milk scarcity.

To date, it is not known to what extent the range development project might increase or decrease the supply and variety of wild plant and animal foods customarily consumed by Fulani, especially during the hunger months. However, it is clear that milk consumption will be affected; subsistence cultivation of millet and maize grain staples may also decline. Nevertheless, the range/livestock plan does not concern itself with human nutrient needs. Instead it is oriented toward providing immediate gains in calf growth rates and improved cattle production on a managed rangeland. The livestock plan stipulates that young calves receive all the maternal milk supply as yield is quite low in the predominantly unimproved Zebu breed of the Sahel, averaging 1.5 to 3 liters per day (Redon 1962). The potential nutritional impacts of the entire project tilt heavily toward the improvement of cattle at the expense of the nutritional health of their owners.

133

The Range/Livestock Project Design

Agricultural scientists from the United States have drawn up five major components for project implementation. Their aim is to improve the forage and water supply for the herds by adjusting cattle numbers to the carrying capacity of the grasses, and improve cattle health and reproduction in order to permit regular offtake of calves for marketing. In order to achieve these objectives the design team set certain requirements for the range perimeter:

a) Rangeland conservation is based on elimination of bush fires through construction of firelands. Pastures will be divided up and provided with water tanks sufficient to cover the needs of limited numbers of cattle during the dry season. Cattle will be culled each year to suit the carrying capacity of the grass cover which varies with rainfall.

b) Cattle herding patterns will be assigned each village, and the herds must be kept there permanently rather than returning to the village from pasture each night. Units of about two hundred animals to a pasture will be dispersed over the land by trained hired herders. Calves will run with the herd.

c) Animal health will be maintained by quarantine and innoculation. Breed improvement measures will also require culling of diseased, old or sterile animals. Infection from other animals will be prevented by banning transhumance or migration of stock on the perimeter.

d) Cow's milk will be devoted to hastening calf growth in the early stages and calves will be kept with their mothers permanently. However, in a later stage, dairy herds to provide milk for human consumption will be located near villages.

e) The human constituents of the project will consist of current Fulani inhabitants of the Diery who will participate in the implementation by use of their cattle and labor. They will be grouped according to village on a permanent basis tied to demarcated pastures. Outsiders will not be allowed to introduce their cattle on the perimeter.

Anthropological Implications

The plan described above forms a total system which takes account of rangeland and animal production needs primarily, human needs only secondarily. Cultural and nutritional factors, especially mechanisms for altering Fulani social organization in cattlekeeping and food-getting, have been largely ignored. The plan depends on rural education by Senegalese government extension agents to convince the Diery Fulani to adapt their way of life to the needs of the project. Anthropological observations suggest that real obstacles to the implementation of this "applied" agricultural development will soon appear.

Obstacles may be classed as *cultural* if perceived by the Fulani in terms of their existing economy and social structure, and as *ecological* if the existing precarious equilibrium between food sources and human nutritional needs is

134

upset. This analysis treats these elements and their interactions in relation to food supply as part of the nutri-structure, posing the following dilemmas within the project design:

Cattle, Fertilizer, Fires – Cow manure used to fertilize soil for grain cultivation will no longer be available as cattle will not be permitted to approach areas of human habitation where plots are located. Instead, commercial fertilizer will be distributed to community compounds to replace manuring. This will require a timely supply, transport, a system of distribution, and adaptation of chemical fertilizer to local soils. Also needed is retraining of the subsistence cultivators in the use of fertilizer and intensive cropping practices which are alien to the Fulani way of life. Traditional slash-and-burn techniques provide ash, and bushfires clear new land for cultivation. Once banned, other methods must be substituted immediately. Even if carefully handled, this changeover may bring temporary decrease in grain harvests and require massive food donations to supplement grain production until there are improved yields. Fulani object strongly to the loss of manure and the ban on burning. They have already raised these objections with the Regional Livestock Service as reasons for not cooperating in the project. If their grain harvests decrease, numerous Fulani may be forced to emigrate to regions of uncontrolled cultivation outside the project perimeter.[4]

The Milk Gap – Human use of milk for daily consumption and ceremonial purposes will be curtailed by the diversion of cow's milk to young calves and the total separation of the herds from the settlements. Since dairy herds are not a major priority of the plan and will not be formed before the range is in operation, at least initially the Fulani will have to do without a milk supply. As shown above, this would cause deficiencies in human nutriture. It would also bring about organized resistance to the dispersal of cattle on the pastures. The questions concerning milk use have already become a source of friction between the project planners and the Diery herders; limiting the human use of cow's milk to suit calf needs represents a classical nutri-structural dilemma of human versus animal nutrition.

Micro-social Structure of Milking and Herding – Even should a dairy herd eventually provide the "technical solution" to the milk gap, there remains the question of alienating cattle from their owners. Mystical values are attached to the ownership and management of cattle and milk carries great symbolic weight. Using milk from a common dairy herd may not be accepted easily by the compounds which compose a community, as each extended family prefers milk from its own cows. The traditional division of labor in cattlekeeping assigns herding responsibilities according to sex and age of compound members, i.e., men herd, women milk. This set of rules regulating group dynamics would be disrupted by the new system of hired herders and milkers. The social response may be a boycott of the project by the people who view it as producing chaos in the extended family by disrupting the established social system of herding, milking, and managing animals.

Conclusions

The project attempts to convert collective bushland into limited pasture, shifting cultivation into permanent agriculture, and cow's milk into calf food. This shift would seriously affect human nutrition, especially among the already weakened vulnerable groups of pregnant and lactating women, infants, children and the aged. It could even more rapidly generate resistance to cooperation as it threatens unacceptable change in customary practices and tends to unravel the tightly knit social system. This interaction between the existing food-chain and sociology of Fulani cattlekeeping represents a major nutri-structural obstacle to implementation of the project design. Initial objections by Fulani husbandmen focus on their conservative economic and cultural beliefs about food needs and values. In addition, the analysis suggests there is a precarious ecological interaction amongst human groups; cattle and the land. With few margins of safety from drought, there is evidently no incentive for change in customary transhumance in the Diery.

Other defects in the range/livestock development plan are as follows: Existing health facilities in the Bakel district are totally inadequate, yet the project contains no human health component in its programming or budget. Educational activities by government extension agents budgeted in the project may be used, in part, toward improved human hygiene, child nutrition, etc. But without the provision of an adequate diet for this grain and milk-based culture, education alone will not be very convincing.[5]

The project plan suffers from a classic means-ends conundrum. Its ultimate purpose is stated clearly in the original proposal as intended to raise the standard of living of the small stockraisers of the Sahel by means of increasing cattle production on improved ranges. While Western management may be technically possible on empty lands, attempts at implementation in the Diery can be expected to encounter mass opposition from the Fulani inhabitants. Vocal opposition may be expressed by the religious and political leaders of the region whose high rank and privileges are based on conserving the traditional status quo. Interviews with indigenous leaders indicate a preference for the gradual re-establishment of cattle herds after the drought losses, rather than attempts to bring about radical change in land-use and cattle-raising techniques. The latter has been urged only by outsiders who see external benefits from improved cattle production, government officials, foreign experts and the Soninke cattle-buyers along the Senegal River.

At the administrative level the attempt to implement this project may well lead to conflict among the poorly coordinated, inadequately staffed government agencies of the Bakel District, as each belongs to a different Ministery competing for resources at the national level. Fulani resistance would also entail legal and political disputes in the district and bring pressure on the government to alter the project design. The Agency for International Development and its associated American contractor for technical assistance could be drawn into these conflicts. Perhaps the Americans will be blamed by the Fulani (and scapegoated by Senegalese government officials) for failures to improve the cattle or the people's well-being. This could prove embarrassing diplomatically, and might hamper other hoped-for attempts by technical assistance donors to respond to the drought by improving the lands, livestock and lives of thousands of Sahelian pastoralists.

At a wider economic level, the project conflict pits Fulani subsistence dairying against Senegalese government policy which designates the Sahelian region for commercial beef production intended for urban consumers. In the best of all possible worlds improved animal production could perhaps fulfill both needs. But in the Diery the risks of change come high to the pastoralists. Cattleflesh on-the-hoof represents Fulani productive capital, and milk and manure products are essential to their food supply. The range/livestock project is dedicated to marketing cattle for meat by altering the connection of the grazier to the herd. It will be more problematic to transform this fundamental relationship than to carry out technical aspects of land-use reform.[6]

Recommendations

The thrust of this paper is to reorient the project design for implementation along more modest lines in keeping with the perceived needs of the Fulani. To succeed at all it must provide for the nutri-structural needs first, and then gradually attempt to co-opt the existing social organization into beneficial range/livestock development. Unlike the current design projections, which claim a "theoretical" economic return on the multi-million dollar investment within three to five years, attention to human needs does not offer short-range profits. Furthermore, it cannot promise a vertically integrated cow-calf operation for meat export to the urban areas. Short-sighted attempts to transform the bushlands into a range for cashcropping cattle ignore the excessive human risks. This suggests the importance of including human constituents in the ecological assessment needed for the redevelopment of the Sahel. Long-range outcomes through maintaining and improving the nutritional equilibrium of small-scale husbandmen may be more valuable than quick technological fixes for the livestock.

As originally suggested by May, rural health services and systematic nutritional surveillance are recommended as part-and-parcel of project work in the Diery. These should include: the provision of safe year-round water points for human consumption separate from livestock watering areas; the use of scientific technology to complement traditional methods of cattle raising already adapted to the region; the study of bush foods and local food crops for development of acceptable dietary supplements for children and adults; an index of food resources reflecting the loss of food crop acreage (as well as animal food products) to cash crops to determine over time the amounts of and kinds of dietary supplements needed to "plug the food gap" (May 1974).

A pragmatic development plan should include economic, social and nutritional health indicators to monitor the effects of change in technology. By working closely with the Fulani population and understanding their needs, innovative use of existing techniques and provision of substitutes for lost sources of food can make for continuity in the society while changes are introduced by rangeland developers.

Notes

1 The idea for this paper emerged from discussion with the late Dr. Jacques May to whose memory it is dedicated. Dr. May, killed with his wife in an auto accident in Tunisia in June, 1975, was to have taken an active role in Senegalese rural health and nutrition programs starting in the autumn of 1975. When he died the rural health project died with him.

2 Potential donors include IBRD, FED, U.S. AID, IDRC. The Senegalese agencies involved are, the Livestock Service, the Water and Forestry Service, the Agronomic Service, the Ministry of Rural Development and the Ministry of Planning.

3 The Soninke are a riverain Sahelian population who today occupy the frontier between Senagal on the East bank and Mauretania on the West bank of the Upper Senegal River. The Soninke practice seasonal agriculture on fertile soils irrigated by the annual river floods, as well as dryland cultivation in the direction of the Diery. The densely populated Soninke villages are highly organized political and economic units which have exported their young adult labor supply for generations as cash-earning migrants. Today they constitute the largest number of Black African workers in France, and approximately forty percent of their male labor force is absent year-round. Soninke cattle buyers use accumulations of cash sent home by migrants to purchase cattle and extend credit to Fulani herdsmen (See F. Kane and Lericollais, L'Emigration en Pays Soninke, ORSTOM, 1974).

4 One permanent village council of elders made an unanimous decision not to participate in the range/livestock project upon learning of the design requirements. This caused consternation among Senegalese officials who sought to explain it away as an exceptional case. However, later the District Administrator and director of the Livestock Service also raised the same objections. Many Fulani reject the notion of attaching themselves to a single village and its pastures.

5 There is one doctor and a few nurses for all of Bakel District which contains over 50,000 inhabitants. None of the health services are located in the Diery and no regular visits are made there by health providers. In addition there are no government schools in the Diery, as all schools are located in the towns and larger villages near the river and major roads. Even where elementary schools are accessible, the Fulani avoid sending their children as they fear the alienating effects of Western education on their offspring's attitude toward traditional family ties. They rely on religious Koranic schools maintained in the larger Diery villages by Toucouleur Islamic teachers. These holy men and local fetish priests also provide herbal and mystical cures for illnesses of man and beast in the Diery.

6 I am indebted to Professor Michael Horowitz for his critique of this paper. In a personal communication Horowitz makes the salient point that a fundamental defect in the proposed range/livestock project is its inherent inflexibility, i.e., inability to "respond to sudden, unanticipated changes: ecological, sociological, political, etc. The system ties the herder to a piece of land, excludes him from others and thereby threatens his major survival mechanism, mobility."

References

Calvet, H. and J. Valenza
1973 Intensive Fattening of Senegalese Peuhl Zebus with Rice Straw. Rev. d'Elevage Medicale Veterinaire Pays Tropicaux. 2661: 105-16.

Cantrelle, P. and T. N'Doye
1964 Le Moyenne Vallee du Fleuve Senegal, Paris.

Denis, J. and A. Thiongane
1973 Characteristics of Reproduction in the Zebu. Rev. d'Elevage Medicale Veterinaire Pays Tropicaux, 26(4): 49A-60A.

Diallo, M.
1973 Rapport Sociologique sur l'Elevage-Senegal Orientale, IBRD.

Diallo, M. S.
1972 Current Status of Husbandry Development Project in Senegal. Bulletin Official Int. Epizootechnique, 77(1): 107-111, Jan.-Feb.

Diallo, M. S., A. D'Ao and A. N'Doye
1973 Commercialization of Bovine Meat in Senegal. Rev. d'Elevage Medicale Veterinaire Pays Tropicaux, 26(4): 99A-111A.

Diop, S., P. Gaye, R. Baylet, M. Ly, and E. M. Tour
1973 Clinical and Epidemiologic Considerations on the Cholera Epidemic in the Department of Bakel (Senegal). Bull Soc. Med. Afrique Noire Langue Française, 17(4): 670-674.

Dupin, H. and T. N'Doye
1962 Les Disponibilities Alimentaires en Proteines au Senegal, Medecine d'Afrique Noire, Vol. 9, No. 2, Jan. 15.

Frantz, Charles
1973 Ecology and Social Organization among Nigerian Fulbe. IXth International Congress of Anthropological and Ethnological Sciences, Inc.

Hardin, Garrett
1968 The Tragedy of the Commons. Science, 162, p. 1234.

Hunter, John M., (editor)
1974 The Geography of Health and Disease, University of North Carolina, Studies in Geography, No. 6, Chapter 1-2, Chapel Hill, North Carolina.

Ingenbleek, Y. and P. Malvaux
1974 Iodine Balance Studies in Protein-Calorie Malnutrition. Archives of Child Disease, 49(4): 305-309, April.

Ingenbleek, Y. and C. Beckers
1973 Evidence for Intestinal Malabsorption of Iodine in Protein-Calorie Malnutrition. Amer. J. of Clin. Nutrition, 26(12): 1323-30, Dec.

Kane, F. and A. Lericollais
1974 L'emigration en Pays Soninke, ORSTOM.

Malumfashi, Ahmed Tijjani
1969 Problems Involved In Settling the Fulani, Livestock Development in the Dry and Intermediate Savanna Zonnes, Zaria: Institute of Agricultural Research, Ahmadu Bello University, pp. 49-54.

May, Jacques M.
1968 The Ecology of Malnutrition in the French-Speaking Countries of West Africa and Madagascar, New York, Hafner, Chapter 1.

May, Jacques M.
1974 The Geography of Nutrition, In: John M. Hunter, ed., The Geography of Health and Disease, Chapel Hill, North Carolina, p. 41.

N'Diaye, A. L. and C. Ba
1972 Animal Husbandry and Cooperation in Tropical Africa. The Example of Senegal. Rev. Elev. Med. Veterinaire Pays Tropicaux, 25(3): 433-443.

N'Doye, Thianar
1968   Proceeding of the West African Conference on Nutrition and Child Feeding, Dakar, March 25-29, p. 7.
Redon, A.
1962   Note sur la Valeur productive du Zebu du Senegal. Elevage et Medecine Veterinaire des Pays Tropicaux, Vol. 15, pp. 265-271.
Scrimshaw, N. S., C. E. Taylor and J. E. Gordon
1968   Interactions of Nutrition and Infection, Geneva, WHO, pp. 44-46.
Smith, Susan E.
1973   The Environmental Adaption of Nomads in the West African Sahel: A key to Understanding Prehistoric Pastoralists, IXth International Congress of Anthropological and Ethnological Sciences.
Smith, V. E.
1970   Agricultural Planning and Nutrient Availability. Nutrition Reviews, June, Vol. 28, No. 6, pp. 143-150.
Stenning, D. J.
1959   Transhumance, Migratory Drift, Migration: Patterns of Pastoral Fulani Nomadism. Journal of the Royal Anthropological Institute of Great Britain and Ireland, 87: 57-73.
Teitelbaum, J. M.
1973   Land Use and Nutri-Structural Change Among Berbers of the Moroccan Inter-Atlas, Nutritional Anthropology Section, American Anthropology Association Meeting, New Orleans.
USAID
1974   Bakel Range/Livestock Design Team Scope of Study.
U.S. Public Service, Nutrition Program.
1968   Proceedings of the West African Conference on Nutrition and Child Feeding, Dakar, Senegal, March 25-29, U.S. Government Printing Office, Washington, D.C. See: Report on Nutrition in Senegal. 1968, pp. 117-121, by: Thianar N'Doye, Nutrition and Industry, pp. 244-254.
Vigreron, M.
1972   Emergency and Conditions for Regional Nutrition Increase. Bull. d'Academie Nationale de Medecine, (Paris), 156 (10): 312-317, April.

The "Last Course":
Nutrition and Anthropology in Asia

Shirley Lindenbaum, Department of Anthropology, New School for Social Research, New York City.

In his *History of Bengali Language and literature,* Sen notes the Hindu tolerance of doctrinal differences for persons avowing Jesus Christ to be the Son of God, or Mohammed to be the only Prophet, but an intolerance of a breach in the rules regarding eating. The concern for infringements of eating rules is so great that even a petty transgression is considered a matter for severe penance or excommunication (Sen 1954:87). Food, it seems, is an "incendiary" matter. In India, groups are defined by what they agree to eat together (Tantrics) or by what they agree not to eat together (Muslims, Jains, Buddhists and Hindu Castes). Much of the anthropological literature regarding food in Asia, in general, has focused on diet as a boundary marker or else on the way hierarchical relationships are expressed through the acceptance of, or refusal to take, food from others.[1]

From a different perspective, Thai beliefs have been examined concerning the edibility or non-edibility of certain animal species (Tambiah 1969). Thai villagers' relation to certain animals expresses both an affinity with and a separation from the animal world. Thus, humans must act ethically toward the ox and buffalo and should not, for example, work them on the Buddhist sabbath. Both animals are considered edible, subject to the observation of certain rules. In addition, an impure act of an ox or buffalo (e.g., straying into the polluted zone of the wash place at night) has, by metaphorical transference, a bad consequence for humans which must be dispelled by ritual. The animals' behaviour corresponds to improper sexual relations among inmates of the house. Moreover, the rules applied to such animals are the same as those which apply to some humans. The incest rule in a Thai village, for instance, requires that any person's great-grandchildren should not intermarry. Another rule requires that buffaloes reared under the house should not be used for sacrifice on behalf of members of the house. A homology exists between the two situations: livestock and women are not to be "consumed" at home but are reared for exchange. Ideas about proper human relations are, then, pinned to rules about the edibility of animals. Dietary regulations thus provide a clue to the ritual attitude toward the animals, to the linking of eating rules with rules about sex, and to the incorporation of nature into a single moral universe with humankind and/or its separation from it.

Despite an awareness that cultural and social systems are not only

141

thought but lived, and that the structural properties of symbolic systems bind individuals and groups to moral rules of conduct (Tambiah 1969:457), there has been less attempt among anthropologists to investigate what might be called the vulgar physiological dimension of symbolic structures. The discussion that follows takes two examples from Bangladesh and examines some nutritional and health aspects of certain symbolic categories. Several issues are presented, further illustrating the interaction of social and biological factors in nutritional anthropology.

Symbols and Survival: male and female

A number of categories, both symbolic and real, are associated with the basic distinction between the sexes in Bangladesh (Lindenbaum 1968). Men are associated with the right, i.e., the preferred side of things; women with the left. Village practitioners state that a basic physiological difference between the sexes makes it necessary to register a man's pulse in his right wrist, a woman's in her left; and they invariably examine patients in this way. Most villagers wear amulets to avert illness caused by evil spirits. Men tie the amulet to the right upper arm, women to the left. Similarly, palmists and spiritualists read the right hands of men and the left hands of women. In village dramas, where both male and female parts are played by male actors, the audience may identify men gesturing with the right arm, women with the left. During religious celebrations there are separate entrances at such public places as the tombs of Muslim saints or Hindu images. In popular belief, girls are said to commence walking by placing the left foot forward first, men the right.

In some instances, this right-left association indicates more than the social recognition of physiological differences, carrying, as it does, additional connotations of prestige, honor, and authority. Women who wish to behave respectfully toward their husbands say they should, ideally, remain to the left side while eating, sitting or lying in bed. The same mark of respect should be shown also to all social superiors, to the rich, and today toward those who are well educated.

Thus, the right-left dichotomy denotes not only male-female, but authority versus submission. It has, in addition, connotations of good-bad and purity-pollution. Muslims consider the right side to be the side of good augury, believing that angels dwell on the right shoulder to record good deeds in preparation for the Day of Judgment; while on the left side, devils record misdeeds. The left side is associated with the concept of pollution. Islam decrees that the left hand be reserved for removing bodily impurities, especially for cleaning after defecation. The left hand, therefore, must never be used for conveying food to the mouth or for rinsing the mouth with water before the proscribed daily prayers. In Hindu history, the left is the position of heterodox theology, of anti-Brahman, egalitarian movements which are organized around powerful female deities. The Vamacharis, medieval Tantrics of

142

the left-hand path, fixed on the most extreme reversals to state their counter-offensive against caste-organized society: eating from skulls, holdings rituals in cremation grounds, and practicing human sacrifice and occasionally cannibalism (Campbell 1974:360). Their invitation to pollution attempted to show that it did not exist. Left-handedness among small children in present-day Bangladesh is understandably discouraged.

A second set of symbolic categories overlaying the right and left concerns the distinction between "two" and "one". Male precedence is expressed both in ritual and in law. At the time of Aqiqah, the naming ceremony for Muslim children, parents sacrifice two goats for a male child, one for a female. Among the semi-nomadic boat-dwelling Bede, where women petty traders have mobility and economic independence, the female still merits only secondary ritual recognition. At the birth of a son, A Bede father donates to the community 1 rupee, but for a newborn girl, 8 annas (half a rupee). Similarly, at a naming ceremony for Hindu children, boys receive 5 names, girls 3. In Muslim legal affairs, brothers inherit a share valued at twice that of their sisters; and a Muslim marriage requires two witnesses, although if two men are lacking, then one man and two women (Al Hadis, Book 2:652).

The symbolic shorthand of these right-left, two-one categorizations reinforces the roles of men and women in a social and hierarchical fashion. It is a cultural code for the political and social realities of village life. Bangladesh is a society with a strong preference for males; the social importance of women depends on their producing a predominantly male population. Since daughters ultimately leave home to reside with their husbands, it is clearly in the mother's interest to produce male children. A difference in the age at marriage (men are on the average 15 years older than their wives) means that many women can expect to spend the latter part of their lives as widows, dependent on sons rather than husbands.[2] Ideally the last child should be a boy; he can, then, care for his mother before the rise of competing demands from his own wife and children (Lindenbaum 1976).

Thus, mothers favour sons, and the bond between mother and son in literature and in life is close and affectionate. More attention is given to the ailments of male children, and the male child receives preferential nutrition. Along with his father he eats first; and, if there is a choice, luxury foods or scarce foods are given to him rather than to his female siblings. The result is a Bangalee population with a preponderance of males and a demographic picture in which the mortality rate for females under 5 years of age is in some years 50% higher than that for males (Mosley et. al., 1970), a statistic not unrelated to the cultural code of right-left, two-one.

A recent epidemiological survey in Bangladesh (Sommer and Loewenstein 1975) confirms that the higher mortality among female children is related to their poorer nutrition. Some 8,292 children between the ages of 1 and 9 were screened to estimate their nutritional status. The screening technique was that of the QUAC stick, which calculates midarm circumference for height on a simple measuring stick, a way of estimating protein,calorie malnutrition. The survey demonstrated that there was a higher incidence of moderate-to-severe malnutrition in female children than in male children. Furthermore, a follow-up study 18 months later showed a higher mortality as well in female children, and the mortality rate of the malnourished group was more than twice that of the group of children as a whole. In an Indian study, Gopalan and Naidu (1972) also noted a decline in the sex ratio of the 1 to 12 year age range between 1901 and 1971, due to the higher mortality of girls between 1 and 5. The most important cause of this toddler mortality was said to be malnutrition underlining again the connections between ideology, differential nutrition, and survival.

Hot and Cold

A second symbolic code in Bangladesh concerns the distinction between hot and cold, a system of classification widely reported in the anthropological literature.[3] Foods are classified according to their heating or cooling effect on the body, a belief related to the humoral theory of disease expounded by Hippocrates and Galen. Incorporated into Ayurvedic and Arabic medicine, the idea was transmitted by the Arabs to Spain and by the Spaniards to the New World. As it travelled, it underwent such modification that the form of the theory in Latin America is now no longer the same as in Asia. Within Asia, too, there are interesting divergences. In Thailand, for instance, eggs are regarded as "cooling" (Hanks 1963:39), while in Bangladesh they are among the "hottest" of foods.[4] In general, Bangladesh consider meat, eggs, ghee (clarified butter), fish, honey and some oils (mustard, nut) to be heating. Vegetables and fruit (especially the marrow *lau*, lemon and cucumber), curd and some oils (sesame) are regarded as cold.

Illnesses, too, are classified as hot and cold, the system providing a basis for determining dietary selection and medicinal care. Hot illnesses must be neutralized by cold food and medicines, and vice versa. A person suffering from the effects of excessive heat (all forms of fever) should be bathed in cold water and given cold foods to eat. Moreover, a weak person must limit consumption of hot foods since they are difficult to digest; but, as health improves, more hot foods may be taken.

There is in addition, a fund of information about the specific effects of certain specific foods. For several days after childbirth, women must eat no meat, eggs, fish or hot curries which would cause indigestion; rather they are expected to keep mainly to rice, bread, tea and cumin seed. These are easily digested, the latter especially having the property of making things dry. Mothers increase their supply of breast milk by eating *koi, magur*, and *shing* fish. They give the newborn child a first meal of honey and mustard oil, 'hot" foods which are believed to provide strength and keep the infant free of colds. Jackfruit, sweet pumpkin, the seeds of *kau* fruit (Garcinia cawa) and some *sag* (green leaf vegetables), especially pea *sag*, are thought to

144

cause loose stools. English potatoes, on the other hand, make stools firm; and prawns and *hilsa* fish (Hilsa ilisha) supposedly constipate. Sour foods are thought to irritate wounds (e.g., circumcision and vaccination), whereas tamarind is believed to cause loss of sexual power. Hot foods should be eaten in cold weather, cold foods in summer. *Panta bhat,* for example, a preparation of left-over cold wet rice, is suitable in summer, while in winter dry foods such as *cirra* (beaten rice) and *muri* (puffed rice) are preferred. Attention should be paid not only to the prevailing season and climate but to the temperament and constitution of the individual. Men of hot temper should restrain themselves from eating excessively "hot" foods lest their tempers become testier.

While these hot-cold categories are conceived as based on physiological effects on the body, little attention has been paid to an empirical test of what are generally regarded by Western observers to be ideas detached from reality.[5] A recent study in Andhra Pradesh, however (Ramanamurthy 1969), makes a preliminary evaluation of the subjective states of four individuals given hot and cold diets for periods of 10 days. Hot foods were generally those which, when consumed, were reported to produce a subjective feeling of burning eyes, burning micturition and a feeling of warmth all over the body. The subjects' feces and urine were analyzed for biochemical differences while on each diet. When consuming hot foods, the acidity of the urine proved to be much higher than when consuming cold foods, a finding thought to be the possible cause of the burning sensation during micturition. Urinary excretion of sulphur was also found to be higher on hot foods than on cold foods, despite the fact that an analysis of the diets for sulphur content did not reveal any significant differences between the two diets. The high excretion of sulphur was thought to be a possible cause for the high acidity of the urine. In addition, nitrogen retention was found to be lower on hot foods than on cold foods, although again the total nitrogen content was the same in both diets. The study would be improved by giving the same diet to non-Indians, to control for subjective symptoms; and, before these preliminary findings can be accepted, much more extensive documentation will be necessary. If substantiated, however, it would indicate some physiological basis for perceived differences among foods, a discrimination that until now has been considered somewhat fanciful.[6]

Despite regional differences in India concerning the classification of certain foods as hot or cold, animal milk is generally considered to be heating and, in undiluted form, a danger to infant health. Cow's milk is therefore broken down, generally in a mixture of half-milk and half-water, a custom frequently cited as a danger to infant nutritional status (Jelliffe 1957, 1968, Anand and Rao 1962). When the child develops an infective diarrhea, classified as a "hot" illness, milk foods are stopped completely; and the diet changes to cool foods such as barley water. If this regime is prolonged, the infant may develop frank kwashiorkor, reported in West Bengal to be called "barleywater disease" (Jelliffe 1957:136).

Indian populations normally discriminate among various kinds of animal milk. In Bangladesh, buffalo's, cow's, and goat's milk are ranked in a descending order of heat. Thus, buffalo's milk is diluted in a ratio of 1 part milk to 2 parts water, and cow's milk in a ratio of 1:1; while goat's milk – like mother's milk – is thought to require no dilution at all. In Andhra Pradesh cow's milk is preferred to buffalo's milk, and again the dilutions are greater for buffalo than for cow's milk (Anand and Rao 1962:180). In West Bengal (India) cow's milk is considered less digestible than goat's milk, a belief Jelliffe attributes to "sympathetic magic" since the green watery cow's stool more closely resembles that of the diarrhetic child than does the hard solid stool of the goat (Jelliffe 1957:136).

Yet Indian mothers appear to be making observations of some physiological merit when discriminating among animal milks. For, as it turns out, the indigenous "heat" ranking of buffalo's, cow's, and goat's milk in India matches their reported lactose content, buffalo's milk being richest in lactose and goat's milk the poorest. On the other hand, curd, a form of milk considered to be "cold" has a negligible lactose content due to the conversion of lactose into lactic acid by bacterial fermentation (McCracken 1971:480).

Further, when mothers completely withdraw animal milk from the diet of an infant suffering from diarrhea, there is again some physiological benefit unknown at the time Jelliffe made his observations in West Bengal. The manner in which dietary carbohydrates are digested and absorbed has been elucidated only within the last decade (Gray 1973:121). Some infants have an intolerance to various complex carbohydrates, the ingestion of which is associated with or followed by episodes of diarrhea. If these infants are maintained on a diet with a high concentration of carbohydrates, their symptoms persist or are aggravated. When carbohydrates are removed from the diet, the infants gain weight and tend to thrive (Sunshine and Kretchmer 1964:38). In particular, in some infants, chronic diarrhea, malabsorption syndrome, and failure to thrive are related to decreased levels of intestinal lactase, the enzyme which hydrolyzes lactose, the disaccharide in milk.

Intestinal lactase and other disaccharidase activities are concentrated in the brush border of the mucosal epithelium of the small intestine. If the activities of these enzymes are impaired, unhydrolyzed dietary disaccharides remain in the intestinal lumen where they exert an osmotic effect and produce diarrhea (Sutton and Hamilton 1968). A series of recent studies have examined carbohydrate intolerance in infants in some detail (Lifshitz, et. al., 1971a, 1971b; Coello- Ramirez, et. al., 1972). The majority of patients exhibited lactose intolerance during the most acute stages of illness. Moreover, in infants with severe diarrhea, there was bacterial proliferation in the upper segments of the small intestine. The number of organisms did not correlate with the duration of diarrhea prior to study nor with the nutritional status of the patient. Rather, the severity of the infection was related to the capacity to tolerate carbohydrates. Lactose tolerant infants had less bacterial overgrowth from the duodenum than other diarrheal patients, and the number of

146

organisms increased with the severity of carbohydrate intolerance. Massive bacterial overgrowth was found in patients with severe impairment of the absorption of all dietary carbohydrates.

It was suggested, therefore, that in severe diarrheal disease there may be a cycle of infection of the upper small bowel, impaired absorption of carbohydrates, and bacterial catabolism of unabsorbed sugars leading to diarrhea. This, in turn, leads to further bacterial proliferation and to increased interference with the absorptive mechanisms of the intestine. The diarrhea can be improved whenever milk feedings are replaced by intravenous fluids, or when specific dietary therapy is given by elimination of the unabsorbed carbohydrates (Coello-Ramirez, et. al., 1972:240). In the absence of antibiotic therapy, which might shorten the course of illness, infant diarrhea must be controlled by careful dietary regulation. Since lactose intolerance is frequently present, a milk formula containing other disaccharides as a source of added carbohydrate is recommended (Lifshitz et. al., 1971a). Carbohydrate malabsorption seems to be the principle factor in the perpetuation of diarrhea, and a rapid return to normal diet is recommended when there is evidence that the administration of specific monosaccharides and disaccharides does not incite diarrhea.

This recent information matches the cumulative observations of Indian populations concerning the heating and cooling effects of certain forms of animal milk. The Indian data are coded into a symbolic set and preserved as a kind of "systemic wisdom".[7] Moreover, lactase deficiency occurs not only among infants suffering from diarrhea but is present in a significant portion of the adult Indian population (McCracken 1971:490). Milk may thus be diluted to aid digestion as well as to increase the volume of the produce before marketing. This is not to suggest that all cultural codes can be shown to encapsulate adaptive behavior. Infants suffering from diarrhea are, in addition, deprived of foods which they may be able to tolerate, a behavioral choice with grave nutritional consequences. The two examples discussed, however, do suggest that there is something curiously appropriate about the homologous relationship between the most mentalistic of anthropological data, cultural symbols, and the actual physiological state. Cultural codes should be closely examined, for they may contain hidden biological messages. As Keesing notes (1974a:90), the issues that concern anthropologists are only partly questions about cultures as ideational systems. We want to understand how human groups organize and sustain their social life, how biology and experience interact. Nutritional anthropology clearly gives weight to both aspects, and in pursuit of the schema defining the appropriate content and consumption of food in various societies, another meaning may be added to the concept of "the effectiveness of symbols" (Levi-Strauss 1963).

Future Research in Nutritional Anthropology

The focus of anthropology is shifting from a narrow definition of humans as makers of culture, to one in which biological, psychological, and social factors are treated as interacting variables within a unitary system of analysis. Among cultural patterns, continual feedback between body and brain occurs so that each is seen to shape the progress of the other (Geertz 1973:48). The two examples discussed above reveal some of the relationships between a society's system of ideas and individual physiological conditions. The data from Bangladesh are not unique in this respect. Cassel's material (as quoted by Freedman, p. 5) concerning the rules which prevent Zulu women in Natal from consuming milk and eggs matches that from O'Laughlin's account (1974) of the prohibitions which prevent Mbum Kpau women of southwestern Tchad from eating chicken, eggs, goat, partridge and all kinds of game birds. Within this byzantine web of social codes lies the explanation for the politics of protein. A pattern emerges of differential male and female dietary regimes, held in place by symbolic and sacred ideas about the proper roles of men and women. Rosenberg's survey (1973) reveals how widespread is this phenomenon of sex-differential diet, a means of prestige ranking with real nutritional impact. Female deprivation of milk and animal protein is more than just a political issue, having consequences for both fertility and sexual dimorphism (Gopalan and Naidu 1972; Stini 1971). More over, the shift to a predominantly vegetarian diet resulting from the agricultural revolution is regarded as a relatively recent event, affecting human evolution and variability, with prejudicial implications for most of the world's people who are now forced to be vegetarians. Since animal proteins offer the eight essential amino acids in best complement, the trend toward dependence on a monocrop is seen to present many societies with a dietary dilemma – how to supply adequate protein for the special needs of infancy, gestation, and lactation (Newman 1975). Symbolic codes telegraph and monitor the distribution process.

Population and Food

If nutritional research in the 1940's reflected primarily concern for national fitness in a time of global fighting, and research in the 1950's suggested the possibilities and consequences of interference with the traditional food habits of colonial peoples (Freedman), the political interests of the 1970's are directed at the related issues of population size and the production of sufficient food. It is here that anthropologists with an interest in nutrition can join health scientists with an interest in anthropology. Recent research already demonstrates this characteristic blend of sociology, anthropology, and biology. Birth statistics from Bangladesh, for instance, show a marked seasonal swing. Such a pattern appears to result from the combined effect of a seasonal termination of lactational amenorrhea, so that more fecund women are at risk during the cool months of the year, coupled with increased coital frequency during the cool season. Since the time period also coincides with and follows peak harvest of the major rice crop, it has been suggested that

148

the cause for more frequent termination of lactational amenorrhea between November and March has to do with better nutrition for the lactating mother, along with changes in her occupational role (Chen, et. al., 1973). Anthropological research might further document and confirm such observations. The notion would be consistent with explanations that have been offered for population growth among sedentary !Kung in South Africa, which indicate a connection between diet and the amount of body fat required for ovulation (Kolata 1974).

Subclinical Malabsorption

Anthropology and medicine also have a common interest in the subject of intestinal malabsorption (Lindenbaum 1973). The small intestine is the primary organ for the absorption of all essential nutrients. Studies performed in Bangladesh during the past decade indicate that many people have an intestinal disorder which is usually asymptomatic and manifested by abnormalities of small intestinal morphologic appearance, and often associated with impairment of absorptive function. While the etiology of this subclinical intestinal disorder is unknown, its existence is well documented, as is its onset soon after birth. Moreover, the presence of malabsorption has nutritional implications which could be determined by an interdisciplinary investigation. It is possible that the impairment of absorptive function contributes to the short stature and low body weight of Bangalees over one year old compared, say, to their American counterparts. (The decreased body size of populations in India [Malhotra 1966] and New Guinea [Malcolm 1970] has previously been suggested to be an adaptive response to limited intake of protein and calories). The presence of subclinical malabsorption, perhaps, plays a role in precipitating frank malnutrition in children with borderline nutrient intake. It is possible, too, that the subclinical malabsorptive state is not necessarily pernicious. Changes in the structure and function of the small intestine could be viewed as adaptations to increased exposure to fecal contamination, even playing a role in protecting the population from lipid overload and its possibly harmful cardiovascular consequences. That is, malabsorption may even protect against "overnutrition".

Co-operative research by anthropologists and health scientists could be concerned with the implications of energy loss resulting from the inability of populations to absorb nutrients from the foods they produce and consume, a nutrient loss of potentially massive proportions since impaired intestinal absorption is not limited to Bangladesh but has been reported also from India, West Pakistan, Southeast Asia, the Caribbean, South America, Africa and the Middle East (Lindenbaum 1973:54). An alternate approach to the problem of malnutrition among impoverished people, then, may be to protect against bacterial infection rather than to introduce radical changes in the technology of food production, a solution with lesser costs in energy expenditure and environmental modification.

Zinc Deficiency

For interdisciplinary research, a number of challenges remain. A recent review of the literature (Sever 1975), for example, points to the importance of zinc in human development and indicates that, although zinc is widely distributed in foods, a number of diets appear to be deficient or marginal in this mineral. In addition, a physiological loss of the element occurs in bleeding and sweating which may lead to low levels of body zinc. Zinc deficiency has been shown to markedly retard growth and sexual development, and it is thought that the deficiency syndrome is only one end of a continum of growth-related problems associated with low levels of physiologically available zinc. In addition, maternal zinc deficiency may be involved in certain malformations of the central nervous system.

While dietary intake of zinc may be sub-optimal, the zinc content of some foods may be, as well, physiologically unavailable. Thus phytate, which occurs in some cereals and legumes, binds zinc – particularly in the presence of excess calcium – and forms nonabsorbable complexes. As a result, the deficiency syndrome is more frequent in the villages of Iran, where flat bread is unleavened and has a higher phytate content than the leavened bread consumed in the urban areas. A similar relationship may be discovered between certain central nervous system malformations in Bombay and dietary reliance on chupattis, which are also reported to be high in phytate (Sever 1975:54).

Pica and Iron Deficiency

Iron deficiency is the commonest cause of anemia in the world today. It is more common in women that in men due to blood loss during menstruation and to multiple pregnancies in which iron is lost to the fetus. Dietary phytates, which are present in some breads, have also been shown to impair iron absorption and are thus an important contributing factor. The relationship between pica and iron deficiency remains intriguing and unresolved. There is a strong association in some cultures between the anemia and consumption of certain unusual items such as laundry starch consumed by southern-born Blacks in the United States and clays eaten in Africa, Turkey and India. It has been shown that laundry starch and various clays bind iron in the gastro-intestinal tract and interfere with its absorption, suggesting that the ingestion of these foods is the cause of the iron deficiency. On the other hand, certain picas have been clearly shown to be the result rather than the cause of iron deficiency anemia. Pagophagia or the craving to eat ice, for example, disappears within days after treatment with iron. It remains to be resolved by further investigation whether other picas, such as those for starch and soil, are the cause or the result of iron deficiency. The contribution of a variety of psychological and social factors may also be further examined (Sayers, et. al., 1974; Coltman, 1969; Reynolds, et. al., 1968; Hochstein, 1968).

150

Thiamin Deficiency

While beriberi, due to thiamin deficiency, is still a major health problem in countries where polished rice is the staple (Vietnam, Thailand, Malaya, Burma), the deficiency state also occurs among populations where both thiamin and caloric intake is considered adequate. Thus, in some north and northeastern provinces of Thailand, the habit of chewing betel nut and the eating of raw fermented fish contributes to thiamin deficiency, since both betel nut and raw fermented fish contain antithiamin factors. Tea drinking and chewing fermented tea leaves, as well as the ingestion of raw clams containing thiaminase, are reported to have the same effect. Some problems of malnutrition, then, do not result from inadequate consumption of nutritious foods but from the counter effect of substances in the foods themselves which render them physiologically unavailable. In some cases the problem may be corrected by educating consumers. Simply cooking fermented fish, for instance, destroys the thiaminase activity and results in significantly improved nutritional status (Vimokesant, et. al., 1975).

The Nutrition of Widows

In the Indian subcontinent widows, like ascetics, retreat from the consumption of luxury goods and gain merit by frequent fasting and by eating small allotments of the least nutritious foods. Since nutrition profoundly affects fertility, the structure of Indian populations could be investigated for the orchestrated deployment of kinds and quantities of foods to different segments of the population. Research in this area might show that the lower fecundity[8] of widowed women in Bangladesh is not due solely to the tendency to underreport their age, or to their past childbearing performance, but as well to frank nutritional deprivation. Since the strictest nutritional and behavioral regulations concerning reproduction also operate among the most prestigious social groups, where production of numbers would serve only to fragment material and ritual estate (Douglas 1966; Lindenbaum 1975), closer attention to the relationships among diet, caste, and stages of life might reveal previously hidden aspects of the biological structure of populations.

Energy Protein Malnutrition

Anthropologists can join in correcting the record on the role of protein in human undernutrition. The concept of a worldwide protein gap, derived from the diagnosis of kwashiorkor as a protein deficiency state has recently been challenged. Moreover, undue emphasis on kwashiorkor rather than marasmus resulted in the international distribution of the surplus of dry skim milk available in the United States after the 1939-45 war, and of protein-rich food mixtures after 1964, when the supplies of skim milk began to dry up (McLaren 1974). Current research in India confirms that the growth

151

and development of undernourished children can be significantly accelerated by calorie supplements that are virtually free of protein. The practical approach to malnutrition among Asian children, it is suggested, lies in bridging the calorie gap with an improvement and increase in present dietaries, rather than in distributing elaborately processed protein-rich formulations which are both unnecessary and expensive (Gopalan et al., 1973) and which may be culturally unacceptable. It has been recently shown that milk can be utilized by many individuals who are clinically "lactose intolerant", and that severity of digestive discomfort is dose-related, diminishing as the quantity ingested becomes smaller and if the milk is combined with other foods in cooking. Thus, the frequently cited limitations on the use of powdered milk by recipients of American aid may have as much to do with culture as biology (Almy 1975).

In Summary

The biosocial view of nutrition presented here suggests that anthropologists can contribute to the field in several ways. Traditional ethnographic data may be re-examined for its inherent physiological implications. The symbolic status of individuals in a society, for instance, may be mirrored by the amount and kind of food allotted to them, and this in turn may affect their mortality rate in childhood. Similar considerations may affect the fecundity of widows later in life, and the performance expected of ascetics and of individuals of low caste. All reveal the links between culture and the biological structure of populations. The possible physiological meaning underlying the hot-cold classification of foods has also hardly been examined, but it is proposed that in one particular case, seemingly irrational recommendations concerning milk intake in infants with diarrhea may be justified in the light of recent discoveries regarding mechanisms of carbohydrate absorption.

Nutritional anthropologists can contribute in a more pragmatic sense by gathering data which may solve some of the problems associated with food intake. In the future, nutritional anthropologists will also be more concerned with evaluation and implementation of the problems of inadequate food production and of energy-protein malnutrition in many countries. It is here that the applied aspect of nutritional anthropology reveals its strength. For even in the case of human undernutrition, dietary factors are but part of the issue (McLaren 1974:95). The etiology of malnutrition involves poverty, bad housing, poor hygiene and lack of information about the value of foods and of family planning. These factors in turn relate to wider economic and political issues which conspire to produce deprived segments in the world population. Nutritional anthropologists should focus then, not on food alone, but on the interlocking physiological and social factors responsible for gross differences in human survival.

Notes

1 See Mandelbaum 1970:196-201 for a review of the literature.
2 67⁰/₀ of women over 50 are widows.
3. See Medical Anthropology Newsletter 6:2:1975 for a list of Selected References.
4 Alland (1975:70) suggests that analysis of the hot-cold systems of classification in Southeast Asis should form a code which has ramifications for ecological adaption in economic and nutritional terms.
5 Jelliffe (1957:135) refers to the classifications as "scientifically irrational".
6 It is believed also that the eating of cold foods can cause the consumer to catch a chill.
7 A phrase borrowed from Roger Keesing's (1974b) observation that "symbolism, by stating relationship and proposing abstract messages at multiple levels, contributes to integration, to systemic wisdom, and to correcting the distortions of purposive consciousness."
8 Fecundity is defined as "women who had given birth during the year or had been pregnant ... currently pregnant, lactating, experiencing post-partum amenorrhea, or regularly menstruating". Stoeckel, et. al., 1972:194.

References

Al-Hadis of Mishkat-ul-Masabih
1963   English Translation and Commentary by Fazlul Karim. East Pakistan.
Alland, Alexander
1975   Adaptation. Annual Review of Anthropology 4:59-73.
Almy, Thomas P.
1975   Evolution, Lactase Levels and Global Hunger. The New England Journal of Medicine, 292:1183-4.
Anand, D. & A. Rama Rao
1962   Feeding Practices of Infants and Toddlers in Najafgarh Area. Indian Journal of Child Health 2:172-181.
Campbell, Joseph
1974   The Masks of God: Oriental Mythology. New York: The Viking Press.
Chen, Lincoln C., Shamsa Ahmed, Melita Gesche & W. Henry Mosley
1973   A Prospective Study of Birth Interval Dynamics in Rural Bangladesh. Population Studies 28:277-297.
Coello-Ramirez, P. & Fima Lifshitz with Vilma Zuniga
1972   Enteric Microflora and Carbohydrate Intolerance in Infants with Diarrhea. Pediatrics 49,233-242.
Coltman, C. A.
1969   Pagophagia and Iron Lack. Journal of the American Medical Association, 207:513.
Douglas, Mary
1966   Population Control in Primitive Groups. British Journal of Sociology 17:263-273.
Geertz, Clifford
1973   Interpretation of Cultures. New York: Basic Books.
Gopalan, C. & A. Nadamuni Naidu
1972   Nutrition and Fertility. Lancet, November 18, 1077-1079.
Gopalan, C., M. C. Swaminathan, V. K. Krishna Kumari, D. Hanumantha Rao, & K. Vijayaraghavan
1973   Effect of Calorie Supplementation on Growth of Undernourished Children. The American Journal of Clinical Nutrition 26,563-566.
Gray, Gary M.
1973   Drugs, Malnutrition and Carbohydrate Absorption. The American Journal of Clinical Nutrition 26:121-124.

Hanks, Jane Richardson
1963 Maternity and its Rituals in Bang Chan. Data Paper No. 51, Southeast Asia Program, Cornell University, Ithaca, New York.
Hochstein, Gianna
1969 Pica: A Study in Medical and Anthropological Explanation. *In* Essays on Medical Anthropology, Thomas Weaver, Ed. Southern Anthropological Society Proceedings No. 1, University of Georgia Press.
Jelliffe, D. B.
1957 Social Culture and Nutrition. Pediatrics 20:128-138.
1968 Infant Nutrition in the Subtropics and Tropics. Geneva: World Health Organization.
Keesing, Roger
1974a Theories of Culture. Annual Review of Anthropology 3:73-98.
1974b Review of Gregory Bateson: Steps to an Ecology of the Mind. American Anthropologist 76:370-372.
Kolata, B. G.
1974 !Kung Hunter-Gatherers: Feminism, Diet and Birth Control. Science 185:932-934.
Levi-Strauss, Claude
1963 The Effectiveness of Symbols. *In* Structural Anthropology. New York: Basic Books.
Lifshitz, F., Pedro Coello-Ramirez and Miguel Leon Contreras-Gutierrez
1971a The Response of Infants to Carbohydrate Oral Loads After Recovery From Diarrhea. Pediatrics 79:612-617.
Lifshitz, E., Pedro Coello-Ramirz, Guillermo Gutierrez-Topete, & Maria Cinta Cornado-Cornet
1971b Carbohydrate Intolerance in Infants with Diarrhea. Pediatrics 79:760-767.
Lindenbaum, J.
1973 Nutrition: Role of Malabsorption. *In* Disaster in Bangladesh: Health Crisis in a Developing Nation. Lincoln C. Chen, Ed. New York: Oxford University Press.
Lindenbaum, Shirley
1968 Woman and the Left Hand: Social Status and Symbolism in East Pakistan. Mankind 6:537-544.
1975 The Value of Women. *In* Bengal in the Nineteenth and Twentieth Centuries. John R. McLane, Ed. Michigan State University, South Asia Series, Occasional Paper no. 25, pp. 75-83.
Malcolm, L. A.
1970 Growth and Development of the Bundi Child of the New Guinea Highlands. Human Biology 42:293-328.
Malhotra, M. S.
1966 People of India including Primitive Tribes – a Survey on Physiological Adaptation, Physical Fitness, and Nutrition. *In* The Biology of Human Adaptability, P. T. Baker and J. S. Wiener, Eds. Oxford: Clarendon Press. pp. 329-355.
Mandelbaum, David G.
1970 Society in India. University of California Press.
McCracken, R. D.
1971 Lactase Deficiency: An Example of Dietary Evolution. Current Anthropology 12:479-517.
McLaren, Donald S.
1974 The Great Protein Fiasco. Lancet, July 13, 93-96.
Mosley, Wiley H., A. K. M. Alauddin Chowdury and K. M. A. Aziz
1970 Demographic Characteristics of a Population Laboratory in Rural East Pakistan. Population Research, National Institutes of Child Health and Human Development.

154

Newman, Marshall T.
1975   Nutritional Adaptation in Man. *In* Physiological Anthropology. Albert Damon, Ed., New York: Oxford University Press.

O'Laughlin, Bridget
1974   Mediation of Contradiction. Why Mbum Women Do Not Eat Chicken. *In* Woman Culture and Society. Michelle Rosaldo and Louise Lamphere, Eds. Stanford University Press.

Ramanamurthy, P. S. V.
1969   Physiological effects of "Hot" and "Cold" foods in Human Subjects. Journal of Nutrition and Dietetics 6:187-191.

Reynolds, R. H., H. J. Binder, M. B. Miller, W. W. Y. Chang, and S. Horan
1968   Pagophagia and Iron Anemia. Annals of Internal Medicine 69,435.

Rosenberg, Ellen
1973   Ecological Effects of Sex-Differential Nutrition. Paper presented at 72nd Annual Meeting, American Anthropological Association, New Orleans.

Sayers, G., D. A. Lipschitz, M. Sayers, H. C. Seftel, T. H. Bothwell & R. W. Charlton
1974   Relationship between Pica and Iron Nutrition in Johannesburg Black Adults. South African Medical Journal 1655-1660.

Sen, Dinesh Chandra
1954   History of Bengali Language and Literature. University of Calcutta.

Sever, Lowell E.
1975   Zinc and Human Development: A Review. Human Ecology 3:1:43-57.

Sommer, Alfred and Matthew S. Loewenstein
1975   Nutritional Status and Mortality: a Prospective Validation of the QUAC stick. The American Journal of Clinical Nutrition 28:287-292.

Stini, William A.
1971   Evolutionary Implications of Changing Nutritional Patterns in Human Populations. American Anthropologist 73:1019-1030.

Stoeckel, John, Alauddin Chowdhury and Wiley H. Mosley
1972   The Effect of Fecundity on Fertility in Rural East Pakistan (Bangladesh) Social Biology 19:193-201.

Sunshine, Philip and Norman Kretchmer
1964   Infatile Diarrhea Associated with Intolerance to Disaccharides. Pediatrics 34:38-50.

Sutton, Robert E., & J. R. Hamilton
1969   Tolerance of Young Children with Severe Gastoenteritis to Dietary Lactose: A Controlled Study. The Canadian Medical Association Journal 99:980-982.

Tambiah, S. J.
1969   Animals are Good to Think and Good to Prohibit. Ethnology 8:423-459.

Vimokesant, S. L., D. M. Hilker, S. Nakornchai, K. Rungruangsak, and S. Dhanamitta
1975   Effects of Betel Nut and Fermented Fish on the Thiamin Status of Northeastern Thais. The American Journal of Clinical Nutrition 28:1458-1463.